CAPITAL FOR PRODUCTIVITY AND JOBS

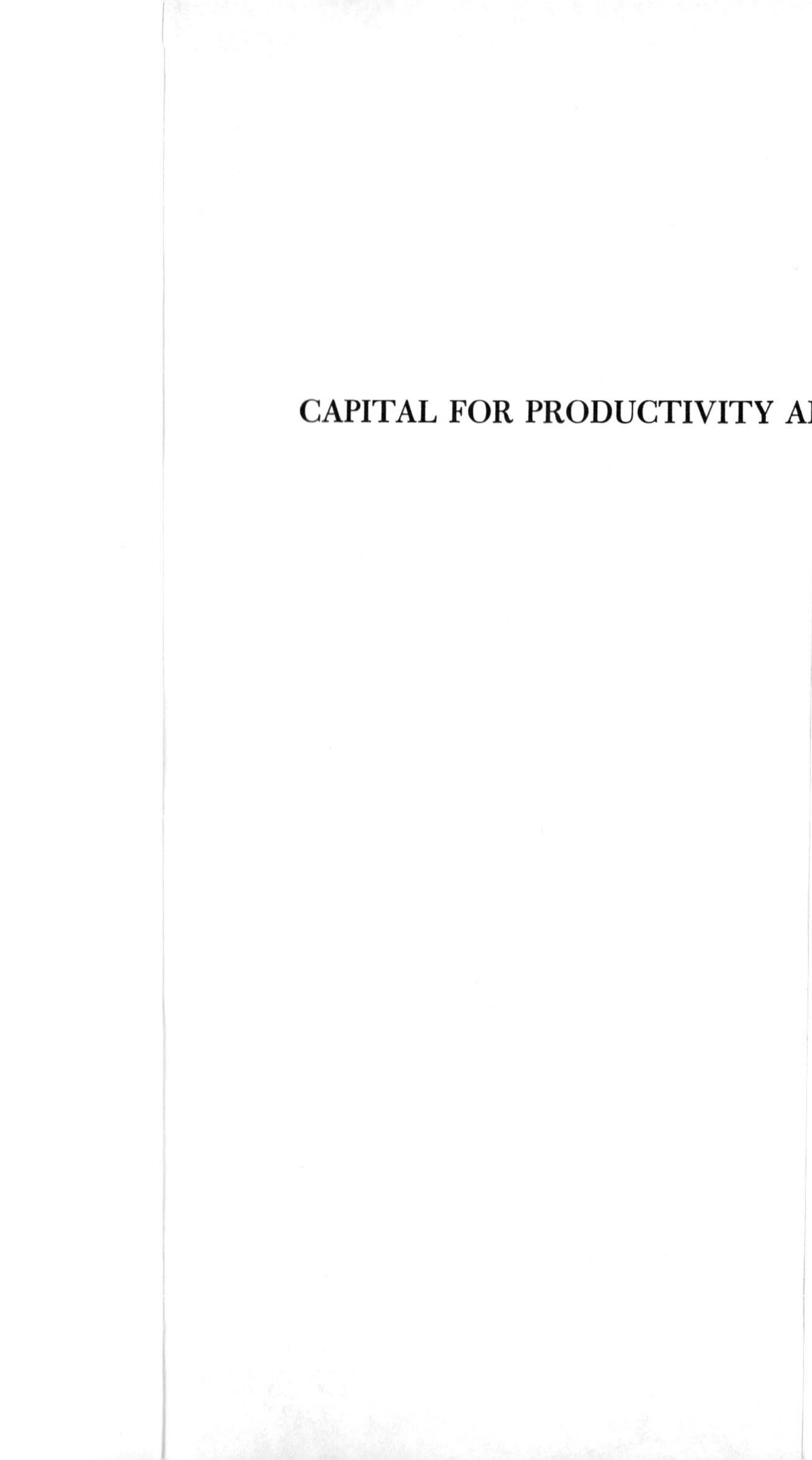

CAPITAL FOR PRODUCTIVITY AI

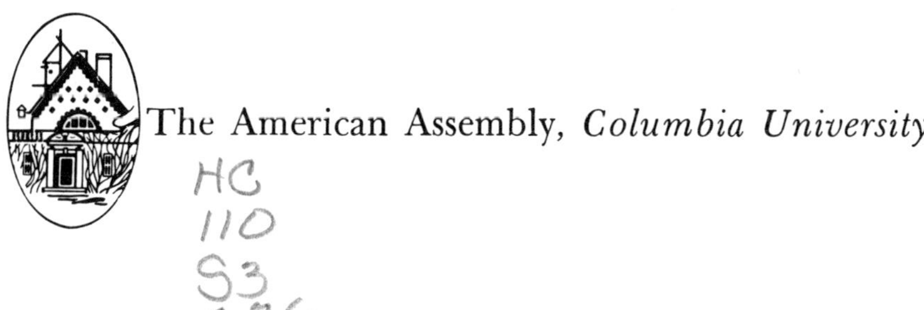

The American Assembly, *Columbia University*

CAPITAL FOR PRODUCTIVITY AND JOBS

Prentice-Hall, Inc., *Englewood Cliffs, New Jersey*

Library of Congress Cataloging in Publication Data
MAIN ENTRY UNDER TITLE:

Capital for productivity and jobs.

(A Spectrum Book)

At head of title: The American Assembly, Columbia University.

Papers prepared for the 51st American Assembly, held at Arden House, Harriman, New York, Oct. 28-31, 1976.

Includes bibliographies and index.

1. Saving and investment—United States—Congresses. 2. Investments—United States—Congresses. 3. Industrial productivity—United States—Congresses. 4. Full employment policies—United States—Congresses. I. American Assembly.

HC110.S3C36 332'.04 77-23330

ISBN 0-13-113498-1

ISBN 0-13-113480-9 pbk.

10 9 8 7 6 5 4 3 2 1

PRENTICE-HALL INTERNATIONAL, INC. (*London*)
PRENTICE-HALL OF AUSTRALIA PTY, LTD. (*Sydney*)
PRENTICE-HALL OF CANADA, LTD. (*Toronto*)
PRENTICE-HALL OF INDIA PRIVATE LIMITED (*New Delhi*)
PRENTICE-HALL OF JAPAN, INC. (*Tokyo*)
PRENTICE-HALL OF SOUTHEAST ASIA PTE., LTD. (*Singapore*)
WHITEHALL BOOKS LIMITED (*Wellington, New Zealand*)

Table of Contents

Preface

Savings benefit our society because the total return from the investment of these savings provides a significant improvement in living standards. Business investment in research and development contributes to the advancement of knowledge, and expenditures on plant and equipment embody that knowledge in the production process. Investment in education and on-the-job training creates a more productive and adaptive work force. Investment by government in roads, health, sewer and water facilities, and so on also fosters employment, productivity growth, and environmental improvement. Investments in decent housing are essential to our welfare.

Such was the collective opinion of the seventy-two Americans who comprised the Fifty-first American Assembly at Arden House, Harriman, New York, October 28-31, 1976, on *Capital Needs of the United States*. In their final report (which may be had from The American Assembly) they gave reasons why the national environment for saving, investment, and expansion of production and jobs has gone wrong, and came up with a number of prescriptions to relieve the malaise.

The chapters in this book were designed by Messrs. Eli Shapiro and William L. White as advance reading for participants in the Assembly. But the problem clearly affects the lives of all of us, and the volume is offered to other interested parties in the hope that it will help us wrestle with the many problems standing in the way of a working, productive, and healthful America.

The American Assembly, a national nonpartisan public affairs forum, takes no stand on matters it presents for public discussion. The opinions herein belong to the authors themselves. Nor are the donors to this American Assembly program to be asociated with the authors' views. Generous gifts from seventeen foundations and corporations were made on the basis of the merits of the program and not because of any effort to make a particular point of view prevail.

Clifford C. Nelson
President
The American Assembly

CAPITAL FOR PRODUCTIVITY AND JOBS

Eli Shapiro and William L. White 

Introduction: The Public Policy Issues

During the past few years there has been a growing interest on the question of whether the United States economy will engage in a high enough level of investment to assure continued growth in productivity and high levels of employment. The sluggish behavior of productivity in the early 1970s and the very large employment requirements needed to reduce the unemployment of the mid-1970s and to provide for a growing labor force accentuated these concerns. The turbulent financial markets in 1972 through 1974 gave rise to further questions about the ability of financial markets and institutions to finance the "required" investment outlays.

This combination of events has given rise to an extensive literature on what has come to be called "the capital shortage." The existing studies and analysis of this issue differ as to the existence or extent of the problem, the causes of the problem, and the merit of the alternative courses of action available to provide solutions to the problem. Some see the problem as real and extending widely throughout the economy; some see the issue as a false one or one limited to very specific sectors within the economy. Some definitions of the capital shortage reflect an assumption that investment needs are large in

---

ELI SHAPIRO *is Vice Chairman of the Travelers Insurance Company and Alfred P. Sloan Professor of Management at M.I.T. Author and editor of a number of major works on saving and banking, Dr. Shapiro has been consultant to the U.S. Treasury Department and director of several business corporations.*

WILLIAM L. WHITE *is Professor of Business Administration at the Harvard Business School. Co-author of* Money and Banking, *he has written widely on business financing and capital markets and has served as adviser to public and private agencies related to commerce.*

order to provide for productivity growth; others see large investment needs in order to provide for employment growth; still others see it as arising from the need to spend large sums on energy development, conversion, and conservation and on efforts to improve our environment. Some see the capital shortage as a shortfall in the proportion of national income which is saved. Still others see it as a problem arising from inadequacies in the structure and operation of the financial system.

This book summarizes and analyzes the assumptions and findings of many of these earlier studies. It is critical of much of this material. In an attempt to gain public support for certain actions, most often restraint on federal expenditures and business tax changes, several different groups advanced overly dramatic and precise forecasts of investment "needs," "supplies," and "gaps." Much of the subsequent discussion centered on the accuracy or lack of accuracy of the estimates. After more intensive analysis, most of these conclusions seem to be significant overstatements. Rather than continue to chase after precise forecasts of needs, supplies and gaps, discussion is now turning to an analysis of those forces which could keep investment outlays from rising as much as their return to society would suggest they should. Analysis of this issue has made clear that the inflation, the instability in the level of economic activity, and the deviations from high employment that took place during the late 1960s and early 1970s were *the* most important factors restraining saving and investment during that period and that the critical factor that will determine the overall volume of saving and investment in the U.S. over the next decade will be the success we have in achieving high rates of employment at a relatively stable price level. Moreover, this new line of analysis is directing attention to the problems posed to investment expenditures by the difficulties of pricing goods and services in ways which allow a sufficient return to investment, by tax policies which discriminate against investment, and by inflexibilities in financial markets which limit investment.

The object of this book is to encourage this change in emphasis by critically evaluating the earlier arguments and by showing how policies which are designed to isolate and offset the forces which restrain investment expenditures can increase investment expenditures and increase our economic well-being. In spite of the fact that many of the arguments which have advanced to support the notion of a capital shortage are faulty, there are good reasons to believe that investment outlays are likely to fall below what we shall call "appropriate" levels. The challenge for public policy is to determine those forces which could keep investment outlays from achieving these levels and to take action to keep these results from happening.

The Structure of the Arguments

The arguments surrounding the concern about a capital shortage can be classified into two groups—those which accentuate real or physical shortfalls and those which stress aspects of the problem which arise in the financial markets.

REAL ASPECTS OF THE INVESTMENT PROBLEM

One of the earliest statements reflecting a concern about a shortfall of investment relative to production requirements appeared in testimony Federal Reserve Board Chairman, Arthur Burns, delivered before the Joint Economic Committee on August 3, 1973. When commenting on the sharp acceleration in prices which had taken place during that year, Chairman Burns argued that recent price developments

> . . . however, have also been aggravated by severe capacity constraints on the production of major industrial materials. Calculations by the research staff of the Federal Reserve Board indicate that in the first half of this year the rate of capacity utilization in major materials-producing industries —including petroleum refining, production of aluminum, steel, cement, synthetic fibers, paper, paperboard, and the like—was at the highest level since the second quarter of 1951.

The August 1973 Federal Reserve *Bulletin* contained an article which presented data on a previously unpublished index of capacity utilization in major materials industries. This article documented in fuller detail the extent of the shortage of unutilized capacity in these industries. While many analysts had been concerned about capacity shortages in specific industries, these data suggested the problem was more severe and more widespread than most observers had thought.

Chairman Burns went on to say

> In many of these industries, there has been very little growth of productive capacity in recent years. Environmental controls have held up construction of new plants, have led to shutdowns of some existing plants, and have prevented the activation of some older standby capacity. Moreover, investment in new capacity was discouraged by the relatively low profits of our domestic nonfinancial corporations between 1966 and 1971. Productive capacity in the paper industry and also in petroleum refining

> appears to have grown less than 2 percent per year during the past several years. In the cement industry productive capacity has shown little or no growth over the past 5 years. Not a single new cement plant has come into production during the past year and a half, and only one new petroleum refinery has been opened since 1969.
>
> These are sobering facts. Lack of sufficient attention to investment incentives in these industries and to the special problems they face as a consequence of environmental control programs, has resulted in shortages of many basic materials needed by American Industry to expand production. For want of steel, or aluminum, or industrial chemicals, or adequate fuel supplies, business firms in various lines of activity have been unable to increase production rapidly enough to meet the demands of their customers; unfilled orders have mounted; and delivery delays have lengthened. Price pressures originating in short supplies of major materials have thus been generalized to semifinished and finished goods.

In September of 1974, the New York Stock Exchange published a study entitled, "The Capital Needs and Savings Potential of the U.S. Economy: Projections through 1985." This study projected business investment and residential construction spending through 1985 and found it likely that they would comprise a larger share of GNP than had been the case during the period from 1961 to 1973. It also projected that federal and state and local governments would have continuous financing needs. Its estimates of business and personal savings were such that there was a gap of $650 billion or $45 billion per year between their *ex ante* projections of uses of funds and savings during the 1974–85 period. The implications of this study were that some sectors, such as housing, small businesses, and even some larger businesses, would be unable to achieve their projected levels of investment due to the difficulty of obtaining finance or to the expense of this finance. The Stock Exchange study argued that unless policies were adopted which closed this gap by expanding the availability of savings, unemployment would be higher, productivity growth would be lower, and the economy would experience severe financial difficulties.

The study's proposals to deal with the problem were a reduction in federal spending, corporate income tax reduction through an adjustment of depreciation allowances and an increase in the investment tax credit, and a reduction in federal personal taxes on dividends and capital gains. It was argued that the rapid inflation rate was reducing private savings and that the reduction in federal spending was necessary to bring the inflation under control. The corporate tax changes were designed to increase the profitability of investment and the level of business savings, while the reduction in personal taxes on dividends and capital gains were meant to stimulate the flow of private savings into equity investment in the business sector.

In April 1975, Barry Bosworth, James S. Duesenberry, and Andrew S. Carron (BDC) published "Capital Needs in the Seventies." This study paralleled the NYSE study in that it projected what it thought would be likely or necessary levels of investment expenditures and compared them with the likely level of savings in the economy. It differed from the NYSE study in several of the particulars of both its procedures and in its conclusions, however. The BDC Study dealt at length and in some detail with projections of investment expenditures for residential construction; state and local government capital spending on sewers, water resources, and mass transport, and private sector capital spending on pollution control and energy production. It assumed business investment needs would increase because of the needs for additional capacity in the basic materials industry and the pollution abatement and energy needs. In addition, residential construction and state and local government capital expenditures were projected to increase as a fraction of GNP. In the aggregate, total investment outlays would have to increase as a fraction of GNP. The study projected personal savings rates to decline slightly and the share of corporate profits in GNP to rise modestly. Given these assumed levels of investment and private savings, the study concluded that overall investment and savings would be balanced only if the federal government had a substantial budget surplus by 1980. And, more importantly, the study concluded that this surplus could be obtained, in large part because federal tax revenues under a progressive income tax could be expected to rise faster than aggregate GNP. Thus, the BDC study concluded that there was likely to be an increased need for investment in the economy, but that there was no *ex ante* shortfall of savings. Private and public savings levels seemed sufficient to meet these estimated investment demands.

In testimony before the Senate Finance Committee on May 7, 1975, Treasury Secretary William E. Simon argued the other side of this issue. He stated:

> In my testimony this morning, I want to draw upon an abundance of documentary evidence showing that the United States has not been keeping pace in its capital investments and that we must devote more of our resources to this purpose if we are to achieve our most basic economic dreams for the future. To sumarize, the record shows that:
>
> —During the 1960s, the United States had the worst record of capital investment among the major industrialized nations of the Free World.

–Correspondingly, our records of productivity growth and overall economic growth during this period were also among the lowest of the major industrialized nations.

–As other nations have channeled relatively more of their resources into capital investment and have acquired more modern plants and equipment, they have eroded our competitive edge in world markets.

–Our record on capital investments reflects the heavy emphasis we are placing on personal consumption and government spending as opposed to savings and capital formation.

–Our record also reflects a precipitous decline in corporate profits since the mid-1960s.

–While the U.S. economy remains sufficiently large and dynamic to overcome our investment record of recent years, our future economic growth will be tied much more directly to the adequacy of our capital investments.

–Estimates of future needs vary, but it is relatively clear that in coming years we will have to devote approximately three times as much money to capital investments as we have in the recent past.

–It is an economic fact of life that increased productivity is the only way to increase our standard of living. For the sake of future economic growth—jobs, real income and reasonable price stability—the inescapable conclusion is that government policies must become more supportive of capital investment and that we must make a fundamental shift in our domestic policies away from continued growth in personal consumption and government spending and toward greater savings, capital formation and investment.

Some analysts have concluded that it will not be possible to meet our future capital investment needs. I disagree. I firmly believe that we are capable of achieving our basic investment goals, but I also believe that they represent one of the most formidable economic challenges of the decade ahead.

Table 1 contains some of the data which the Secretary used to advance his position.

The Secretary's testimony argued that capital investment, particularly business fixed investment, was a major determinant of the pace of productivity growth and the rate of increase in our standard of living. Moreover, it was critical that public policy turn to actions which expanded incentives to invest as well as to take steps to curtail the growth in personal consumption and government spending in order to free the resources required for this increased pace of investment.

In May 1975, the Secretary of Labor, John T. Dunlop, commissioned a study which evaluated another aspect of the question of the likely adequacy of investment expenditures in the economy. Secretary Dunlop took note of the existing concerns about the adequacy of capital formation and established a study group to "explore the pos-

Table 1.

	Investment as a Percent of Real National Output, 1960-1973 *		*Productivity Growth, 1960-1973 (Average Annual Rate)*	
	Total Fixed **	*Non-residential Fixed*	*Gross Domestic Product per Employed Person*	*Manu-facturing Output per Manhour*
United States	17.5	13.6	2.1	3.3
Japan	35.0	29.0	9.2	10.5
West Germany	25.8	20.0	5.4	5.8
France	24.5	18.2	5.2	6.0
Canada	21.8	17.4	2.4	4.3
Italy	20.5	14.4	5.7	6.4
United Kingdom	18.5	15.2	2.8	4.0
11 OECD Countries	24.7	19.4	5.2 †	6.1

Source: U.S. Department of the Treasury.

* OECD concepts of investment and national product. The OECD concept includes nondefense government outlays for machinery and equipment in the private investment total which required special adjustment in the U.S. national accounts for comparability. National output is defined in this study as "gross domestic product," rather than the more familiar measure of gross national product, to conform with OECD definitions.

** Including residential.

† Average for 6 OECD countries listed.

sible connection between the capital formation issue and the nation's ability to achieve the objectives of either the Joint Economic Committee of the Congress or of the Administration with respect to a target rate of unemployment by 1980 and 1985." The group was to project the levels of investment which would likely be necessary in order that the economy operate at slightly less than a 5 percent rate of unemployment by 1980 and a target rate of unemployment of 4 percent by 1985. Further, the group was to present a set of policy recommendations which would cause that level of investment to be forthcoming.

The group concluded that private investment would have to represent a slightly larger share of Gross National Product (GNP) in the future in order to permit the economy to move rapidly toward high employment without experiencing excessive inflation.

Thus, another element had been added to the argument that the United States economy had to increase its rate of investment. Without that increased rate of investment, it was argued that the demand for output would not grow fast enough to reduce the unemployment rate to acceptable levels and provide jobs for the rapidly expanding labor force. Increased investment outlays had been argued by others to be necessary to alleviate capacity bottlenecks, or to stimulate productivity growth, to meet pollution control requirements, and to meet expanded needs in areas such as water and sewage treatment facilities and mass transportation. Now, increased rates of investment were necessary for an additional reason: to provide the demand for output which would provide the demand for jobs which was necessary to achieve our employment objectives.

The group went on to conclude that any analysis which projected a full economic recovery before 1980 inevitably must assume either a reduction in federal tax rates for individuals and corporations or substantial federal surpluses to avoid the so-called "crowding-out" of private investment.

> For those analyses which take what we believe to be the more productive paths of reduced tax rates, the problem of directing savings into equity forms appears paramount. In other words, the ability of corporations to attract risk capital, through either internal or external sources, is a necessary factor in increasing the rate of investment.

The group came to this conclusion from an analysis of the financial position of the corporate sector and the implications of this position for the ability of this sector to finance any significant expansion in investment. Their analysis concluded that there had been significant deterioration in profitability as well as in returns on investment in the past ten years. The group concluded that this was the primary cause of recent corporate financial weakness. Further, this weakness, in the absence of tax changes, was the only clearly visible obstacle to the financing of the investment necessary to reach 4 percent unemployment by 1985.

Thus, another major element of the group's findings was its highlighting of the necessity to recognize and alleviate the problems which had developed in the financial structure of business firms as an essential part of any program of assuring the growth in business investment.

In early 1975, Benjamin Friedman published a study entitled "Financing the Next Five Years of Fixed Investment" in which he, too, focused on the importance of financial variables in the outlook for investment outlays. Friedman's study, like the others mentioned, projected an increase in the level of necessary investment expenditures.

He concluded, however, that this pace of investment would require a substantially enlarged volume of external financing for business corporations, including increases in equity issues, corporate bonds, commercial mortgages, and bank loans. Because of this he concluded that "to an unusually great extent, financial considerations may act during this period as effective constraints." "These financial constraints," said Friedman, "may well constitute a greater determinant of the basic course of U. S. economic events than has been the case at any time during the post-World War II era."

It is to these financial elements of the capital formation outlook that we now turn.

FINANCIAL ASPECTS OF THE INVESTMENT PROBLEM

Concern over developments in financial markets first arose during the years 1972 to 1974 as a result of the enormous volume of external financing required by business firms. These sharply increased financing requirements and the escalation of interest rates which took place during this period gave rise to concerns about the ability of financial institutions and markets to supply a sufficient volume of funds to business. Special concern was raised about the sources of finance for smaller firms and firms with lower credit quality ratings.

As business financing fell off sharply in 1975, these concerns were replaced by the fear that the explosion in the financing requirements of the United States Treasury would "crowd-out" private borrowers. It was thought this crowding out in financial markets would seriously limit the ability of business investment and housing expenditures to lead the economy out of recession. Moreover, over the longer run, it could limit the capital formation that was necessary to assure the productivity growth and employment which would support rising standards of living and keep the United States economy competitive in world markets.

The third area of concern was that of a potential mismatch between the needs of investors and the preferences of savers. An important part of this image of the problem was a concern that the excesses of the early 1970s had left some financial institutions in positions that would make it difficult for them to play their necessary roles in financing the legitimate needs of an expanding economy.

The very large volume of business financing which took place in 1973-74 was the result of several forces. Business expenditures on fixed assets expressed as a percent of GNP remained at historically high levels throughout this period. Business inventory investment in physical units persisted at a relatively constant and moderate rate during this period as well. However, the inflation, which was especially pronounced in industrial material prices, caused the replacement cost of the inventories used in production and sales to substantially exceed their original production cost. Thus, business firms found themselves forced to finance extraordinarily large increases in the book value of their inventories. As a result, the total operational needs for finance of business firms grew dramatically in 1973 and 1974, as is shown in Table 2.

At the same time, internal funds (profits after tax, including inventory profits, less dividends, plus depreciation) grew only moderately. While inventory profits soared, operating profits (total profits excluding inventory gains) fell dramatically. In spite of this fact, dividend payments grew steadily. During 1974, for example, operating profits after tax less dividends amounted to only $2.5 billion compared with a figure of $15 billion in 1972. The more rapid growth in operating needs than in internal funds resulted in a sharp expansion of external needs. The drop in equity prices in 1974 made the sale of new equities very costly; as a result most of this external need was funded through the issuance of debt. Business borrowing from banks rose to annual rates of $30 billion in 1973 and 1974, compared to about a $5 billion rate in 1970-71. Corporate bond issues, after a decline in use in 1973 relative to 1970-72, rose sharply in 1974.

Faced with a very large volume of financing requirements and a growing concern about the economic outlook, lenders became much more quality conscious when granting credit. With the overall level of interest rates rising rapidly in response to the acceleration in inflation, these concerns over credit quality meant that riskier borrowers had to pay very high rates of interest in order to attract funds. For many companies of medium or small size, raising funds seemed almost impossible.

As is shown in Table 2, the financial position of the business sector changed significantly in 1975 and 1976. Inventory investment, which had been a major source of the increase in total operational needs, turned negative in 1975. This was the first period of negative inventory accumulation measured at book value since 1960. Expenditures on fixed assets fell slightly as a fraction of GNP. Even though operating profits fell so fast in the early parts of 1975 that internal funds declined, external needs collapsed. As the inventory decline ended, and a moderate pace of inventory accumulation began, profits

TABLE 2. NONFINANCIAL BUSINESS CORPORATION FINANCIAL NEEDS AND SOURCES
(All data are flows as a percent of GNP)

	1954-57	*1958-60*	*1961-67*	*1968-70*	*1971-72*	*1973-74*	*1975*	*1976* **
Total Operational Needs	9.7	9.0	10.2	10.5	11.1	12.9	8.7	10.7
Plant & equipment	6.9	6.5	7.0	7.8	7.4	7.8	7.1	6.8
Inventory	0.9	0.4	1.1	1.1	1.2	3.1	—0.3	1.6
IVA	0.4	—	0.1	0.4	0.5	2.1	0.8	0.8
Real	0.5	0.4	1.0	0.7	0.7	1.0	—1.1	0.8
Other *	1.9	2.1	2.1	1.6	2.5	2.0	1.8	2.2
Internal Funds	7.3	6.9	7.8	7.3	7.2	8.0	7.6	8.0
External Needs for Operations	2.4	2.1	2.4	3.2	3.9	4.9	1.1	2.6
Liquid Asset Increase	—	0.3	0.4	0.4	0.6	0.7	1.2	0.7
Debt Issues	2.1	2.0	2.5	3.2	3.5	5.1	1.6	2.5
Short term	0.6	0.6	1.0	1.2	0.9	2.9	2.6	2.1
Long term	1.5	1.4	1.5	2.0	2.6	2.2	—1.0	0.4
Equity Issues	0.2	0.4	0.2	0.3	1.0	0.5	0.6	0.8
Profits before Tax	8.8	7.5	8.7	7.3	6.4	7.1	6.2	7.4
Operating profits	8.4	7.5	8.6	6.9	5.9	5.1	5.4	6.6

Source: Federal Reserve Board, *Flow of Funds Data* and *Survey of Current Business.*

* Includes expenditures on residential construction, foreign direct investment, net trade credit, net miscellaneous financial assets and liabilities, and discrepancy.

** Annual rate for first half of year.

increased sharply and internal funds rose. This kept external needs in late 1975 and early 1976 at quite low levels. Corporate bond issues continued high, but were largely offset by bank loan repayments. In 1975 and early 1976, businesses were restructuring their balance sheets by replacing short-term debt with longer term debt and rebuilding their stocks of liquid assets. Their net external financing needs were quite small, however.

The question for the future is whether the very large external financing requirements of business which were observed in 1973-74 are indicative of those which should be expected, or whether these financial requirements were the results of a set of circumstances that are not likely to occur again. It is clear that the circumstances had little historical precedence. The rapid inflation during that time increased financial needs at the same time that it reduced the supply of internal funds. The overall need for finance arising from operational requirements had never been so large, nor had operating profits ever fallen so low.

It is clear that some of the investment, especially that in inventory, was the result of the concerns about capacity and raw material shortages which were rampant in 1972-74, and which abated significantly by 1975-76. However, there are arguments which suggest that business investment outlays will have to grow sharply to meet those capacity shortages that do exist and for the many reasons advanced in the earlier sections of this introduction. On the other hand, the shortfall in operating profits appears to have come as a surprise to many business firms. Many of these firms have since taken steps to assure that their accounting and pricing systems more adequately reflect replacement costs, and are using LIFO methods for valuing inventories in order to avoid the income taxes that inventory profits imply. However, the outlook for business profitability is far from certain. Foreign competition or pressure from domestic price controls may keep the profitability of domestic corporations from rising to levels which would provide enough internal finance to allow business firms to avoid experiencing another sharp increase in the proportion of their funds they must raise externally.

If business firms continue to commit large sums to investment at the same time that they continued to generate levels of retained earnings as low as those experienced in 1972-74, business external needs would continue to be large. Thus the outlook for the volume of business external financial needs depends critically on the behavior of business investment relative to its profitability.

The meaning of the recent fall in corporate profits for the outlook for future corporate profitability is discussed at some length by Feldstein in Chapter 5 of this volume. The connection between business investment and corporate profitability is explored by Eisner in Chapter 2.

The United States Treasury was a borrower in private financial markets in every year from 1960 to 1975 except for 1969. Prior to 1975, these financing needs posed little problem for other financial sectors. The needs were small on average compared to the needs of housing or business, and the Treasury's needs expanded to high levels only during recessions when the financing needs of the other sectors were small or declining. In 1975, the Treasury's needs expanded to very high levels even when expressed as a percent of high employment GNP. The bulk of these needs arose because the economy was in recession. As income fell and unemployment increased, tax receipts fell sharply, expenditures on unemployment compensation rose significantly, and caused the actual budget deficit to increase by about $33 billion. In addition, personal and corporate tax cuts designed to stimulate the economy's recovery increased the budget deficit somewhat further.

As the economy expands and moves closer to high employment levels of output, much of these financing requirements will disappear. There are two sets of circumstances which could cause the Treasury's financing requirements to continue to be large even as the economy expands. One would be an expansion of federal spending programs or a reduction in tax rates which imply a deficit at high employment levels. The other circumstance could arise from difficulties in the notion of the high employment budget. If the changing structure of the labor force (more women and teenagers) and the existence of more liberal unemployment compensation systems raised the overall level of unemployment at which significant inflationary pressures arise above the 4 percent levels commonly assured in computing the economy's potential output at high employment, then our current estimates of high employment output may overstate our true potential. Also, if productivity growth has taken place more slowly of late, or if the rise in the costs of energy, or if the introduction of additional pollution control requirements has reduced the economic potential of some of our industrial capacity, our current estimates of the level of output which the economy could produce at high employment and reasonably stable prices may overstate its real potential. Overstating the level of high employment output leads to an overstatement of the revenue the existing tax structure would generate at high employment and understates the size of the financing requirements implicit in any set of spending and tax policies.

Thus, while most of the financing requirements that the Treasury is now experiencing arise from the recession and should disappear as the economy expands, the Treasury could remain a large borrower if we adopted fiscal policies which enlarged the deficit at high employment or if we based budget projections on a too optimistic level of high employment GNP.

The third aspect of the capital shortage as a financial problem arises from a concern that there is a potential mismatch between the financial needs of business and the financial preferences of household sources. Business is said to need long-term finance while savers prefer short-term financial assets; business is said to need equity while individual savers show a much greater interest in holding debts. Concern over these possibilities is greater the more one feels that financial institutions and markets are not well positioned to bridge these differences at reasonable cost to borrowers and competitive returns to savers.

The forces which give rise to these concerns can be seen from an examination of the savings and financial asset choices made by households. There have been a number of trends which have dominated household savings behavior over the past thirty years. As can be seen in Table 3, these trends continued and were exaggerated in the early 1970s. First, households have allocated the vast bulk of their annual accumulation to debts as opposed to equities. Within debts, households have accentuated claims on intermediaries (demand, time, and savings deposits, savings through insurance, or pension funds) rather than lend their funds directed to corporations or governments. Finally, households reflecting their interest in safety and liquidity allocated the bulk of their financial assets accumulation to relatively short-term deposits and savings accounts.

In part, these household choices reflect the opportunities open to them. For example, since corporations were able to meet most of their needs for equity through the retention of earnings, their new issues of stock were relatively small and households were not offered large amounts of new equity issues to buy. Since certain institutional investors, such as pension funds, were shifting the composition of their portfolios toward equities at the same time that corporations were issuing only modest amounts of new equity, it was especially unlikely that households would be major net accumulators of new equity issues. Also, since a large fraction of the demand for debt financing arose in

TABLE 3. HOUSEHOLD ACQUISITION OF FINANCIAL ASSETS BY TYPE
(All flows are expressed as a percent of GNP)

	1954-57	*1958-60*	*1961-67*	*1968-70*	*1971-72*	*1973-74*
NET ANNUAL INCREASE IN:						
All Financial Assets	6.4	6.4	7.3	7.4	9.4	9.8
Deposits	2.7	3.0	4.6	3.9	7.5	5.5
Demand deposits Currency	0.2	0.4	0.7	1.0	1.0	0.8
Time and savings	2.5	2.6	3.9	2.9	6.5	4.7
Directly held debts	1.3	1.4	0.8	1.7	–0.3	2.0
Contractual retirement savings	2.2	2.4	2.4	2.4	2.6	2.6
Life insurance reserves	0.7	0.7	0.7	0.6	0.6	0.5
Pension plan reserves	1.5	1.7	1.7	1.8	2.0	2.1
Equities	0.3	0.1	–0.2	–0.5	–0.4	–0.2
Investment Co. shares (mutual funds)	0.2	0.3	0.4	0.5	0.1	–
Corporate equities (directly held)	0.1	–0.2	–0.6	–0.9	–0.5	–0.2
Other	–0.2	–0.4	–0.2	–0.1	–	–0.1

Source: Federal Reserve Board, *Flow of Funds Data.*

the home mortgage market where thrift institutions play a major role as lenders rather than in the corporate or government bond market, one would have expected household savers to be induced to direct their savings flows to these thrift institutions.

On the other hand, this past behavior of households may also reflect a basic belief that their share of the retained earnings of corporations gave them about enough additional equity investment, and that they preferred the liquidity and safety of deposits and savings accounts more than they liked the higher return which was available on such direct debts as corporate bonds, mortgages, and government securities.

As the external financing needs of business expanded sharply in the late 1960s and early 1970s, this predisposition of the household sector toward acquiring deposits as opposed to direct debts meant that commercial banks were a much more readily expandable channel for financing business than was the public bond market. The commercial banking system grew very rapidly as financing demands arose in the business sector with its long working arrangement with the banks and because banks had a savings product with great appeal to household savers. Attempts to lure more household funds into the bond market, on the other hand, were more difficult. Household purchases of corporate bonds did increase significantly in 1973-74, however, as the data in Table 3 show. These purchases required such things as sharply increased interest rate spreads between bonds and deposits, and shorter maturity bonds. Given the interests of households in safety and liquidity, the public bond market was a real alternative only for large, high quality borrowers. The fall in real or operating profitability and the fall in the level of stock prices made equities a relatively unattractive way to raise money in the eyes of corporate treasurers and a relatively unattractive investment for households. Looking back, the fact that business financed the bulk of its expanded external financing needs through an increase in debt, mainly short-term debt, was not too surprising given the past behavior of household savers.

Business' response to their reduced profitability was an attempt to better assess their costs and to raise their margins. They looked more critically at the prospective profitability of investments. Higher rates of profitability would help to redress the equity shortage in two ways. They would increase retained earnings and they would make new equity issues more attractive to investors.

Banks also responded to the very rapid expansion in their assets. Early in the period of very rapid growth, they began pricing their loans on a floating rate basis. This passed much of the uncertainty over interest costs on to their loan customers. However, the growth in assets was much more rapid than that in capital—in part, because the loan growth was so explosive and, in part, because the banks were not sure how much of the loan growth was permanent. Moreover, as the economy moved into recession in 1975, some of the businesses with large loans outstanding experienced serious financial problems and even bankruptcy. Many of the loans which financed real estate ventures had to be rescheduled and the difficulties of New York City and New York State seriously eroded the value of the municipal securities portfolio of a large number of major banks. Finally, the world-wide recession gave rise to concern about the quality of the very large volume of foreign loans which banks had made.

The banks are continuing to respond to these difficulties. They are more concerned about the quality of the assets they acquire and are trying to assure themselves that the rates they charge on loans and earn on investments are large enough relative to their cost of funds to warrant the risks they take.

The tastes of savers have always been different enough from the needs of real investors that financial institutions are a necessary part of the American financial scene. The events of 1972-74 exaggerated these differences and put financial institutions under great pressure. The markets and institutions show considerable flexibility, however. Corporations have made their bonds more attractive to households by shortening their maturities. Mutual funds which specialize in bonds, and thereby provide diversification and liquidity to bond portfolios, became more popular with household investors. Banks managed their margins so as to provide themselves with more risk taking capacity.

Just as there is evidence which suggests to some that certain of the financial road-blocks to capital formation are being resolved, there are arguments that the severity of the actual investment needs may well have been somewhat overstated. For example, the shortfalls in capacity which appeared in specific industries in 1973-74 were in part the result of two events which may well not be repeated. First, all the major economies of the world were experiencing a period of strong economic expansion during this period of time. Such a simultaneous boom had not occurred before. These boom conditions increased domestic and foreign demand on United States capacity at the same time they limited the availability of imports. Second, the United States experienced its first devaluation in the postwar period during this time. This event made United States exports much more competitive in world markets than they had been prior to the devaluation. American industry, particularly the basic materials industries, experienced expanding market shares in a rapidly growing world economy at the same time there was a strong economy at home. To the extent that these factors played a major role in the domestic capacity shortages which existed at that time, and may not be repeated, these capacity shortages are less indicative of the basic insufficiency in United States investment and more the result of the unusual features of the time.

In addition, there has been considerable dispute over the preciseness of the linkage between capital investment and productivity growth which plays so important a role in some of the arguments expressing concern over the adequacy of investment. While almost all analysts agree that business investment is an important factor in this process, there is considerable evidence that other factors are also important. Thus there is disagreement over how much to stimulate what types of capital formation in order to stimulate productivity growth. This topic is discussed at some length in Chapter 1 by Fabricant.

Moreover, the data which is often used in international comparisons of capital investment and productivity has been criticized on the grounds that it substantially overstates the actual amount of investment undertaken in countries other than the United States. The argument goes on to state that when proper adjustments are made to take account of international price differences, investment relative to GNP in the United States for the 1950s and 1960s is not lower than in other industrialized countries. Thus, the connection between productivity growth and investment is less precise than some have argued, and the data on the international position of the United States not so adverse as some have tried to make it. (See, for example, "Investment Ratios and Economic Growth Rates," H. Cheng, *Business Review,* Federal Reserve Bank of San Francisco, Spring 1974.)

As the chapters by Fabricant and Eisner make clear, there is considerable dispute over the proposition that there is a special linkage between investment spending and employment levels. Both of these authors deal critically with this argument as it was advanced in the study commissioned by the Department of Labor which was referred to above.

Perhaps the strongest argument advanced by those who oppose the notion of a capital shortage is that such an idea pays much too little attention to the automatic responses of a market oriented economy. In such an economy, the existence of actual or potential capacity shortages not only give evidence of the need for investment, but they also create pressure for price increases in the products involved. With effectively functioning markets, these price increases result in increased profitability, which makes investment outlays more attractive and which also provides a part of the funds with which to finance these outlays. In addition, the rise in the price of the products in industries with relatively small amounts of excess capacity causes some decrease in the demand for these products as users substitute other products where economical. The automatic responses of the market act to reduce the extent of the shortage by expanding supply and curtailing demand.

This description of the evolution of the discussion surrounding a possible capital shortage has attempted to make clear the wide range of arguments advanced in support of such a shortage, the existence of a substantial body of opinion taking the contrary position and the large number of public groups who have spoken out on this issue.

The Chapters in This Volume

The other papers in this volume examine specific elements of the capital shortage argument. The chapters have two purposes. Each chapter is to evaluate the existing literature as it relates to the chapter's area of specific concern. In addition, each author has been asked to report his own conclusions with respect to the appropriate definition of the problem and public policy prescription for its solution.

The first of these chapters, entitled "Perspective on the Capital Requirements Question," written by Solomon Fabricant, is an analysis of the presumptions which lie behind many of the analyses of the real or physical capital shortage question. Fabricant is quite critical of much of this work. He rejects the presumption that the productivity growth or employment projections on which the calculations are usually based are suitable goals. He doubts the implicit assumption that capital formation is *the* determinant of productivty growth and employment. He quarrels with the assumption that capital bears a definite or fixed relation to output and employment. While deploring the tendency to overstate the issue, Fabricant agrees that we need to be concerned about the prospective rates of productivity growth and levels of employment. He proposes we turn away from the tendency to set numerical goals and to look for their achievement primarily by enlarging the scope and scale of government. Instead, he proposes we concentrate our attention on correcting those forces which cause private incentives to be dissipated and private decisions to be interfered with by inflation, mistaken laws or regulations, and imperfections of competition.

The next three chapters deal with aspects of the demand for investment in the years ahead. The first, written by Robert Eisner and entitled "The Outlook for Business Investment," examines this subject in the light of such factors as capacity needs, employment and productivity objectives, profitability and the special issues of energy development, conversion and conservation, and mandated investments in the areas of environmental improvement and job safety. Like Fabricant, Eisner is quite critical of the numerical estimates of physical and financial capital needs. He sees business investment as endogenous rather than predetermined, and depending critically on profitability and the outlook for demand. Eisner argues that the government has its most profound effect on business investment through its policies which bear on macroeconomic stability. He recommends against fiscal policies which he sees as designed to subsidize investment, such as the investment tax credit, accelerated depreciation, and the capital gains exclusions, and in favor of governmental policies which encourage investment only by fostering macroeconomic stability and allowing the market forces of profit and cost to determine the amount and composition of investment.

It is followed by a chapter written by Sherman Maisel, entitled "The Investment Demand for Housing," which examines the recent history and changing share of housing investment in GNP and the likely future course of housing investment in the light of such factors as demography, the growth of apartments, inflation, the rise in financing costs, social pressures, and the pressure for rehabilitation of urban housing. Maisel argues that the problem of housing differs considerably from other types of investment. He finds that the demand for investment in residential housing is likely to grow more slowly than national output. Thus, the overall level of housing demand for saving and resources is not a problem. Fluctuations in the rate of housing construction and a fear that the thrift system which has played so large a role in financing housing in the past cannot stand the type of pressures experienced over the past ten years do present problems, however. Maisel reviews the possible solutions to these problems but finds the forces resisting change to be quite significant.

The final chapter dealing with the investment outlook looks at a different aspect of the problem. It addresses the less tangible, but quantitatively as important, areas of investment in human and knowledge capital. This chapter, written by Richard Freeman and entitled "Investment in Human Capital and Knowledge," is an analysis of the significance of these forms of investment in total capital formation and their effects on productivity, growth, and employment. Freeman finds investment in these areas to have been among the most important sources of productivity growth. After having risen more rapidly than other forms of investment, however, these intangible forms of capital are no longer an expanding share of the nation's capital stock nor a leading area of annual gross capital formation. The return to a major component of human capital, college education, appears to have fallen among the young. The return to a major component of knowledge capital formal research and development, has been found to be quite high in various studies. As the rate of growth of human and knowledge capital decelerates and the return of the former drops, the contribution of these inputs to growth is likely to be less in the future than it was in the past.

Governments play a major role in human and knowledge investment, and Freeman argues they have not done a good job of managing that role. He proposes a major overhaul in the R & D and educational policy-making process to reduce the deleterious effects of what he calls hurky-jurky governmental policies on the job market for R & D personnel and other high-level specialists. He points to the major shift in the nation's research budget from military to civilian research and to the need to better manage the federal assistance to civilian research activities. Finally, he makes several proposals to deal with the declining return to some types of education.

The next chapter, written by Martin Feldstein and entitled "National Saving in the United States," is an analysis of whether the existing structure of incentives to save results in the "correct" level of national saving. Feldstein finds that while the overall level of saving has not changed appreciably relative to GNP, the composition of saving has changed substantially. Personal and corporate saving have become a larger share of the total while the federal government has shifted to the position of a dissaver. Feldstein's central argument is that several forces cause Americans to save less than they "should" and that this results in a significant loss in economic welfare. He argues that while the usual arguments in favor of a capital shortage are incorrect, one can make a convincing case that the present tax on corporate income and the present social security system do create a savings "shortage." By driving a wedge between the true profitability of investment and the profitability which is seen by private investors, these forces induce savers to accumulate much less savings than they would desire to do. Feldstein proposes a shift from taxes on capital income toward taxes on labor income and a change in the structure of benefits and financing of social security in order to allow American savers to obtain the benefits that additional investment would bring.

The final two chapters deal with two of the policy issues we shall raise. The chapter, "Regulation and the Achievement of Productivity Growth and High Employment," by Leonall C. Andersen, is concerned with the role which regulations and regulatory policy can play in achieving these objectives. He concludes that current regulations impose a considerable cost on the economy, primarily by resulting in a less efficient use of resources in production. He also finds regulations to have retarded the growth of employment and of human capital formation. Andersen presents a strategy for regulatory policy which has two elements. Regulation should rely first on enhancing market forces. It should foster information flow to influence consumers and rely on the influence of product liability laws to influence producers. Governmental regulation should be used only when self-regulation fails. Also, when regulating the government should consider, more carefully than it has, the costs of regulation as well as the benefits.

The chapter by Daniel M. Holland, entitled "The Role of Tax Policy," is an analysis of the effects which the existing tax system exerts on the efficiency with which we use our existing resources and upon the level and composition of saving and investment. It evaluates the potential effects which would arise from several revisions in our tax structure. In spite of the fact that tax changes figure prominently in proposals to deal with the "capital shortage," Holland finds that the empirical evidence to date suggests that major changes in the tax structure (so severe as to be ruled out politically) would have only a modest effect on the rate of saving and investment. The effects of likely changes in taxes, he argues, would be still weaker. However, he concludes that a meaningful payoff in terms of efficiency and productivity could come from tax changes which would induce a more efficient utilization of the capital stock we now have. He finds the corporate income tax a major source of distortion and inefficiency in this regard. He proposes a full integration of the corporate and personal tax—an abolition of the corporate income tax *and* the taxation of corporate earnings (both distributed and undistributed) currently as part of stockholders' personal income—on the grounds that it would enhance economic efficiency as well as make the tax system more equitable.

The Policy Issues

The choice between current consumption and current saving and investment is one of the most important facing a society. Saving benefits our society because the capital formation that it allows is the primary determinant of the productivity growth that generates rising living standards. Business investment in research and development contributes to the advancement of knowledge, and expenditures on plant and equipment embody that knowledge in the production level of saving and investment and result in their allocation to less than the most productive uses. Public policy must be designed to offset these forces.

The primary determinant of the overall amount of saving and investment that the U.S. economy will engage in over the next decade will be the level of aggregate demand over this period. Unemployment of labor and capital reduces investment. Therefore, maintaining high levels of employment in our economy is critical to engaging in a large volume of saving and investment. The increased saving and investment that will result from a fuller utilization of labor and capital will create a significant increase in our capital stock and be of enormous value to our economy, especially as it adapts to the changing costs of energy and the increased concerns about the need to protect the environment.

Reasonable price stability will be essential to the achievement of these sustained high rates of employment. Inflation results in more than serious inequities within the economy. It results in a reduction in the total volume of investment, and it directs the allocation of investment away from the uses that would benefit productivity and society he most.

Improving our ability to maintain high employment and a reasonbly stable price level is *the* most important element of any program o stimulate saving and investment and *the* most critical public policy ssue in the area of capital for productivity and jobs.

Other factors of central importance are government tax and exenditure policies and the pricing and regulatory practices used in roduct and financial markets. While these factors have an effect on he overall level of saving, they also exert a significant impact on the llocation of saving to different investment uses and on the efficiency ith which we use the capital stock we have accumulated.

Tax policies drive a wedge between before-tax and after-tax returns savers and limit saving and investment. Reducing this wedge would nhance rewards to savers so that at high levels of income and employent we would enjoy greater saving and investment. By treating difrent types of income or expenditures differently, tax policies exert nportant effects on the allocation of saving and investment. While ther objectives such as tax equity and the distribution of income are ntral to the development of appropriate tax policies, the effects of ese policies on the total and allocation of saving and investment has be one of the central public policy questions relating to capital rmation.

process. Investments in education and on-the-job training more productive and adaptive work force. Investment by th levels of government in such diverse areas as research and ment, roads, health services, and sewer and water facilities al productivity growth and environmental improvement. Inves residential construction provide decent housing for our pc All of these forms of investment contribute to improved li dards in important and interrelated ways.

The relationship between investment and productivity fixed or precise that one can use it to forecast a "need" for i which is helpful in forming an idea as to whether there is ment "gap" or shortage which requires action. This is tru because so many different types of investment contribute tivity. Also, economic relationships are most often not fixe ible and adaptive. Technological requirements do allow sc tution between capital and labor or among different types and labor. Production choices can and do respond to th costs of different factors of production. Moreover, there is c uncertainty over the relationship between expenditures types of investment and their subsequent effects on produc reasonably precise definitions of needs, gaps, or shortages been advanced may well be useful devices to focus publi but they do not seem to be the kinds of things which can by more detailed serious analysis.

While investment expenditures are critical for prod creases, it is not true that specific levels of investment are order to achieve a given overall employment objective in run. Over the longer run, investment has its distinctiv workers through its effects on productivity and their living rather than through its effects on the level of emp the near term, however, the demand for employment is somewhat more rigidly related to specific types of exp workers find it difficult to shift occupation or location or find it difficult to change the labor intensity of their pro cesses. Because of this, there is some sense in the notion o "balance" in the composition of expenditures in the short ment expenditures (in business and elsewhere) would ha role in this balance. Even in the short run, though, on overstate the importance of specific amounts of specific ty ment in determining the level of employment.

A number of forces other than private choices act to

Government expenditures exert significant effects on the level of saving and its allocation to investment. Expenditures in areas such as national defense and police, fire, and public safety help create the stability so essential to high volumes of saving and investment. Without meaning to suggest that their value is solely in their economic impact, government expenditures in education and health contribute in substantial ways to the enhancement of productivity. Other government programs reduce saving and investment, however. As Martin Feldstein points out in Chapter 5, the way we currently manage the social security system may well result in a significant reduction in saving and overall economic well-being. These are but a few examples. A thorough examination of the impact of government expenditure policies on saving and its efficient allocation to investment would be a critical part of the analysis of the forces affecting productivity.

Some forms of government regulation in product and financial markets are of great social value. Nevertheless, the effectiveness of the market system in allocating resources and determining investment decisions has been seriously limited by the imposition of a wide variety of regulatory practices. Private industry has, in fact, often requested this government regulation. These imperfections in the market system have been with us for a long time. Their consequences have been exacerbated by inflation and recession and by the significant changes which are taking place in the costs of energy and raw materials. It is especially important in these circumstances that we take maximum advantage of the assistance that a market-determined set of prices can give as we attempt to allocate our resources among competing uses. Our interest in improved productivity requires us to examine the regulations and other factors which affect the structure of prices and, thereby, resource utilization.

An efficient allocation of financial resources among alternative uses is also critical to an efficiently operating real economy. Our financial markets and institutions have shown resilience and adaptability as well as a capacity to serve our nation well. Yet, regulation often limits the competition for savings among institutions and their freedom to allocate funds to different uses. It inhibits the efficient utilization of saving and reduces the returns to savers. In times of rising rates of inflation and rising market rates of interest, these restrictions cause behavior that threatens the solvency of some financial institutions and drastically reduces the ability of financial markets and institutions to function as rational allocators of capital. Reducing economic instability and inflation would bring a substantial improvement in the ability of our financial institutions and markets to efficiently allocate capital. We must continue to implement changes that enable financial institutions to compete more freely for savings and that provide them with the opportunity to allocate saving in response to the most productive opportunities available in the economy.

In sum, the public policy issues involved in the question of capital for productivity and jobs lie in three areas—fiscal and monetary policies that help to create conditions of high employment with reasonable price stability in order to achieve a high level of saving and investment, government expenditure and tax policies that do not discriminate against saving and that foster its allocation to the most productive uses, and regulatory practices in product and financial markets that encourage competition and strengthen the ability of the market system to allocate resources.

Solomon Fabricant 

1

Perspective on the Capital Requirements Question

One Point of View

A PRELIMINARY WORD

Do not underestimate the difficulty of the question that has been put before us here—the manifold question, what capital is required for a reasonable rate of productivity growth, and also a reasonably remunerative and reasonably full level of employment, and how to assure the formation of this capital in the years ahead. I do not believe that our discussion, careful as preparation for it has been, and impressive as is the roll of participants, can yield an answer on which we would all agree. We lack the firm knowledge and the unanimity of values essential for agreement.

To face this hard fact of life—to place the question in its proper perspective—is already to have made some progress. Perhaps we will agree on some points of fact and policy here and now. More hopefully we may agree on the research, education, and governmental organization that can help eventually to provide the tested knowledge, coherence of values, and effective procedures essential for further progress.

The reasons for this view will be spelled out in the pages following. But the reader may rest assured that I have not hesitated to present my own opinions, for what they are worth, on how to deal—

SOLOMON FABRICANT *is a director and member of the Senior Staff of the National Bureau of Economic Research and Professor Emeritus of Economics at New York University. Author of many books covering a range of economic subjects, Dr. Fabricant has been consultant to many groups in and out of government and has served on two Presidential commissions.*

now—with the problems with which we are concerned. Indeed, summaries of these opinions follow immediately.

THE WRONG APPROACH

Let me say directly, at the risk of being blunt, that I doubt whether it is helpful to estimate, or try to estimate, the capital that will be required for productivity growth and high employment, and the capital that will be forthcoming, in order to determine the difference between capital requirements and supply in the years ahead. The estimates of capital shortage or surplus are estimates of a difference between two prospective aggregates, each vulnerable to error in the underlying assumptions and data. For this and other reasons, I do not think much of the approach that has become rather conventional in recent discussions of the capital requirements question.

More specifically: (1) I reject the presumption that the productivity growth or employment projections on which the calculations are usually based are suitable goals. (2) I doubt the implicit assumption that capital formation is *the* determinant of the productivity growth and employment that will materialize. (3) I quarrel with the additional assumption that capital bears a definite and fixed relation to output and employment—that there is little or no room within present or future technological and institutional arrangements to adapt output or employment to the capital available, or to adapt capital to the output or employment people want. (4) It appears to me, also, that the investment required for energy independence, pollution control, and improved occupational safety and health would be uncertain even if the standards to be met—and the means by which they were to be met—were settled rather than being subjects of great current controversy. (5) Further, I suspect the accuracy of the available data for the particular purpose of making the calculations. (6) Finally, I deplore the tendency, fostered by the conventional approach, to set specific numerical goals and timetables, to treat them as achievable, and then to look for their achievement primarily by enlarging the scope and scale of government—more government regulation, more direct government financing, more government intermediation.

THE RIGHT APPROACH

Whether or not the calculations turn up indications of a capital shortage, we need to be concerned about prospective rates of productivity growth and levels of employment. We do not need dubious calculations to prompt us to ask what to do, and spur us to do what needs to be done. Without estimates of capital shortage, for example, we may reasonably conjecture that interest rate ceilings in an inflationary regime make for uncertainty and inefficiency, not to mention inequity, and thus adversely influence the formation and distribution of capital.

There is already plenty of evidence—at least to suggest—that private incentives are being dissipated and decisions interfered with in one way or another, by inflation, mistaken laws and regulations, and imperfections of competition. These are the incentives and decisions which were fundamental to the growth of productivity and remunerative employment in the past, and fundamental, I believe, also in the future—incentives and decisions to save and invest, to move funds more efficiently from savers to investors, to conserve more expensive and substitute less expensive factors of production within available technology, to devise new technologies in order to increase the output obtained from a unit of labor and capital, to seek out and enter new markets, to develop new materials and more efficient forms of organization, and to seek and to offer employment.

The obstacles to higher productivity and employment relate not only to capital. There can be deleterious effects on employment, for example, from a minimum wage set too high, at least for some prospective workers, and from peculiarities in the unemployment compensation system, such as those to which Martin Feldstein has drawn attention. But a systematic survey would, I am sure, provide a long list even if it were limited to the obstacles affecting capital and finance.

True, many of these obstacles were designed to meet other national goals. We should ask whether the social benefits once sought are still provided, and if so whether these benefits still exceed their cost. And if the answer is not clear enough, we should ask for the data and knowledge needed to narrow our differences of opinion on the benefits and the costs.

With the obsolete or otherwise undesirable obstacles to enterprise eventually lowered, if not removed entirely, with the economy more stable than it has been, the private decisions of savers and investors, producers and consumers, workers and employers could be made more freely, more confidently, and more rationally than now. The energy and knowledge of individuals and business concerns would be put to more effective use—not only in furthering their own private interests, but also in helping others in the community through the more rapid rate of productivity increase and the higher level of remunerative employment that would be generated. Indirectly, also, the values our people place on economic growth and employment, and other social goals as well, would become clearer through the freer choices they could make in the market place and in the other ways they could better dispose of their time and money. This would not make political decisions on these goals unnecessary, but when necessary, the decisions would be better founded.

Some Major Difficulties

If the reader is to appreciate the views I have just summarized, he must understand, first of all, why people can differ so widely on the question to which this meeting is addressed.

COMPETING NATIONAL OBJECTIVES

The accumulation of capital is not itself the objective. Our concern here is with the rate of productivity growth and the level of remunerative employment. But these are not the only national objectives. A better distribution of income, for example, is also an important economic objective; and there are noneconomic goals, of which national defense and political and economic freedom are not the least. One issue, then, is the productivity growth rate and employment level that can or should be considered "reasonable," taking into account other—and, to some degree, competing—national objectives.

Our various national objectives are not always as inconsistent or as competitive as is often supposed. Greater economic freedom favors increase in productivity, as Adam Smith argued long ago. And fuller employment helps to improve the distribution of income. Yet to a degree, the goals are competitive. How much productivity growth or employment we really want, then, depends on how much we care to pay for them in terms of a slower approach to, or perhaps even some retreat from, our other national goals.

People will differ on what the price should be and whether or not it is worth paying. In a word, the desired rate of productivity growth and level of employment are part of the question. The productivity growth we want is not necessarily the 3 percent per annum of the postwar period, or the somewhat lower rate of the past decade. The employment level we want is not necessarily the level implied by the 4 percent rate of unemployment in mid-1955, the "full-employment" base used by the Council of Economic Advisers in 1962 (and since) to calculate potential GNP.

CAPITAL IS NOT THE ONLY SOURCE OF PRODUCTIVITY GROWTH AND HIGH EMPLOYMENT

Another issue is the amount of capital that is "required" to attain any specified rate of productivity growth or level of employment under stated and presumably possible, likely or desirable conditions. The volume of capital formation will certainly influence these. But so will numerous other factors. They range from the composition of the labor force to the economies associated with large-scale production. If capital is taken to mean only tangible capital, as it often is, also to be counted among the "other factors" are various forms of intangible capital, such as technology.

In substantial degree, the several factors are necessary complements to one another. Sophisticated equipment cannot be maintained and run without trained workers. To some degree, however, capital and the other factors are also substitutes for one another. Output may be raised—up to a point—by adding more capital *or* by improving the quality of labor. This means that determination of the quantity of capital required is not a straight-forward engineering calculation. It depends on the relative costs of the several factors of production, as well as on the techniques of production.

Further, policies directed specifically at increasing capital formation may appreciably affect—favorably or unfavorably—the other sources of productivity growth and high employment. For the economic system *is* a system. It is not easy to push or pull one element of the system without causing changes in related elements. And when the policy actions proposed relate to taxes, there may well be multiple direct as well as indirect effects on the other factors.

A sound assessment of the volume of capital required, and a sound choice among the policies to attain it, then, cannot finally be made without due regard to the role of the other factors. People will differ on what is sound. Here also our private interests often clash and we often attach different relative values even to the goals we all favor.

LIMITED KNOWLEDGE

There will be differences among us also because of limitations on our knowledge. What we know of the historical facts, and of the interrelationships among the facts, falls short of what we need to come to reasonably firm conclusions about investment and savings and their bearing on productivity and employment.

The widely used GNP measure of national output, for example, does not cover most household production or the quality of the air we breathe and the water we drink. And not all that is covered—especially governmental and other services—is measured satisfactorily. Economists have barely begun, to cite another example, to establish the relative importance of the various forms of intangible capital. And even the measurement of tangible capital for the present purpose leaves something to be desired, as is indicated by the variety of measurements turned out in recent years.

Further, quantitative projections of capital requirements necessarily rest on the expected relation between the projected rates of growth of national output or of employment and the stock of capital. As I mentioned, these ratios depend on technology and the relative prices of all factors of production. We have only rough ideas of the current magnitude, not to mention the future magnitude, for example, of the increase in capital facilities that is technically needed, at a given level of output, to offset—or contribute to—a given decrease in labor input.

The same can be said, of course, of the projections of capital supplies, and thus also of the extent to which projected supplies will exceed or meet or fall short of projected requirements. And it can be said as well, how, in the end, demand and supply will be reconciled, or if not reconciled, of the form in which the gap between them will appear. What, for example, is the propensity to save out of a given income? Economists know more now than they used to know about this relationship. But this, in significant part, means that they now realize how little they used to know. Even today, we have only some more or less inconsistent hypotheses of the effect on the savings rate of Social Security and prepaid medical care, both of which have been widespread for some time. And the future will bring changes in the propensity to save in ways difficult to foretell.

Involved is not only technological change in the sense used in describing improvements in manufacturing processes, but also change in financial institutions and markets. Some of the latter changes are caused by new laws and regulations, or revisions (or enforcement) of old, deliberately designed to improve the working of the economy, as in the case of bank deposit and mortgage insurance. Some arise as incidental effects of economic growth and development, as in the case of urbanization, and the relative increase in the importance of the service industries. Some arise from financial innovations developed and introduced by enterprising men, to which William Silber, in the New York University project on capital markets in 1975-85, rightly draws attention. We can be sure that industrial and financial innovations will take place. When making projections, however, no one can confidently predict just what the innovations will be and just when they will become operative.

It may seem surprising, in view of these uncertainties, that the various projections of capital requirements and supplies gathered together by Gary Fromm, for example, and presented to a Congressional Committee by Henry Wallich in March 1976, do not differ more radically. The reason, I think, is plain. The data used and the assumptions made in preparing the various estimates are similar, despite the range of possible choices. This, I suspect, partly reflects the fact that few estimators like to end up with extreme projections, that is, with projections that differ substantially from those of others. Partly also it may be the burden or inconvenience of preparing alternative estimates derived from a variety of assumptions and a variety of data—not all possible assumptions, of course, but also not only the "conventional" assumptions; not all possible data, but at least more than those limited to the national accounts—and trying to attach to each some probability of its materializing. In short, there is a strong element of convention in the preparation of economic projections, just as there is in the financial accounting of business enterprises. And the former, as much as the latter, is not necessarily more realistic as a result.

Especially surprising is the rather general presumption that the business cycle, of which we were all forcefully reminded by the recession of 1973-75, may be ignored in the several projections of the decade ahead. Fromm notes that only one of the eight studies summarized by him explicitly anticipates another recession during the next ten year period. It is no less premature now than it was in the early 1970s to follow what seems to have become another convention —that somehow the private economy has been freed of the characteristics, inherent in its nature, that make for cyclical fluctuation—that business cycles are entirely due to mistakes of government—that the assumptions about government policy embedded in the projections preclude the onset of recessions.

Which Capital?

In most discussions of the possibility of a capital shortage, it is tangible capital to which reference is being made. In the Department of Commerce study presented in the January 1976 *Economic Report of the President,* it is only the fixed tangible capital of business which is considered. But there are inventories as well as plant and equipment. There is intangible as well as tangible capital. And these various forms of capital are held by households, nonprofit organizations and governments, as well as by business.

That the tangible capital of business enterprises is a major form of capital, well worth the strong interest in it, is obvious. The other forms are not negligible, however, as is evident—even after plenty of allowance for unavoidably rough edges around the estimates—in the calculations provided in a study at the National Bureau of Economic Research by John Kendrick. Indeed, in 1969—the latest year for which his data are available—the net tangible assets of business (valued in 1969 prices) constituted little more than about 20 percent of the nation's total capital. (It would be even less had I not excluded from the total certain items of investment in human capital, particularly the cost of rearing children, about which I have some qualms.)

The percentage was low first because intangible capital, "produced" by research and development, by education and on-the-job training, was very substantial. In fact, it was not much smaller than the stock of tangible capital. Intangibles accounted for 45 percent of the grand total of all capital. Second, of the stock of tangible capital, business held only about 40 percent. Families held 36 percent, and government—even excluding military assets—the other 23 percent.

These estimates, it should be remembered, are valued net, after deducting accumulated depreciation, obsolescence, and depletion. Apart from the usual errors of estimate already mentioned, there are various conceptual and other questions that get considerable attention in professional discussions of the contribution of capital formation to productivity growth—precisely one of the subjects with which we are concerned—and we had better be aware of them.

One question relates to the estimate of depreciation and other capital consumption. There is a certain arbitrary element—or at least an element of judgment—in the choice of the period or of the "lifetime" of the assets over which they are presumed to lose value; and of the time pattern of this loss, which may be according to a straight line or on some "accelerated" basis. The resulting estimates may differ significantly. It is not for nothing that business financial statements are required to state whether the depreciation reported is the same as the depreciation accepted for tax purposes.

The other question concerns the choice, for measuring the contribution of capital to change in productivity, between gross capital assets, before deducting reserves for depreciation, and net capital assets, after such deduction. To avoid getting involved in technical details, let me say only that I would choose net capital assets. Kendrick, whose capital estimates I have cited, would choose gross. And Denison, on whose analysis our discussion of the sources of productivity growth will rest, prefers a weighted average of the two, with gross more heavily weighted than net. Here too, it can make a significant difference which is used. Between 1948 and 1969, the gross stock of tangible assets used by business firms (excluding residences operated commercially) rose at an average annual rate of 3.5 percent; for the net stock, the average rate was 4.2 percent.

Whichever estimates are used, it is important to note that the rates of increase over the postwar period of the different types of capital varied widely. For the educational capital used in business, for example, the rate was about 0.6 percent per annum according to Denison—much less than the rates for tangible capital previously mentioned. (However, this does not mean, as we shall see, that the contribution to growth of output or output per manhour of tangible capital relative to that of educational capital was in the same proportion.)

This variation in the rates of growth of different forms of capital is important because the sources of the funds that finance different types of capital, and the capital markets through which the funds flow to investors, are also different. This is why there can be, as some put it, a shortage of capital for some purposes, such as housing, at the same time that there is capital being offered for other purposes. As might be expected, the institutional and other obstacles to the free flow of funds between markets and uses have not remained constant. Changes in regulations, for example, do take place, even if with a lag, and even if not sufficiently to meet such problems as those caused by inflation. And the innovative activities of financial entrepreneurs are stimulated by the opportunities opened up by the differences among markets. Adaptations of this sort will surely occur also in the years ahead, but how rapidly and in what way is uncertain, as I have already noted. And there are strong differences of opinion on what to do to improve the situation. Here is another reason why the question before us is so difficult.

Capital and Productivity

IMPORTANCE OF PRODUCTIVITY GROWTH

We are concerned about the rate of productivity growth because it is the major source of the economic growth that enables us to raise our standard of living.

During the post-World War II period, for example, the nation's private product (excluding government, for which an adequate measure of output is not available) rose at an average annual rate of 3.4 percent, according to the U. S. Bureau of Labor Statistics. The number of persons working rose by only slightly over 1 percent per annum. Offsetting half of this increase in numbers was an annual reduction in hours per person of almost 0.5 percent. Total hours worked by all persons therefore increased by only 0.6 percent per year. Our measure of growth in productivity (output per manhour) is, then, the difference between 3.4 and 0.6, or 2.8 percent per year. We can say, with some qualification for interaction between employment and productivity, that by far the big factor in increasing output was not more or harder work but more productivity. Its contribution was not the same in other periods, but in every earlier period of similar length, productivity was a major factor and in the great majority of periods it was the preponderant factor. When the calculation is shifted to a comparison of output per hour with hours of work per capita (instead of total manhours), in accounting for the increase in output per capita (instead of total output), the importance of productivity becomes even more dominant.

When we are concerned about productivity, it is natural to be concerned about capital. No record, statistical or otherwise, of any country fails to show an upward trend in productivity and at the same time an upward trend in tangible capital per worker. This is by no means a coincidence. There are good economic reasons why the two would move up together. Increase in productivity and the income it brings generate capital formation. And capital formation helps to increase productivity. Indeed, the classical economists concentrated largely on tangible capital as the source of productivity increase.

On this, economists have learned better. As we shall see later, more sophisticated analysis, using more comprehensive and better statistical data, makes clear that increase in tangible capital is a source, but not the only or even the dominant source of increase in productivity.

RETARDATION IN PRODUCTIVITY GROWTH

Concern about productivity growth was heightened by the halt in this growth during the recession of 1973-75. For the first time in twenty-five years, productivity declined for as many as six quarters, two in 1973 and all four in 1974.

The cyclical turn that came early in 1975 has already restored productivity to its previous peak level and a bit more. However, the index is not yet up to the value it would have reached had growth continued at its long-term average rate. On the basis of earlier cyclical experience, we may expect that the increase in productivity will continue. Whether the advance will push the level up to the trend line, before the next recession occurs, is still a question, however.

It is a question that troubled observers even before the recent recession began. Some felt that during the past decade or so, the rate of productivity growth had fallen to a lower level. Others, broadening the perspective to the entire postwar period, asked whether productivity growth had not been undergoing gradual retardation. According to calculations made by the National Commission on Productivity in 1975, the rate of increase in output per manhour in the private economy did tend to decline gradually during the postwar period. The trend rate of increase was about 3.6 percent per annum around 1947, 3 percent around 1960, and by 1974 it was down to 2.4 percent.

Similar cyclical declines in the rate of productivity growth occurred also in other industrialized countries, and there is some evidence also of retardation in their trend rate of growth. But their average rates of productivity growth have generally been higher than that of the United States. Here, of course, is another source of concern about productivity growth in the United States—our position in international trade, and still more important, our political and military position.

SOURCES OF PRODUCTIVITY GROWTH

Concern about the relatively slow rate of productivity growth in recent years has, as might be expected, generated several explanations. One of these being stressed is a low rate of tangible capital formation. Before saying more about these rather casual explanations, it is well to acquaint ourselves with more carefully prepared quantitative estimates of the sources of productivity growth in the United States during the postwar period.

These, for 1948-69, are readily derived from the valuable researches at the Brookings Institution by Edward Denison. His estimates apply only to the private business sector for reasons already alluded to. Government is excluded because output measures are not available; and household "production," largely of housing services (which are included in the official estimates of GNP and in the BLS series), is excluded because the national accounts do not cover the household labor that supports the production of housing services.

During 1948-69, the tangible capital of business firms—inclusive of inventories, plant and equipment, and land—rose at a rate of about 2.9 percent per annum, significantly less than the rate of 3.7 percent for total business product. A portion of the resulting increase in the stock of tangible capital was used to outfit, so to speak, the growing labor force employed by business enterprises—a labor force growing at the rate of 1 percent per annum, in terms of number of persons and 0.6 percent in terms of manhours. Tangible capital per manhour available for raising productivity, then, rose at a rate of roundly 2.3 percent.

It should not be presumed, however, that the percentage increase in productivity would equal, or even come near to equaling, the percentage increase in tangible capital per manhour. The resulting increase in output per manhour depends on what each additional unit of tangible capital adds to output, given the other factors of production (including intangible capital) as well as on the increase in the number of units of capital. As do other economists, Denison assumes that tangible capital is compensated in accordance with what it adds to output, an assumption reasonable in the circumstances—that is, under competition and with regard to long-term changes. On this assumption the marginal product of tangible capital may be inferred from its rate of compensation recorded in the income statistics compiled by the Department of Commerce. According to these figures, the income received for the use of tangible capital, during the postwar period, approximated 20 percent of the national income. Each 1 percent increase in tangible capital per manhour may then be expected to raise output per manhour by two-tenths of 1 percent. The contribution to productivity growth of the increase in tangible capital, so measured, is 2.3 multiplied by 0.2, or a bit under 0.5. This is about a sixth or seventh of the increase in productivity over the period under consideration. The rest, 2.7 percent, of the 3.2 percent rate of increase in productivity, is to be attributed to other sources.

What other sources? The identification and weighing of these depends on the availability of data and the willingness of the estimator to use his judgment when the evidence is less than adequate. Although necessarily rough, Denison's estimates are better and more detailed than most, and deserve the attention they have attracted.

Improvement in the quality of labor, brought about through formal education, is one such source. Another, negative in sign, resulted from a shift in the age-sex mix of the labor force toward less qualified workers. Together, these changes in the quality of labor yielded a contribution to growth of productivity of about 0.4 percentage points. Economics resulting from increase in the scale of operations, an entirely different type of factor, provided another 0.5 points. A net decline in the intensity of demand, reflecting differences in the stage of the business cycle in 1948 and 1969, tended to reduce productivity growth by 0.2 percentage points. Offsetting this was a contribution of the same magnitude resulting from the improved efficiency associated with the reduction in hours per person at work. Better resource allocation, reflecting a shift of employment from farm and nonfarm self-employment to more productive activity elsewhere (as measured by market values), contributed 0.4 percentage points.

The total of these contributions is 1.8 percent. The remaining 1.4 percentage points are accounted for by Denison under the heading of advances in technology and other sources "not elsewhere classified."

Education and technology could of course be classified as intangible capital, as Kendrick has done. The other sources distinguished by Denison would then be those accounting for the efficiency with which tangible and intangible capital is utilized.

Questions about the accuracy of the data and of the assumptions—questions of which Denison is well aware and takes the trouble to discuss—arise here, of course, as they do in making projections of capital requirements and supplies. Some sources of productivity growth have been omitted, or rather included in the "n.e.c." category. Of these, on-the-job training and net improvements in the health of the labor force are shown separately in Kendrick's capital estimates. Land constitutes another questionable item. Denison, skeptical of the available data, assumes no change in its physical volume, which means that he assumes no contribution by land to total growth and a negative contribution by land to growth in output per manhour.

There are also questions about interrelationships among the various sources and the extent to which their separate contributions can be determined. To some extent, as already mentioned, inputs complement one another. Some technological change is embodied in tangible capital in order to be put to use in production. On this reasoning, the contribution of technology depends in part on the rate of increase in capital. On the other hand, the contribution of tangible capital, in Denison's form of analysis, is being credited with some of the contribution of technology (and other factors) that reduces the real cost of capital goods. In either case, however, the question is largely one of how to classify some of the contributions to productivity growth between two types of capital—technology, an intangible form, or plant and equipment, a tangible form.

The several inputs are also, in some degree, substitutes for one another. Doubling the rate of increase in capital (the rates of increase in other inputs constant), for example, would not double capital's contribution because of diminishing returns.

There are, finally, questions concerning the data utilized in the calculations. One is about the choice between gross and net assets, and another about the choice among different depreciations formulas, questions which I have already raised. Still another is the choice among various input-stock ratios, discussed at some length in the technical literature, which I have not mentioned. The estimates of capital's contribution to productivity growth depend on these choices. The results will be different, and often significantly different.

Variation in the Tangible Capital-output Ratio

The figures cited for the period 1948-69 indicate a decline in the ratio of tangible capital to output. This is not unusual. Presumably during this period, as in other periods, the decline reflects the net balance among several factors. One is the substitution of tangible capital for labor under pressure from a rising price of labor relative to the price of the services of capital goods. This tends to increase the capital-output ratio. Working in the other direction, however, is increase in the efficiency with which both labor and capital are used in production. This tends to reduce the capital-output ratio. Perhaps another factor tending to reduce the capital-output ratio is the rise of the service industries, which are presumed to require or to use less tangible capital per worker than, say, manufacturing. But this tendency is less clear and in any case, less strong, for some service industries use more capital per worker than do some manufacturing industries.

That the tangible capital-output ratio is unstable is indicated also by the fact that changes in it occurred within the postwar period, and in similar short periods before World War II, allowing (as we should) for cyclical fluctuations. During the shorter periods distinguished by Denison, for example, his estimates of potential national income (which reflects an adjustment for the business cycle) rose in the nonresidential business sector by 2.2 percent per annum between 1929 and 1941, while reproducible tangible capital remained constant, on net balance. During 1941-48, the two rates of change were, respectively, 3.0 and 1.7 percent; during 1948-53, 4.5 and 4.0 percent; during 1953-64, 3.2 and 2.9 percent; and during 1964-69, 4.9 and 4.8 percent. Inclusive of land, the rates of increase in tangible capital would be smaller in every subperiod. In other words, the tangible capital-output ratio declined during these subperiods at rates ranging from 2.5 to 0.1 percent per annum. It is hardly necessary to retell the story in terms of changes in the tangible capital-labor ratio. It is sufficient to say that this ratio also varied appreciably from one period to another.

Change in industry mix, as has already been mentioned, could alter the national tangible capital-output ratio even if that ratio were constant in every industry. But the ratio has not been constant. One of the interesting contributions of the National Bureau's large project on capital formation and financing under Simon Kuznets' direction during the 1950s bears on this point. In the case of manufacturing and mining, for example, the tangible capital-output ratio, measured in a variety of ways, first rose for some decades and then declined. In the regulated industries, the general trend was rather sharply downward, with the rate of decline diminishing over time.

If the trends within industries were fairly smooth—and did not change direction—one could project them into the future, as the Department of Commerce has done in its study of fixed capital requirements. And one could try, further, to allow for increases in the capital-output ratio arising from efforts to achieve energy independence, to reduce pollution, and to meet higher standards of occupational safety and health. But the trends are not smooth and do change direction. And the additional capital that is required for energy, pollution control, and improved working conditions is still uncertain. Inevitably, therefore, troublesome doubts arise concerning the results of these calculations.

Earlier I mentioned recent speculations about the causes of the retardation of productivity growth during the postwar period. Unfortunately, these speculations are hardly more than off-the-cuff theorizing, with few exceptions. Not surprisingly, therefore, they are somewhat inconsistent with one another. A shortage of tangible capital in the past decade is generally included in such a list. But it includes also, to illustrate current thinking, such factors as the influx of new and inexperienced workers, deterioration of workers' attitudes, a tendency toward slackness on the part of management, the cumulation of imperfections of competition in labor and commodity markets, and increased government interference. Even the more formal estimates made in this connection, particularly of recent changes in tangible capital per worker or manhour, yield inconsistent results. In its Fourth Annual Report (March 1975), the National Commission on Productivity and Work Quality noted that according to the Bureau of Labor Statistics the tangible capital-labor ratio in the private economy grew more rapidly during 1966-72 than during 1947-66; but other statisticians, using different concepts and measurements, show little change in the capital-labor ratio during 1966-72 and a slightly higher change during 1950-66. The Commission concluded that one cannot, with any confidence, assess the impact of tangible capital formation on the recent trend of productivity.

The points I have been trying to make are, I think, reasonably sound. Tangible capital is an important factor accounting for productivity growth. But there are other factors, and they also are important, to judge from the quantitative analyses of Denison and other careful students of economic growth as well as the speculations concerning the retardation of productivity growth during the postwar period. Further, both the systematic and the intuitive analyses are consistent with my other main point, namely that factors affecting productivity, including tangible capital, change in relative importance over time. In short, the concept of a definite and fixed tangible capital requirement, and the estimates of future tangible capital requirements, are of doubtful validity.

Capital and Employment

When we are concerned with the cyclical expansion of employment, the prospective volume of tangible capital formation may hardly be ignored. We might then put our question in terms of the amount of tangible capital formation, along with the other segments of aggregate demand, including consumption and government expenditures, required to reach full employment. For reasons given in the discussion of productivity growth, I would not take these estimates as seriously as some do. But when our concern is with the long-term level of employment and unemployment in the decades ahead, I would not consider the estimates worth making. A quick glance back at the economic development of the United States, or at the world today, would not reveal any correlation between the average stock of tangible capital and the average level of unemployment.

What would be revealed is a close relation between tangible and intangible capital per worker and the level of remuneration of those employed. What workers produce and what they earn depends importantly (though not entirely) on the tangible and intangible capital with which they pursue their tasks. It is this relationship that I wish to emphasize.

There is a second point also worth raising. In the discussion of productivity growth it was noted that capital and labor are, to a degree, substitutes for one another. Capital can displace labor, a possibility that often raises strong resistance against mechanization and other forms of capital formation. My second point deals with this and other problems of adjustment to the developments associated with capital formation and productivity growth.

Effects on Income

The formation of capital, when it means an increase in capital per worker (as it generally does), tends to raise labor productivity. It does so, first, by improving the quality of labor; second, by equipping labor with more and better tools and equipment; and third, by improving the processes of production. Higher labor productivity, in turn, means higher labor income, not only more wages and salaries but also bigger fringe benefits. Only a few decades ago the fringe benefits might have been ignored with little error resulting, but paid vacations, medical insurance, and pensions are now too large to be so treated. If a value could be put on it, one could add also improvement in working conditions.

Improvement in the quality of labor results from investment by families, governments, and business enterprises. There is, of course, the education and training that make up a large chunk of the country's intangible capital. There is also investment in health, which affects productivity. The prepaid medical insurance covered in fringe benefits helps to finance medical expenditures, but so do higher family incomes. There are also public and private investments in water, sewage, and hospital facilities, in medical research, and in such things as safeguards against accident.

Capital tends to raise the productivity even of labor of a fixed quality. An unskilled worker in the United States today, for example, is more productive than the unskilled worker in the United States of earlier generations, and than the unskilled worker in other countries. It is the greater volume of tangible and intangible capital per worker —greater in the United States today than it was before or than it is elsewhere—that enables our unskilled workers to produce more.

The higher productivity of labor leads to higher real incomes by raising money wages and fringe benefits, as employers compete for workers; and by reducing or keeping down (relative to wage rates) the prices of the goods and services produced, as enterprises compete for markets with one another.

Increase in capital is not the only source of increase in productivity, as we have seen. However, defined broadly, as it should be, to include investment in intangible as well as tangible capital, and in research and development as well as education and training, capital is the preponderant source. Capital formation then, is also the preponderant source of the increasingly remunerative rates of income earned by labor.

Problems of Labor Adjustment

There is no doubt that automation, mechanization, or other investment that makes for higher labor productivity can wipe out jobs. The cigar makers before the war, the cotton pickers after the war—history is thronged with workers who could bear witness to the suffering caused by labor-saving developments. But, as I have said elsewhere, theirs is not the entire story, nor even the larger part of it.

It is true that the direct effect of increases in output per manhour—whether because of capital formation or otherwise—is to reduce unemployment. Increase in an industry's output per manhour is identical with a reduction in the number of manhours the industry employs per unit of output. When all other things remain unchanged, this reduction in employment per unit makes for a reduction in the industry's aggregate employment. The bigger the rate of increase in the industry's output per manhour—ignoring its indirect effects—the bigger is the direct pressure on the employment it offers.

But there are indirect effects of productivity increases, and these may not be ignored. All other things, in other words, are not equal. A rise in an industry's productivity also presses down on the price of the industry's product. The more rapidly productivity rises, the greater tends to be the reduction in selling price. If demand is at all responsive to price—and it would be extraordinary if demand were entirely inelastic—output will rise and thus partially restrain the effect of higher output per manhour. Indeed, if demand is sufficiently responsive to the decline in price, the resulting rise in output could even exceed the rise in output per manhour. The number of manhours worked in the industry would then go up, not down.

The historical record informs us that this event is not infrequent. In the long-run, industries in which productivity has risen more rapidly than in the economy as a whole have often raised their employment by a *larger* percentage than did industry generally, and not by a smaller percentage, as might be supposed. We find, correspondingly, that industries in which productivity has seriously lagged have often raised their employment *less* than industry generally or have actually cut employment. On the other hand, there have also been industries in which relatively rapid increases in productivity have been accompanied by relative or even absolute declines in employment. Farming is the outstanding example of our generation.

On the whole, the historical record indicates no general association of relatively high trend rates of increase in productivity with low trend rates of increase in employment, and lagging increases in productivity with accelerating employment. Over the long run a better than average increase in an industry's productivity sometimes meant a better and sometimes a less than average increase in employment. A less than average increase in productivity was sometimes accompanied by a less than average increase (or even a decrease) in employment and sometimes by a better than average increase.

The course of employment in an industry reflects not only what has been happening to the industry's own productivity but also what has been happening to productivity in the country at large. The increase in national productivity and the higher income it has brought, has tended to raise the demand for the output of many industries. Higher national productivity has in this way supported or increased the demand for workers in these industries and often offset the direct effects of the industries' own productivity changes when these effects tended to be adverse to employment in these industries.

Especially great, of course, were the effects of increased income on the output and employment of industries that produce the goods and services that people buy more freely as they grow richer. Although these were often industries in which productivity lagged and costs and prices rose, the record shows that increased national productivity helped sustain and often raise employment in them. People wanted the products of these industries even though those products had become more expensive; with their income advancing, they were able to pay the higher prices. Many of the health service industries provide examples of rising prices accompanied by rising rather than falling demand.

Nor is this the end of the story. Because population and the total labor force increase, industries in which employment is declining relatively may nevertheless be industries in which the absolute number of jobs is stable or even rising.

Further, even when an industry's employment is declining absolutely, unemployment is not necessarily created as a result. When the pace of decline is slow enough, the reduction is absorbed by the normal decline in the length of the workweek, one of the fruits of rising productivity. And normal attrition by retirement also plays a part.

Probably more important, workers often go off voluntarily to a new job in a growing industry because the new job pays better than the old job. For although technological change may destroy jobs, it also creates new jobs to which workers are attracted by better pay even before their old jobs have become obsolete.

Yet it is a fact that technological and other changes within an industry can create serious problems of adjustment. Not everybody whose job has become obsolete is ready for retirement, or has moved off to a new job on the West Coast, or is intellectually and physically able to learn a new trade.

The effects of technological changes on particular groups of workers can be serious, more serious than would be estimated when attention is concentrated solely on the total number employed in an industry. The introduction of a machine may create new jobs for machine tenders and equipment maintenance men, but not for the men whose crafts have become obsolete.

Nor are the problems of adjustment always minor even when the old skills are still in demand. Technological change may demand adjustment not only to new work and working conditions but also to quite different modes of living. When that is the case, as it was in many farming communities after the war, the problem of adjustment becomes especially severe.

The problem of adjustment depends not only on the rate of technological development and the other factors that make labor adjustment necessary, but also on the capacity of the country to adjust. There is evidence that this capacity has grown on net balance. A higher level of education, better transportation and communication, a greater reserve in the form of savings—these, which are identified among the sources of higher productivity, help also to ease the problem of adjustment.

In addition, improvement has taken place in aids to adjustment, including unemployment insurance, employment services, retraining programs, and the like. And there has also been improvement in private arrangements, worked out in labor-management agreements, to study and ease the problems of adjustment to technological change.

Whether or not the difficulties suffered by workers in adjusting to changes in the labor market are greater now than they were in earlier times, most of us would agree that the suffering should be alleviated. The solution, it must be stressed, is not to impede capital formation or technological development, or the other factors that make for higher productivity. Higher productivity is the source of the greater economic welfare we want for ourselves and our neighbors. Nor is the solution to cut hours of work so rapidly as to take the fruits of higher productivity in a larger proportion of leisure and a smaller proportion of goods and services than most of us like. Instead, arrangements must be made whereby society as a whole helps shoulder the problems of adjusting to the rising productivity—to see to it that the problems do not fall only on the backs of those immediately affected. And where legal or other obstacles impede the hiring of young or old or handicapped or minority workers, or workers and employers are induced by the terms of the unemployment insurance or welfare or social security systems to swell the number of unemployed—or the number reported as unemployed—these systems should be subjected to close examination and revision.

Perhaps I should state explicitly what I have just implied, that the standard by which the "fullness" of employment is judged also requires reconsideration. Economists, aware of the changes in the age-sex mix of the labor force that has taken place during the postwar period, of the broadening of the unemployment insurance system, and of the ambiguities inherent in the concept and measurement of employment, unemployment, and the labor force, have recently been drawing attention to this need.

Concluding Remarks

I started out by confessing my uneasiness with the projections of capital requirements and of the other quantities that enter current discussions of long-run economic policy. Perhaps my jaundiced view reflects experience, with projections and forecasts, that is no longer relevant. Maybe I am not up on the current state of the art. But my admission of this possibility means only that I am willing to be convinced; I am not yet convinced. As for my reservations about the accuracy of available data and the limitations on knowledge, it should be understood that these apply to the use of these data and this knowledge in the present connection. For many other purposes I hold no such reservations.

Let me acknowledge further that what I had to say about policy was very sketchy—necessarily so. And to avoid misunderstanding, I want to point out also that what I favor is not altogether contrary to what is imbedded in the policy assumptions underlying the projections, put in to balance expected capital requirements with expected capital supplies. I do not mean to question the value of every proposal linked to the projections. But by the same token, what I believe makes sense is not quite the same as the policies to which most projectors and many others seem to be inclined.

The big difference, I think, is in our attitudes toward the role of government. No one would deny that government has a vital part to play in our nation's economic life. "The practical question," as Arthur F. Burns stated it years ago, "is how that part will be played." As I see it, government's role is primarily to provide the environment within which, in the words used earlier, the private decisions of savers and investors, producers and consumers, workers and employers, can be made more freely, more confidently, and more rationally than they can now be made. This requires that government strengthen competition rather than monopoly; contribute to economic stability rather than to instability; promote domestic peace and tranquility rather than stir up dissension.

A few final words: In the nature of the case, improving the capacity of the economy to deal more adequately with old problems, and adapt better to new developments, is a slow process. It took literally generations of effort before economists could begin to understand the problems of productivity growth and employment and to clarify their concepts of saving, investment, and capital. It took the Great Depression and a world war to bring the country to agreement on the Employment Act of 1946. And as for governmental procedures, fiscal 1977 is the first year in which a budget reform act might help to restrain increases in federal expenditures. Our expectations must be tempered.

Yet we could be more optimistic if objective economic and social research and the provision of statistical data were being undertaken on a larger scale and with greater emphasis on basic questions than the country has so far been willing to finance or allow the time for. It would help if stronger efforts were being made to better the understanding by our people of the operation of the economy, and of what is possible and impossible through government action—and when possible, at what cost. It would help if efforts to rationalize government organization were more vigorously pursued, and differences on the locus of authority more decently composed.

I close on a hopeful note. Some signs do point to a climate of public opinion increasingly favorable in the respects I have just mentioned. There is, after the recent trying experience to track closely short-term changes in inventories, prices, employment, and other important economic variables, a greater willingness to spend money on widening and strengthening the nation's statistical intelligence base. This is bound to improve also the econometric models, and the projections derived from them, that depend heavily on the statistical data available. The Joint Council on Economic Education, which was organized shortly after World War II, is taking steps to extend its activities. And there is at least some talk of a "sunset" bill, or something like it, to subject the accomplishments and costs of various federal spending programs to systematic periodic review, and termination if not reenacted. Nor has the last nail yet been driven into the coffin of the "deregulation program." It will be progress even if—or also if—we back up from earlier steps that we come to recognize were misguided.

Robert Eisner

2

The Outlook for Business Investment[1]

Business investment is and should be endogenous.

By that we mean, the rate at which profit-seeking enterprises acquire additional plant, equipment, and inventories is something that comes out of the interworkings of the entire economic system. At least, that is the way it is under the rules of a free enterprise, competitive system. In such a system, the rate of investment is not imposed as a prior constraint. It is the resultant of the utility-maximizing saving propensities of households and the profit-maximizing production decisions of business.

Capital "Requirements"

It has been widely alleged that future productivity, prosperity and growth as well as critical needs in the United States economy depend upon major business investment. In this connection, there have been many recent efforts to project "investment needs."

A New York Stock Exchange study pointed to a capital "shortage"

ROBERT EISNER *is William R. Kenan Professor of Economics at Northwestern University and Senior Research Associate of the National Bureau of Economic Research. He has written extensively on the determinants of business investment. Dr. Eisner is a Fellow of the American Academy of Arts and Sciences and of the Econometric Society. He is currently Associate Editor of* The Review of Economics and Statistics *and has been a member of the Board of Editors of* The American Economic Review.

1 Parts of this paper have been taken, with revision, from "The Corporate Role in Financing Future Investment Needs," prepared for the forthcoming Congressional Joint Economic Committee volume, *U.S. Economic Growth from 1975-1985: Prospects, Problems and Patterns.*

of some $650 billion by 1985.[2] Treasury Secretary William E. Simon, comparing his estimates of capital requirements in current dollars over the next decade with capital expenditures in current dollars over the last decade, came out with a gap of over $2.5 trillion without however noting the noncomparability of prices. We also have estimates by Bosworth, Duesenberry, and Carron and by Chase Econometrics, Data Resources Incorporated, Reginald Jones, Benjamin Friedman, the Wharton School, the Federal Reserve Board, Allen Sinai and Roger Brinner (for DRI), a special study group of the Bureau of Labor Statistics, and the National Planning Association.[3] Projections of gross private domestic investment as a ratio of gross national product over the years 1974 to 1985, or various subsets of that period, range from 13.9 percent (Chase Econometrics, 1975-80) to 19 percent (Chase Bank, 1975-85, and Wharton, 1982).

Some of the figures in this set are not out of line with past experience. Indeed, the 15.8 percent ratio of gross private domestic investment to gross national product projected for 1980 by Bosworth, Duesenberry, and Carron is just about the mean for that variable in the 1950s as well as in the prerecession year of 1973. It was, however, greater than the mean of those ratios for the 1960s. If we eliminate residential construction and restrict ourselves more narrowly to business investment, we find projections for 1980 higher than the historical record of the 1950s, as the share of residential construction falls.

The historical record of nonresidential business fixed investment is one of relative increase rather than decrease in the last decade. As Table 1 reveals, the mean ratios of nonresidential fixed investment to gross national product, both measured in constant (1972) dollars, were 9.1 percent and 9.2 percent in the three five-year periods from 1951 through 1965. The jump in this ratio to 10.3 percent in 1965 was followed by five more years of relatively high nonresidential fixed investment, so that the ratio of mean investment to mean gross national product in the 1966 through 1970 period was 10.4 percent. Despite the sharp dip in 1975, to 9.3 percent, the ratio of the means for 1971-75 was still at 10.1 percent.

[2] *The Capital Needs and Savings Potential of the U.S. Economy, Projections through 1985*. September 1974, pp. ii, 16.

[3] Arnold Sametz, Paul Wachtel and Harry Shuford, "Capital Shortages—Sectoral and Aggregate," presented at joint meetings of the American Economic Association and the American Finance Association, Dallas, December 28, 1975, and *Journal of Finance*, May 1976. Also See Barry Bosworth, James S. Duesenberry, and Andrew S. Carron, *Capital Needs in the Seventies*, Washington, D.C.: Brookings Institution, 1975.

Table 1. Nonresidential Fixed Investment as a Ratio of Gross National Product, Constant (1972) Dollars, 1946-1975

(1) *Year*	*(2)* *Nonresidential Fixed Investment* *(Billions of Dollars)*	*(3)* *Gross National Product* *(Billions of Dollars)*	*(4)* *Ratio* *[(2) ÷ (3)]* *(Percent)*
1946	42.0	477.6	8.8
1947	48.9	468.3	10.4
1948	51.0	487.7	10.5
1949	46.0	490.7	9.4
1950	50.0	533.5	9.4
Mean 1946-50	47.6	491.6	9.7
1951	52.9	576.5	9.2
1952	52.1	598.5	8.7
1953	56.3	621.8	9.1
1954	55.4	613.7	9.0
1955	61.2	654.8	9.3
Mean 1951-55	55.6	613.1	9.1
1956	65.2	668.8	9.7
1957	66.0	680.9	9.7
1958	58.9	679.5	8.7
1959	62.9	720.4	8.7
1960	66.0	736.8	9.0
Mean 1956-60	63.8	697.3	9.1
1961	65.6	755.3	8.7
1962	70.9	799.1	8.9
1963	73.5	830.7	8.8
1964	81.0	874.4	9.3
1965	95.6	925.9	10.3
Mean 1961-65	77.3	837.1	9.2
1966	106.1	981.0	10.8
1967	103.5	1007.7	10.3
1968	108.0	1051.8	10.3
1969	114.3	1078.8	10.6
1970	110.0	1075.3	10.2
Mean 1966-70	108.4	1038.9	10.4
1971	108.0	1107.5	9.8
1972	116.8	1171.1	10.0
1973	131.0	1235.0	10.6
1974	128.5	1214.0	10.6
1975	111.4	1191.7	9.3
Mean 1971-75	119.1	1183.9	10.1
Mean—all years	78.6	810.3	9.7

Derived from *Survey of Current Business,* Table 1.2, January 1976, part I, and July 1976.

It can hardly be held, therefore, except for the recession that broke out in 1974, that business investment has been suffering. Some may attribute the long boom to special tax advantages in the way of accelerated depreciation and equipment credits. Others may see primary cause in the boom of economic activity through much of the 1960s. The acceleration principle tells us, of course, that we may expect the rate of investment to be positively related to the acceleration of the rate of output or aggregate demand, albeit with some lag. When the rate of real growth in output slackens, investment falls, both in absolute amount and as a ratio of output. These declines may be noted in 1970 and 1971 and again in 1975. One might reasonably infer for the future that business investment will recover sharply as the general rate of output recovers and demand again presses upon existing capacity.

A major study of capital requirements was undertaken for the Council of Economic Advisors under the direction of Beatrice N. Vaccara of the Bureau of Economic Analysis.[4] It projected a figure of $986.6 billion, in 1972 prices, for nonresidential business fixed investment from 1975 to 1980, or 12.0 percent of cumulative gross national product, "in order to insure a 1980 capital stock sufficient to meet the needs of a full employment economy, and the requirements for pollution abatement and for decreasing dependence on foreign sources of petroleum."

The Vaccara-BEA study warrants attention as perhaps the most meticulous, thorough, and detailed estimate of business fixed investment "requirements" for the years ahead. Its strengths permit us to focus on basic, inherent deficiencies of projections of this genre.

First, the Vaccara-BEA study utilizes a Bureau of Labor Statistics estimate of 1980 "full employment" GNP of $1,575.2 billion in 1972 prices and a sectoral composition of that GNP projected by the BLS which predetermines the proportions of gross national product devoted to more and less capital-intensive final demand sectors. Second, capital-output ratios by industry are determined on the basis of estimates of such ratios in 1970 or 1967-70, or projected trend from 1963 through 1967-70. These are adjusted for utilization ratios when the latter are available. As the Vaccara-BEA report acknowledges, no adjustment is made for the effects of possibly changing interest rates, prices, availabilities or costs of obtaining capital. The base estimates of capital-output ratios are indeed themselves subject to a considerable

[4] A Study of Fixed *Capital Requirements of the U.S. Business Economy, 1971-80,* U.S. Department of Commerce, Bureau of Economic Analysis, December 1975.

margin of error, as is noted by a 17 percent discrepancy between the stock estimates of Jack Faucett from which the individual industry figures are derived and corresponding total private stock estimates of the BEA. (These differences are seen as relating primarily to average service life assumptions.)

Third, in estimating capital requirements some assumptions must be made about discards or retirements and consequent need for replacement. The procedures used here are acknowledged in the Vaccara-BEA work to be "summary," and do not allow for adjustment to economic conditions. One should think, for example, that if capital requirements were high relative to saving or capacity in capital goods industries, so that there were anything approaching a "shortage," firms would discard existing plant and equipment less rapidly.

Fourth, requirements for pollution abatement capital are taken from BEA and McGraw-Hill projections and include "a large dose of judgmental adjustment." Fifth, needs for energy-related investment are taken from "Project Independence" programs.

Thus, an estimate of $1,473.4 billion of fixed capital requirements of the U. S. Business Economy from 1971 through 1980, of which the $986.6 billion is the residual need for 1975-80, stems basically from projected expansion needs, given discards or retirements, to meet a specified final product mix in 1980 with previously existing capital-output ratios. On to this total of some $1,283 billion, however, was added $82 billion because of the projected increases in capital-output ratios in some industries, $58 billion related to specified energy-investment needs, and $50 billion related to also specified pollution-abatement requirements.

With all of its ingenious integration of data and application of input-out matrices, the Vaccara-BEA study, cited and leaned upon in the *1976 Economic Report of the President,* is subject to possibilities of serious bias, generally on the high side, as its authors do indeed point out. More basically, this approach ignores the free play of economic forces which makes business investment not something "required" or exogenous, but endogenous as we indicated above. It implicitly denies that the output mix as between more and less capital intensive sectors will be influenced by the cost and availability of capital. If society, through government, really were to impose particularly high requirements for capital for real or imagined needs of energy independence or pollution abatement, and if higher rates of return to investment did not bring forth more aggregate saving or the channeling of more saving to sectors of high investment demand, we should expect the higher cost of capital to make output in more capital intensive industries relatively higher priced and to change the final product mix.

Further, higher rates of interest or higher costs of capital should be expected to lead each industry to use less capital intensive methods of production. This frequently implies utilizing capital which is of lesser durability and is less expensive.

Finally, utilization of existing capital and of labor and other resources will cause an adjustment of "requirements." If capital appears "short," we may expect relative cost and price advantages and hence output increases in industries and sectors where there is greatest opportunity for fuller utilization of existing capital. We may also expect increased demand for labor and other resources which will not only mean full utilization of the existing labor force with the resultant reduction in unemployment and increases in average hours worked but also the drawing into market production of additional workers who will substitute for capital in the production of the nation's output.

A study prepared under the direction of Don R. Conlan in 1975 for John Dunlop, then Secretary of Labor, suggests that more investment is necessary to provide sufficient productive capacity to accommodate a national goal of high employment without undue inflation. But neither higher productive capacity nor higher productivity would seem relevant to attain high employment. All might work who wish to work, in a less productive economy as well as a more productive economy. And if the shortage in capacity is due to a lack of physical capital, one should expect all the more demand for labor to make up for that lack.

As for more investment being necessary to reduce the rate of inflation, one should not forget that investment in any direction, if it is not carried too far, may increase net capacity, but any *increase* in investment increases demand. To the extent inflation is to be explained by demand-supply relations, investment cuts both ways. A steady rate of net investment, as long as marginal returns are positive, brings increased capacity or supply, but steady demand. An increasing rate of net investment may increase demand more than supply and hence actually contribute to inflation. Further, investment tends to raise capacity or supply in the future while increases in investment raise demand immediately.

The study prepared for Secretary Dunlop also suggests "that the capital requirements for each new job in the future are significantly larger than in the past and, in order to achieve the desired employment objectives, serious consideration should be given to increasing the incentives to invest." But again we must insist that any suggestion of fixed capital requirements per job puts the economy in a straight-jacket. This rigidity would appear to have more to do with the analyst's perceptions than even the most modest flexibility and responsiveness that we may expect from the real, market economy that we know.

Inflexibility may reduce the rate of investment and the rate of employment either in the industry affected or in other industries. Some inflexibility may come from government itself, as where regulatory agencies hold prices of certain products, such as electric power, so low that, while the quantity demanded might be very high, firms anticipating continued low prices would not find it profitable to invest in the capacity to meet future needs. Anticompetitive forces in building trades and residential construction, along with restrictive covenants and imperfect mortgage markets, may account for depressed investment and excess capacity in the home-building industry. It is hard to see in any of this, however, evidence of a general shortage of capital to meet the requirements of a growing labor force.

Issues of Financing

Financing is frequently seen as a major concern in the outlook for actual business investment. Benjamin Friedman wrote in 1975, "To an unusually great extent, financial considerations may act during this period [1977-81] as effective constraints on the amount of fixed investment which the economy in aggregate is able to do." [5] In May 1976, however, Allen Sinai reported "There are no financial shortages of any consequence." [6]

Also seeing no general shortages of physical capacity in the near future, Sinai found "an unprecedented surge in cash flow" and generally "enhanced business liquidity . . . used to acquire financial assets and reduce debt." In fact, it turns out that all nongovernment sectors show major increases in holdings of U. S. government securities in 1975: $16 billion for non-financial corporations, $30 billion for com-

[5] "Financing the Next Five Years of Fixed Investment," *Sloan Management Review*, 16, no. 3 (Spring 1975), 52.

[6] "The Prospects of a Capital Shortage in the U.S.," *Euromoney*, May 1976, as reprinted by Data Resources, Inc., as Economic Studies Series Number 24, second page.

mercial banks, and record increases as well for nonbank financial intermediaries, life insurance companies and pension funds. Sinai declared, "The real issue now is whether the growing liquidity base of the U.S. economy will propel the expansion higher and longer than is generally believed." It is interesting to relate this to often expressed concerns as by Conlan of federal finance "crowding out" funds for private investment. It is the huge federal deficits which have made possible the general increase in liquidity, in the form of government securities, here viewed as creating a major potential for increased business investment.

In fact, it is hard to see financial constraints acting as the original cause of reduced investment. Friedman's own estimates of 1977-81 sources and uses of funds by nonfinancial corporate business show roughly one-fifth of average annual flows of $301 billion going to "financial investment," including particularly acquisition of liquid assets and the extension of trade credit. He also foresees a continued substantial reliance on external funds amounting to almost half of the total sources, with a continued rise in the corporate bond-to-equity ratio. Looking at the financing of business investment specifically, Bosworth, Duesenberry and Carron projected $251.5 billion of investment for 1974 through 1980 of which $186.9 would be internally financed and $64.6 would come from external financing.

The data on financing do not suggest critical problems in this area. In general, past patterns and trends are expected to continue. Even if they did not, however, it is difficult on analytical grounds to see serious investment curbs which are *at root* financial. To do so would be to deny the essential efficiency of our capital markets, a major indictment indeed of some of the most fundamental operations of our economic system.

Individual firms may well believe themselves pinched by financial shortages in the face of what appear to them to be attractive investment opportunities. But in any economy where resources are not free, there are opportunity costs to investment. Costs to an individual firm, financial and nonfinancial, reflect market valuation of alternative uses of desired resources. If an individual firm finds that it cannot obtain funds at a sufficiently low cost to warrant their use in investment, this in principle implies that there are other uses of those funds which are deemed more valuable.

Where, in the aggregate, firms feel that they cannot profitably finance as much investment as they wish, households, nonprofit institutions and governments and government enterprises apparently have exercised superior claims to the additional resources which business might elect to have for more investment. This, ultimately, is not a financial constraint but a real constraint imposed by the limitation of resources on the one hand and society's preferences, expressed both individually and socially, on the other.

Productivity and the Rate of Return to Capital

Probably of more moment than financing is the rate of return on capital. A study by William Nordhaus ("The Falling Share of Profits," *Brookings Papers on Economic Activities,* 1: 1974) suggests a drop in the "genuine" rate of return on nonfinancial corporate capital. It fell fairly steadily from its high of 10.0 percent in 1965 to a plateau of around 5.5 percent in the 1970s, before the current or recent recession. This genuine rate of return involves a depreciation adjustment, akin to that now incorporated in the National Income Accounts, and the inclusion of net interest in the numerator and the total value of nonfinancial corporate capital rather than net worth in the denominator.

Part of the decline in the rate of return may be attributed to an increase in the effective rate of corporate taxation on genuine income. For while the widening of tax loopholes, particularly accelerated depreciation and the equipment tax credit, tended to reduce the nominal tax rate on corporate income, the effect of inflation was to add to taxes a large share of inventory appreciation not included in genuine profits.

Inflation also had the effect of increasing the attractiveness to business of debt-financing. The higher interest rates associated with inflation meant increased deductions from taxable income while the erosion of real value of principal, a major loss to bondholders, contributed to a capital gain on the part of holders of business equity.

Daniel M. Holland and Stewart C. Meyers have measured rates of return in terms of market valuations and inclusive of capital gains and losses and the effects on real values of changes in consumer prices. They have reported real returns earned by investors in nonfinancial corporations as averaging over 10 percent per year from 1947 to 1965 but averaging minus 2 percent from 1966 to 1975. While these are in a sense before-tax returns to investors, since much of them consisted of unrealized or lightly-taxed realized capital gains the effective after-tax return to investors may not have been much lower.

Presenting a variety of additional measures, Holland and Meyers find that real rates of return were generally high in the mid-1960s and lower since, but they note that nonfinancial corporations "are better off now than in the mid-1950s." They observe further, "Operating profitability (ROC) is about the same now as then, but the cost of capital is lower. (If there is a capital 'shortage,' it has as yet had no observable effect on the cost of capital.)" ("Trends in Corporate Profitability and Capital Costs," Cambridge: Sloan School of Management, M.I.T., 1976, xeroxed, page 38.)

Evidence of a secularly declining rate of return on nonfinancial corporate capital may be questioned. The 1973 rate was still by Nordhaus calculations approximately equal to the returns for 1953 and 1958, both recession years. The negative returns after 1965 in the market value measure of Holland and Meyers may reflect partly the negative effect on real values of the Vietnam War, with real returns of −11.6 percent in 1966 and −13.9 percent in 1969. And they are dominated by returns of −19.5 percent in 1973 and −29.3 percent in 1974, as an inflationary economy entered its worst decline since the Great Depression of the 1930s.

The rapid upsurge of corporate profits in 1976 may, moreover, be signaling a new boom in the rate of return on capital, following upon some years of recession and prerecession sluggishness. Further, what may be most relevant to investment decisions is the expected rate of return on equity. For many highly levered corporations, real losses to owners of corporate bonds corresponded to substantial capital gains on equity.

To the extent that the rate of return on capital has been declining, however, it may well relate to the "deepening" of capital brought on by a tax structure which, contrary to views expressed by some business spokesmen, has been heavily weighted in recent years in favor of business investment in plant and equipment. And to this extent resources have been channeled into activities with less net productivity. Output, growth and the general welfare may be enhanced more by government, household, and nonprofit institution investment in both human and nonhuman capital, and by business investment in research and development, training, and general administrative skills and efficiency.

The Fundamental Identity beween Saving and Investment

Projections of future investment should take into account the fundamental identity between saving and investment, the nature if not the very existence of which is sometimes forgotten. It may be instructive to note, in our Table 2, projections of an increase of gross private

TABLE 2. SAVING AND INVESTMENT, WHARTON ESTIMATES AND PROJECTIONS, 1976, 1977, AND 1978 *(Billions of Dollars)*

	1976	*1977*	*1978*	*Changes from 1976 to 1978*
Gross Private Domestic Investment (GPDI)	247.7	315.7	361.1	113.4
Personal saving	79.9	82.0	83.9	4.0
Undistributed corporate profits	52.4	69.7	73.3	20.9
Corporate capital consumption adjustment	–15.9	–19.1	–21.3	–5.4
Inventory valuation adjustment	–13.1	–16.8	–17.9	–4.8
Capital consumption allowances	180.2	201.4	228.3	48.1
Gross Private Saving (GPS)	283.5	317.2	346.3	62.8
Federal budget surplus or deficit (–) (NIA basis)	–56.3	–40.1	–20.1	36.2
State and local budget surplus or deficit (–) (NIA basis)	12.3	20.1	23.6	11.3
Total Government Budget Surplus or Deficit (–) (GBS or D)	–44.0	–20.0	+3.5	47.5
Statistical Discrepancy (SD)	6.1	5.8	5.8	–0.3
Net Foreign Investment (NFI) *	–2.0	–12.8	–5.5	–3.5
Gross Private Domestic Saving (GPDS = GPS + GBS or D + SD – NFI)	247.6	315.8	361.1	113.5

Source: Derived from Wharton Mark 4.2 Quarterly Model, Control Update-Present Policies Continued—September 26, 1976. Wharton Econometric Associates, Inc., University of Pennsylvania, Philadelphia.

* Equals net exports minus net federal government transfers and interest payments to foreigners minus net personal transfers to foreigners.

domestic investment of some $113 billion from 1976 to 1978, and how they square with the fundamental identity. We see that gross private domestic investment always equals what we may call gross private domestic saving, or gross private saving plus the government budget surplus (or minus the deficit), plus the statistical discrepancy, minus net foreign investment.

The identity is sometimes forgotten. At other times it is endowed mistakenly with behavioral significance. Thus, it is correct to observe that gross private saving may go to finance gross private domestic investment, to finance net foreign investment, or to finance federal or state and local budget deficits. It is improper, however, to hold all but two of the aggregates constant and then to conclude *from the identity* how changing one would change the other. Thus, it may be correct but quite misleading to say that with given gross private saving (and budget deficit), increasing net foreign investment will decrease gross private domestic investment. For the increase in net foreign investment may result in greater output, income and saving and hence *more* gross private domestic investment.

Similarly, and perhaps more central to public discussion, it is correct but misleading to state that with a given rate of gross private saving, an increase in the federal budget deficit would reduce investment, or that a decrease in the deficit would raise investment.

First, it may be noted that if the federal budget deficit is increased by transferring more funds to state and local governments, there may merely be an increase in the federal budget deficit matched by a decrease in state and local budget deficits or increases in state and local budget surpluses. Second, if an increase in the federal budget deficit is accomplished by a cut in personal income taxes, the immediate effect would be an increase in after-tax personal income and in personal saving. If some of the increase in after-tax income goes into consumption spending, this may further increase income and personal saving or perhaps increase corporate profits and undistributed corporate profits. If the federal budget deficit is increased by a cut in the corporate profits tax, it is readily apparent that the immediate effect is an increase in undistributed corporate profits. Quite similar arguments would apply to increases in transfer payments, such as for social security benefits.

This analysis should make clear that widely expressed arguments that large federal budget deficits are threats to investment or, by absorbing private saving will "crowd out" investment, at least to the extent they are based upon the saving-investment identities, are quite fallacious.

Working behind the saving-investment identity are real factors of resource allocation. These relate not to budget deficits, transfer payments or taxes *per se*. If taxes and transfer payments merely redistribute income or purchasing power, they have no *prima facie* effect upon investment, corporate or otherwise. They will affect the distribution of consumption and the distribution of ownership of assets, both of which may be politically sensitive issues. But, frequent loud arguments to the contrary notwithstanding, they are of uncertain direction in their influence, if any, on the aggregate of investment. However, government actions that affect directly the allocation of resources, such as government purchases of goods and services or categorical transfer payments, as for health care, may affect the composition and even the aggregate of saving and investment. Where the government takes more resources for defense or education or health services, fewer resources are available elsewhere. The remaining resources may still be divided in the same proportions among production of current consumption goods and services and production of capital goods but the total of each may be less than if the government had not reserved some resources elsewhere.

This, of course, applies to a situation of full employment. With less than full employment, government purchases of goods and services or transfer payments may actually bring about more total production, consumption, and saving in the rest of the economy. And finally it should be noted, in connection with the broader view of investment to be considered below, that certain government expenditures, as for education, health, or transportation may involve significant and major public investment.

A Broader View of Investment

These considerations should lead us to a much broader consideration of basic determinants and costs of business investment. One may be seriously misled by too narrow a view, particularly that of an individual firm. Here it may appear that the availability of funds is a simple, overwhelming determinant of the rate of capital expenditures. Even in this instance, one may readily document the fact that most large firms make capital expenditures to the extent that they appear sufficiently profitable. For the giants of American industry that do the bulk of capital spending, funds are available. The question is whether the profitability of their use is sufficient. And the expected profitability of use of funds varies considerably more than their cost.

Where profitable opportunities dwindle it may appear that the high cost of funds is discouraging investment. But were profitability high, that same high cost would not discourage investment. Even availability may be an evidence of expected profitability. Banks and other investors will be reluctant to make funds available if investments do not appear sound, that is, profitable.

Ultimately the total amount of saving and investment in the economy may be seen to depend upon total income and output *and* proclivities to save for future consumption instead of consuming now. As long as employment is less than full and output and income are hence less than the total of which the economy is capable, saving and investment can and would be increased by coming closer to full employment. Given a situation of less than full employment, virtually any increase in output, whether of consumer goods or goods and services produced by or purchased by government, would also generate more saving and investment. The underlying economic relation indicating that higher income implies more saving and investment is relatively unassailable.

The financial counterparts to this underlying real relation may be varied. With a higher national income, there may be greater personal saving, more in the way of undistributed corporate profits, elimination of dissaving by the unemployed, and financial flows in one way or another from the savers to those requiring real capital, to the extent those in these categories are not identical.

Once full employment is attained, the story is a different one. Any attempts now to increase investment, that is output not contributing to current consumption, must involve a reallocation of resources rather than merely the utilization of previously idle people and productive capacity. In such a situation, difficulties experienced by corporations in financing more investment may reflect simply the reluctance of business or government, or nonbusiness investors, to give up their shares of output.

While fiscal and monetary measures may well bring about some alteration in the mix of output for current consumption and investment for the future, much of their effect is rather to alter the composition of invesment itself. Investment may properly and usefully be viewed more broadly as all current output or productive activity which contrbutes to future output. Alongside of the traditionally included business acquisition of plant, equipment and additional inventories, we should then place similar acquisitions by government, federal, state and local, and by nonprofit institutions. We might also note that acquisition of automobiles by households are as much investment as similar acquisitions by taxi companies or firms. Washing machines and dishwashers acquired by households are as much investment as those acquired by laundromats or restaurants.

Not only are durable goods of households, government and nonprofit institutions investment; so too are education and training, whether on-the-job, in school, or in the home. For these also contribute to future output. By many measures, the last dollars spent in education and training have been more productive than the last dollars spent on plant and equipment. In addition, we should include in investment child rearing expenses and provision for health and mobility, all of which make possible future output. And of course few deny that expenditures for research and development have contributed mightily to productivity. Our stock of knowledge is in many ways more valuable than our stock of brick and mortar. Much of the brick and mortar, of course, is conventionally counted as part of gross private domestic investment in the form of residential construction, but relatively little of this residential construction will be included in business investment.

Hence we find business investment a quite minor proportion of total capital accumulation in the economy. In connection with certain on-going research on extended concepts of national income and output, utilizing in large part recent estimates by John Kendrick, we take total capital accumulation in the United States economy during 1969, excluding "net revaluations" or capital gains, to be $671 billion. Against this we may note that all nonresidential business investment, corporate and noncorporate, amounted to only $98.5 billion for structures and equipment and $7.8 billion more for change in inventories. Nonresidential business investment was thus less than 16 percent of all investment in the economy.

Effects of Monetary Policy and Tax Incentives

The outlook for business investment is seen by many to depend considerably upon monetary policy and specific tax incentives for investment that are or may be made available. In general, easier monetary policy is seen as bringing lower interest rates, although this is disputed by "monetarists." They argue that increases in the quantity of money will only temporaily lower interest rates but then raise prices, the expected rate of inflation and the nominal rate of interest as well. Clearly, higher expected rates of inflation bring on higher nominal rates of interest. It is hardly clear, however, that these prevent the lower real rates of interest which are what should be relevant to investment decisions. Further, one may well properly question whether expansionary monetary policy alone, that is the Federal Reserve System bringing about the exchange of noninterest bearing debt (money) for interest bearing debt, will generally cause much inflation.

The main body of economic thinking does perceive a negative relation between the rate of interest and investment and hence a positive relation between easier money and investment. What that monetary policy will be is likely to depend considerably upon the political process. Despite the short-run independence of the Board of Governors of the Federal Reserve System and of the Open Market Committee, one may anticipate that a Democratic administration would have some influence in implementation of its traditional policy of easier money. This would appear particularly likely as long as the rate of unemployment remains high and the economy has not completed its recovery from the sharp and deep recession that began in 1974.

With business investment such a small proportion of total capital accumulation, measures intended to affect investment are frequently poorly judged if one concerns oneself exclusively with business investment. In fact, there is little evidence that tight money and higher interest rates have a direct impact on business investment. They do have profound effects, in large part because of governmental restrictions and institutional arrangements in mortgage markets, on investment in residential housing.

Tight money may choke off investment by relatively smaller and less credit-worthy unincorporated business. It may have very drastic effects on investment by state and local government and school districts. It may also make purchases of some consumer durables more difficult. In its impact on security prices it may affect importantly people's perception of their wealth and hence their own consumption and investment in human capital. There may well be important indirect impacts on business investment from the general movement of the economy in response to monetary policy.

Paradoxically, it is possible that tight money intended to discourage investment may actually increase business investment. For example, to the extent that construction resources are freed from residential housing and government building, they may become more readily available for the erection of new business plant. Corporate fund raisers may well lament the higher interest rates that they pay and yet not note that lower construction costs (or less rapid rising construction costs) or shorter delivery times are a consequence of the tax impact of tight money elsewhere in the economy.

In some quarters, the prospects for business investment in general are seen to depend very much on the extent of tax incentives—some of us call them "loopholes"—designed specifically to encourage business investment. I have long argued that these tax subsidies cost more in tax revenues than they gain in investment.[7] But here too the chain of causation and the ultimate results may be more complicated than generally perceived. To the extent that tax incentives mean tax cuts which bring us closer to full employment by increasing demand, they are likely to raise business investment and other investment as well. An investment tax credit, for example, may influence business investment in considerable part by raising the value of corporate stock, hence increasing the net worth of stockholders, thus leading stockholders to buy more as consumers. This in turn creates pressure on capacity for the production of consumer goods and stimulates investment to meet this pressure.

These indirect effects of tax incentives for investment may be just as well achieved, however, by general tax measures intended to influence aggregate demand. The outlook for business investment in the future will depend most on the general state of the economy. The recession which began in 1974 has been disastrous to all investment. While gross national product in constant (1972) dollars declined 6.6 percent from $1,242.6 billion in the fourth quarter of 1973 to $1,611.1 billion in the first quarter of 1975, the total of fixed investment dropped 23.6 percent, from $192.9 billion in the first quarter of 1973 to $147.4 billion in the second quarter of 1975. From the beginning of 1974 to the third quarter of 1975, while unemployment rose from 5.2 percent to between 8.5 and 9 percent, real nonresidential business fixed investment fell 17.5 percent, from 133.5 to 110.1 in billions of 1972 dollars. A high rate of investment spending will depend very much upon the extent of economic upswing and the expectation that

[7] R. Eisner and M. I. Nadiri, "Investment Behavior and Neo-Classical Theory," *The Review of Economics and Statistics,* August 1968, and Eisner, "Tax Policy and Investment Behavior: Comment," *The American Economic Review,* June 1969; "Tax Incentives for Investment," *National Tax Journal,* September 1973; "Business Investment Preferences," *George Washington Law Review,* March 1974; Eisner and Patrick Lawler, "Tax Policy and Investment," *The American Economic Review,* March 1975.

it will continue. Both of these may well be determined considerably by general fiscal policy.

Given full employment and full utilization of resources, which would contribute vitally to business investment, tax incentives to further stimulate business investment can only increase total investment if they increase the proportion of income saved. If the public is loath to save more, higher after-tax expected returns to business investment will tend to raise interest rates and the opportunity costs of capital generally. They will thus lure resources into business investment at the expense of residential construction, investment by state and local government, and investment in human capital, as well as those forms of business investment such as expenditures for research and development and executive or employee training, which are not benefiting from the particular tax advantages accorded.

The Role of Government

In fact, the outlook for business investment depends considerably upon the role of government. Most fundamentally, government policies bearing on employment and macroeconomic stability profoundly determine the expected profitability of investment. Where aggregate demand is low, excess capacity high, and the expected rate of growth of demand and output uncertain or modest in relation to the existing slack, business investment will be depressed. Where aggregate effective demand and the utilization of men and machines are relatively full, and where demand is expected to continue to increase, business investment demand will be high. Actual investment will then be constrained by the availability of resources for which superior claims are not exercised.

This suggests a second major influence or constraint imposed by government upon the rate of business investment. Under conditions of full employment, government expenditures for goods and services command resources which might otherwise be used for business investment. Any increase in business investment in this condition must require reductions in personal consumption expenditures, decreases in exports, increases in imports or reductions in the allocation of resources to other forms of investment. The latter again include not only residential construction but stubstantial amounts of capital accumulation disguised in conventional income and product accounts as "intermediate" expenses for training, education, medical care, and job mobility.

Government may affect investment as well by influencing the mix of final product and the way in which it is produced. Specific expenditures for goods and services may call for investment in specific capital optimal for that production. Bombers may need certain kinds of machine tools; roads may need cement mixers; schools may need construction equipment. And government may create a demand for new capital goods to meet requirements for protecting the environment.

Finally, government has variously subsidized and encouraged investment in general or particular forms of investment. These include accelerated depreciation for plant and equipment, most notably the allowance of double rate declining balance and sum-of-the-years digits methods for tax purposes beginning in 1954, guideline depreciation offering markedly shorter lives in 1962, the asset depreciation range system making possible still further shortening of lives in 1971, and a gradual acquiescence by the Internal Revenue Service in shorter lives and consequently lower taxes over the years. Further, there has been the equipment tax credit, originally introduced in 1962, variously modified, suspended, reinvoked, ended, reenacted and increased currently to 10 percent plus 1.5 percent more for corporate contributions to employee stock ownership plans.

The tax laws permit and encourage various "tax shelters," which have induced certain kinds of construction. Encouragement to investment in tangible assets or equities in them has also been given by the combination of interest deductibility for tax purposes and the exclusion from taxable income of half of realized capital gains and all of "unrealized" capital gains. Government has in addition offered tax encouragement to specific types of investment as for certain antipollution expenditures.

Serious questions should be raised as to the merit of general government encouragement to business investment in plant and equipment. One may argue that in particular cases there are positive externalities, that is benefits which go beyond the decision-making firm, which justify public subsidy to bring about more private investment than would be freely undertaken. This, it should be pointed out, does not generally apply to investment by firms to reduce the extent to which they themselves are polluting the environment. For in this instance, the preferred solution would be the imposition of taxes to force the firm to choose among the options of paying the social costs of pollution that it imposes or reducing or eliminating the pollution or the activity that causes it. It is not optimal to use public funds or general resources which continue to permit the firm to disregard total social costs in determining its activities.

Government encouragement to business expenditures for plant and equipment is frequently justified as a means of stimulating aggregate demand and employment. It can well be effective in these directions, although in terms of the employment objective there may be more or less substantial leakage in substitution of plant, equipment and new technology for labor. There is no justification, however, for focusing on encouragement of business investment to bring about full utilization of our resources. Neutral increases in demand by general reductions in taxes or increases in transfer payments are to be preferred on efficiency grounds. Production to meet the increased demand could then be undertaken under the normal competitive, profit incentives.

Policy Recommendations

On the tax side, the major current subsidies of the investment tax credit, accelerated depreciation and capital gains exclusions should be eliminated rather than extended. If there is any place in the economy where free market forces should be allowed to operate without bias it is certainly in the field of business investment. If business investment appears profitable it should be undertaken. Otherwise it should not. There is no reason why a tax credit of $10.00 should be used to convert a $100.00 investment with an unprofitable $95.00 after-tax payoff to one with a profitable $105.00 payoff. Similar arguments apply to accelerated depreciation.

The current exclusion of half of realized capital gains from taxable income and the complete exclusion of unrealized capital gains offer a major incentive to investment in corporate equity, along with other kinds of appreciable instruments and property. This tax treatment has the effect of unduly stimulating business investment while biasing resources and productive activity into channels which can create untaxed or lightly taxed capital gains as opposed to ordinary income. The failure to tax unrealized capital gains is also a major source of the so-called "lock-in" effect which reduces the mobility of capital and the freedom of operation of our capital markets.

The six-month holding requirement to qualify for the capital gains exclusion, to increase to twelve months as a consequence of the 1976 tax law revisions, would appear to be a minor consideration in restricting sales as compared to the tax liability on appreciated assets at any time after the initial period. Proposed changes in capital gains treatment that would reduce still further the tax rate on realized capital gains for assets held longer would have the perverse effect of increased lock-in. The holder of appreciated securities who knows that the tax rate will decline if he holds his securities longer would be all the more dissuaded from selling. Indeed he would only sell if he expected his securities to decline by more than the tax saving resulting from selling later. This lock-in tends to restrict the movement of capital from less profitable to more profitable firms and thus reduces overall productivity in the economy.

Some correction to these distortions would be found in at least taxing capital gains at death. Indeed further measures might well be taken to tax unrealized capital gains as they accrue. In the case of listed corporate securities it would be a simple matter for owners to report the last quotation of the year and the capital gain or loss from the previous year. To the extent that capital gains taxes were so extensive as to cause financing problems for their payment, the Treasury could permit delayed payment with, of course, appropriate interest charges. In fact, it is doubtful that such Treasury financing would be necessary, as loans on corporate securities are readily available from private banks as well as brokers.

Full taxation of capital gains as accrued should, if we are to restrict ourselves to taxing income rather than capital, permit deductions from taxable gains of the amount of capital appreciation associated with general price inflation. It should also permit full loss offsets as well as averaging to prevent progressive tax rates from unduly penalizing those whose gains are concentrated in time.

A further measure in the direction of improved financing of investment as well as a more equitable tax structure would be integration of the corporate and individual income taxes. The corporate tax itself would be abolished but individuals would include in taxable income their share of corporate earnings, whether paid out in dividends or not. The payment of dividends would thus be encouraged, all the more so if there were effective taxation of capital gains resulting from undistributed profits. Stockholders would have immediate access to corporate earnings. Businesses with the most profitable investment opportunities would prove the successful bidders for reinvestment of earnings. It may be added, in terms of equity, that inclusion of corporate earnings in individual taxable income would mean a more progressive rather than a less progressive tax structure. Marginal tax rates would be based upon individual earnings rather than set essentially at a flat 48 percent, which is in turn at least partly passed on to all stockholders, the poor widow and orphan and the multi-millionaire alike.

In terms of monetary policy, a number of banking restrictions should be eliminated. Most important, the prohibition of interest payments on demand deposits should be eliminated and restrictions of interest payments on savings accounts should be removed. This would offer small investors the opportunity to earn market rates of interest and hence protect themselves against expected inflation. It should contribute as well to equalizing and stabilizing the availability of savings to corporate and noncorporate investors.

In terms of balanced growth, there should be every effort to make up for the inherent market imperfections in investment in human capital. Since we are not a slave economy, it does not pay businesses to invest adequately in human capital of employees. For however valuable that capital, it is difficult for firms to prevent employees from enjoying the return to this capital with new employers.

The one major role of government in assisting the financing of investment is the indirect one of maintaining a level of aggregate demand sufficient to attain full employment. This may be done by keeping tax rates sufficiently low and transfer payments or government expenditures for goods and services sufficiently high. The historical record as well as sound economic analysis should be absolutely clear. It is not budget deficits or federal debt that create problems in financing or implementing business investment. The greatest deterrents of business capital expenditures are the excess of capacity and general unemployment of resources associated with inadequate aggregate demand. The attainment and maintenance of full employment is certainly the greatest possible governmental contribution to the long-run health and growth of business capital expenditures.

Business capital expenditures will contribute to economic growth to the extent that they are undertaken on the basis of unbiased calculation of their expected returns. It is correct that capital accumulation contributes to future output. In many situations more capital accumulation raises the rate of growth of output.

But this is not necessarily always so. Even in the aggregate, capital may be accumulated beyond the point where it adds to output as much as its own cost of production, that is, beyond the point where, with diminishing returns, the marginal net product turns negative. It is certainly true that distortion of the allocation of resources to particular forms of investment may bring negative net returns. At the least, the tax expenditures and subsidies or other forms of government intervention may lead to a substitution of less productive for more productive investment, thus reducing the rate of economic growth.

Finally, it must be recognized that growth has fuller dimensions than market output. Business expenditures to abate pollution, reduce noise, and generally improve the environment may not add to market output. They may indeed prove to be substitutes for market output. Various public expenditures as well may lead to the production of services not valued or undervalued in conventionally measured gross national product. Such expenditures should also be undertaken only so long as the value of their marginal return is greater than or at least equal to their marginal cost. But where this is true, these capital expenditures, by government, households, and nonprofit institutions, as well as business, should be recognized as contributing to the maximization of social welfare.

Ultimately, it should be recognized that economic growth is not a good in itself. It is not necessarily desirable that we have more in the future than in the present. It is not axiomatic that all of us should sacrifice now in the prospect that our great-grandchildren would live better or that any of us should be forced to sacrifice more when we are young in order to live better when we are older. Unless some countervailing public imperative can be found, it seems best to leave these decisions to individual free choice.

It remains overwhelmingly important that our choice be made within the freedom to work as much as we wish and to realize our full potentials in the way of developing all of our capital, physical and human. Within that context and with proper attention to the "externalities" of the environment in which we all live, so far as there is free competition unshackled by inappropriate government controls and unbiased by tax distortions, business may be expected in its investment decisions to contribute optimally to economic growth.

Sherman J. Maisel

3

The Investment Demand for Housing

Investment in residential housing is a sphere where demand is expected to grow more slowly than national output. Relative to a full employment economy, housing will need a smaller share of total resources, thus making some capital and saving available for other uses. Since 1958 private investment in housing has averaged about 4.3 percent of real GNP. I estimate (see Table 1) that over the next ten years the demand for such investment should be about 3.9 percent of the GNP. In real terms, the amount of required investment in housing should rise from about $58.9 billion (in 1972 dollars) a year during the period 1972-74 to an average of about $68 billion (in 1972 dollars) for the period 1980-85. Since it is smaller than the expected growth of total GNP, the share of housing in production should fall.

The slower growth of the resources required for housing does not mean that there is no saving-investment problem. One does exist because of the probable instability of this demand. From a low in 1970 through a high in 1972 to a low in 1974, monthly housing starts rose by 125 percent and then fell by 65 percent. This was the worst fluctuation in housing construction since 1929. The quarterly share of real GNP invested in housing varied between 3.1 percent and 5.2 percent. This fluctuation created critical pressures on housing re-

---

SHERMAN J. MAISEL *is co-director of The National Bureau of Economic Research-West, and Professor of Business Administration at the University of California (Berkeley). He was a member of the Board of Governors of the Federal Reserve System (1965-72) and has been a consultant to several public and private agencies. Among his recent books are* Managing the Dollar *and* Real Estate Investment and Finance.

TABLE 1. PROJECTED PRIVATE RESIDENTIAL INVESTMENT

	In Thousands of Dwelling Units (annual rates) To Satisfy Demand from:				*In Billions of 1972 Dollars (annual rates)*	
	Household Formation	*Vacancies*	*Replacements*	*Total*	*Total*	*Percent of GNP*
1972-74	1690	—	710	2400	$58.9	4.9
1975-80 *	1420	140	760	2320	53.2	3.8
1976-80 *	1420	360	770	2550	58.4	4.0
1980-85 *	1430	170	950	2550	67.5	3.8

Source: Projected for this study; see text for explanation.

* Fiscal years.

sources, on the overall economy, on housing prices, and on the general level of inflation.

There is general agreement that this instability does not reflect shifts in underlying, long-term supply and demand. Rather, changes in financial conditions and the availability of credit cause starts to fluctuate around their basic trend. Other factors such as profitability and government programs cause some of these movements, but their significance is far less than that of financing.

To evaluate housing's role in investment, saving, and output, we start by analyzing the underlying demand for new dwelling units. This demand is then related to total residential investment requirements. A discussion of the system of housing finance follows, together with its problems and proposals to improve it.

There is some, but not too much, disagreement over the underlying estimates of demand. There is a great deal of conflict over what problems exist on the financial level, what causes them, and what should be done about them.

The Demand for Housing

We project a small increase, from 2,400,000 to 2,550,000, in the number of housing units produced annually between the base period 1972-74 used for this study and the years 1980-85 (all years are fiscal years). The details are shown in Table 1. While the data average over several years, year-to-year differences in basic demand are small. In constant 1972 dollars, projected residential investment increases from $58.9 to $67.5 billion, primarily reflecting some added services or quality in each dwelling unit. Since the rate of growth in both potential and actual GNP is expected to be faster, the share of GNP going to housing investment is expected to fall.

However, the increase in required production compared to 1974-76 would be much larger—from 1,550,000 to 2,550,000 units. Such comparisons reflect a critical problem of residential investment—its sharp fluctuations. The share of GNP going to housing compared to 1974-76 would also increase, but not sharply—by about 10 to 15 percent. The concepts behind these estimates are basic to understanding and the ability to analyze the forces underlying the need for houses and their impact on total demand and production.

HOUSING INVESTMENT IS A DERIVED DEMAND

Three factors dominate and cause large fluctuations in housing production: (a) houses are durable, properly maintained they can last for hundreds of years; (b) the demand for housing investment is a derived demand; (c) most purchasers of houses require large amounts of credit available over long periods.

The basic demand for housing services from which the demand for investment derives is the desire to occupy a particular type of dwelling unit with individual features such as size, quality of construction, maintenance, location, neighborhood, etc. Most services in any year are supplied by the existing stock of houses. The demand for production or residential investment arises only when the existing stock cannot furnish the space demanded (de Leeuw).[1] In units, new production usually ranges between 2 and 3 percent of the existing stock. Since new units contain more amenities and services than existing ones, the annual value of new production is about 5 percent of the net stock. The existing stock can continue to house the population for a year or two even if no units are added. As a result, large variations occur between the underlying, long-run, or basic demand for residential investment and actual production.

A handy method of analyzing the investment demand is first to examine changes in the housing services demanded and then see how they influence production. The forces determining the demand for

[1] All citations in parentheses may be found in the references listed at the end of this chapter.

space and for investment, while related, are different and can move quite separately. A gap between demand and supply can be filled either by appreciation or depreciation of the existing stock, by removals from the stock, by construction of new dwellings, by additions and alterations, or by maintenance and repairs.

Most studies of housing needs or investment demand deal primarily with the number of units demanded. This is only part of the story. In addition, investment will vary with the quality or expenditures per new dwelling. Investment also takes place through additions and alterations, through building of nonhousekeeping residential units, and through value added by brokers. In fact, 20 to 25 percent of annual investment occurs in these other frequently neglected categories.

The Forces at Work in the Housing Market

Fig. 1 diagrams the forces at work and some interrelationships between the markets for housing services and the market for residential investment. At the start of a period, a stock of space exists with a number of structures, each furnishing a given quantity of housing services (Maisel and Roulac).

The left of the figure shows the demand for this space by households, for vacancies, and for nonhousekeeping units. This demand will shift as a result of demographic, social, political, and economic forces. These alter the number of households, the desired vacancies, and the services demanded from an average unit. Depending on the relationship between demand and supply, the number of actual vacancies will alter, as will housing prices and rents.

These movements trigger changes in the supply of space services. Some units will be removed. Others may change in value through appreciation or depreciation. Finally residential investment will occur. The amount of investment in new dwelling units or in the existing stock will depend upon the changes in prices and rents, expectations, construction costs, land costs, subsidies and taxes, and, most critically, the cost and availability of financing.

HOUSEHOLDS

Table 1 projects that household formation will require about 1,400,000 new dwelling units each year for the decade 1975-85. This is the largest share of total demand for new units. The number of households depends primarily upon the size of the population and its age

Fig. 1. Supply and Demand for Housing (Number of Units and Value per Unit)

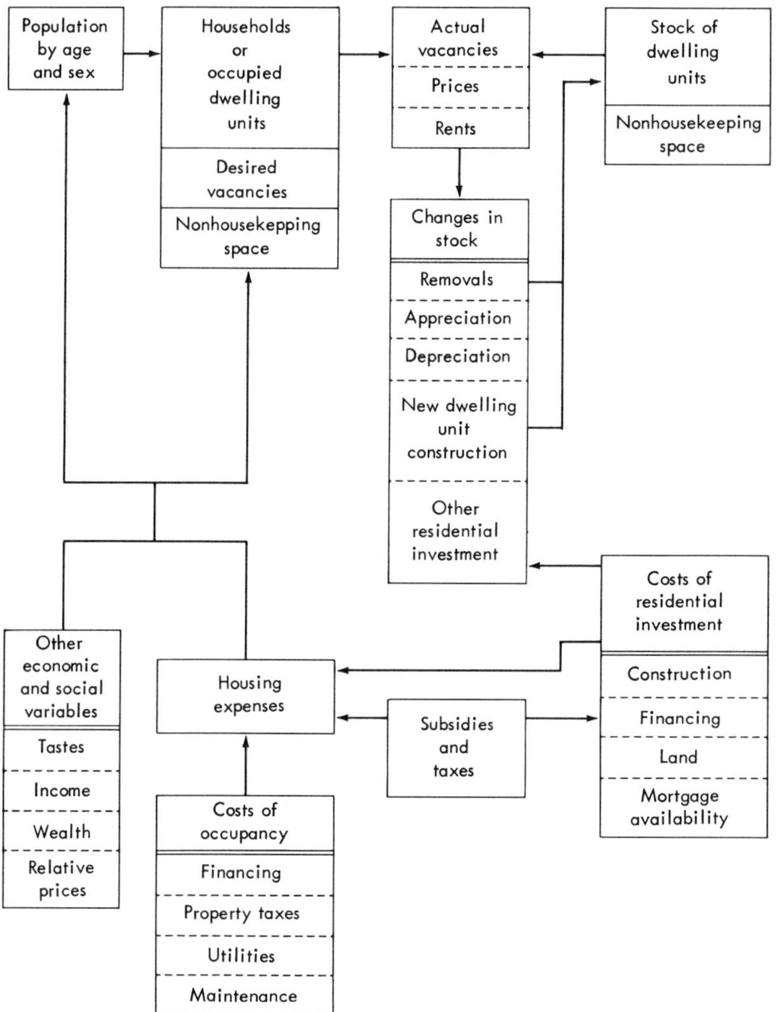

distribution. A given population can, however, form different numbers of households depending upon desires to share units or live separately. The numbers of households formed by a given population is measured by its "headship rate."

Population—The projected increase in households is based on projections of the Bureau of the Census (see Table 2). More than 85 percent of the expected increase in households is based directly on an increase in the population in age groups that form household heads. Errors in such projections over ten-year horizons tend to be small. All those who will head these households are already alive. Demographic errors arise primarily from changes in deaths and migration.

Headship Rates—From 1950 to 1975, almost half of the added households in the United States arose from changes in the headship rate rather than from added population. The largest changes in the demand for dwellings were found among the elderly and young unmarrieds. The number of adults sharing a house with others has fallen steadily, as has the ratio of husband-wife households.

These changes seem to have firm social and economic causes. With Social Security, widowed grandmothers no longer have to move in with their children. With more jobs and income and a change in social mores, young unmarrieds can maintain their own homes. The ability to separate is also influenced by the expense of houses and their availability.

The projection underlying Table 1 shows a demand for dwellings of 250,000 per year from a continuing change in the headship rate. This is less than half the rate of prior periods. The reason is that as higher percentages of the new population have moved into their own units, the numbers available to form new households have fallen sharply.

TYPES OF HOUSEHOLDS

Not only the number, but also the type of households influences the level of housing demand. Single persons and small or young families are more likely to live in apartments or mobile homes than are units composed of mother-father with children. There is a high correlation between a household's type and age and the house it occupies. The projections show almost an even split between the growth of husband-wife families and other types.

TABLE 2. ESTIMATE OF DWELLING UNITS DEMANDED BY TYPE OF STRUCTURE (000)

	Total Stock								
	March 1, 1975			*July 1, 1980*			*July 1, 1985*		
Type of Structure	*By Households*	*For Vacancies*	*Total*	*By Households*	*For Vacancies*	*Total*	*By Households*	*For Vacancies*	*Total*
1 unit	47,500	4,400	51,900	51,320	4,780	56,100	55,800	4,900	60,700
2 or more units	19,820	2,430	22,250	22,800	2,800	25,600	24,450	3,550	28,000
Mobile homes	3,800	—	3,800	4,600	—	4,600	5,600	—	5,600
Total	71,120	6,830	77,950	78,720	7,580	86,300	85,850	8,450	94,300

	*New Construction Adjusted * Annual Rates (000)*							
	July 1, 1976-80				*July 1, 1980-85*			
Type of Structure	*Change in Households*	*Change in Vacancies*	*Replacements*	*Total*	*Change in Households*	*Change in Vacancies*	*Replacements*	*Total*
1 unit	570	160	240	970	810	110	260	1,180
2 or more units	460	200	470	1,130	280	60	530	807
Mobile homes	390	—	60	450	340	—	160	500
Total	1,420	360	770	2,550	1,430	170	950	2,550

Source: Cf. Text. **For Households cf:** U.S. Bureau of the Census, *Current Population Reports,* "Projections of the Number of Households and Families: 1975 to 1990," Washington, D.C.: Government Printing Office, 1975. Series C for under 35; Series B for 35 and over.

* Other units adjusted to higher expected rate of mobile home production.

DESIRED VACANCIES

Many observers are confused when they note a demand for vacancies as shown in Table 1 and Figure 1. Anyone trying to sell or rent a unit is dismayed when he is forced to hold it vacant. However, from an overall point of view, we need vacancies. They furnish flexibility to ease the problem of families who have to or want to move. In addition to units available for rent or for sale, others are vacant awaiting occupancy; some are held off the market—as in estates—while others are held for occasional use, or are temporarily occupied, or are seasonal units.

While the amount of construction needed for added vacancies is the smallest of the three types of demand (about 6 percent for the decade), it contains the largest probable error both in percentage terms and in magnitude. We note that the estimated demand for vacancies for the decade 1975-85 is 1,550,000, but for the nine-year period 1976-85, it is 3,140,000, or more than twice as much. This reflects the low level of production in 1975-76.

Since 1960, the percentage of vacant units in the stock has varied between 8.4 and 10.5 percent, or by approximately 2 million units. In 1960 and 1967, the rate was 10 percent. Many studies assume these were normal years and use this as their estimate of desired vacancies. Others stress the increased interest in recreation and project a large potential increase in vacant second homes. (In 1974, about 2.9 million households owned a second home.) They, therefore, show a need for vacancies of 10.5 or 11 percent.

In contrast, Table 1 contains a conservative estimate of vacancies of 8.8 percent in 1980 and 9 percent in 1985. Use of 10 percent as a need would raise estimated demand for the decade by another million units.

REPLACEMENTS OR REMOVALS

The final demand in Table 1 (shown as removals in Figure 1) is for the replacement of units removed from the stock. A need for 8,500,000 units for the decade is projected, or about one-third of the total.

We lack adequate theory of the forces leading to removals. At least four factors are at work:

1. Some units are lost through disasters such as fire, flood, windstorms, or similar forces.
2. Some units are pulled down because they have deteriorated and are not

worth fixing up. Migration from farms and central cities has left vacant units which eventually are destroyed.

3. Many units are destroyed because their land is required for other uses. Highways or public works lead to a destruction of dwellings. Many have been pulled down as part of urban renewal projects. Others come down because the market replaces them with new houses, apartments, or industrial and commercial buildings.
4. Finally, some units are shown as removals primarily for definitional reasons. For example, the existing stock may be converted to more units when occupied by several families. If then one moves out, a unit is removed. Or if a household living permanently in a motel or hotel with cooking facilities moves out, the unit reverts to hotel status. Those definitional changes were exceedingly significant in the 1930s and 1940s, but have been less so recently.

Many consider the need for replacements as primarily a function of depreciation or age. This is typically not the case. Houses can and do last hundreds of years if properly maintained. Whether or not they are kept up depends upon demand and the cost of maintaining them or of building replacement units.

Removal rates since 1955 have been close to 1 percent of the existing stock per year. This rate is projected as continuing. Conflicting forces are at work. Removals should rise as the stock gets older, particularly because mobile homes have increased greatly in the past twenty years and these are assumed to have a shorter life. On the other hand, rates could fall because it may be relatively cheaper to maintain existing units and because the degree of migration seems to be decreasing. The projection assumes these forces will more or less offset each other.

SUBSTANDARD UNITS

Another possible replacement requirement exists. If national policy determines that under normal market conditions too many substandard units will remain, action can be taken to speed up the removal rate and thus the number of replacement units required. Some projections show a need and therefore a demand over this decade to replace as many as 4,000,000 units beyond prior levels (Joint Center, U. S. President's Commission).

Any estimate of housing deprivation and therefore of needs is extremely uncertain. Past estimates, depending on the observer's definitions, show from 10 to 13 million households living under substandard conditions. These definitions and measurements are quite arbitrary.

We have few accurate measures of the inadequacy of dwellings or neighborhoods or of undue sacrifices made by families. Recently the Department of Housing and Urban Development (HUD) has increased the data collected on these problems. In Annual Housing Surveys, they have asked questions about a unit's physical condition, its equipment, and its occupants' views on neighborhood qualities.

Replies show many people have problems with their dwellings. Most families feel their neighborhood services and street conditions are inadequate. On the other hand, the number who are sufficiently dissatisfied to want to move does not seem large. For example, about 5 percent want to move because of street and neighborhood problems.

More importantly, while some relationship exists between problems and dissatisfaction and family income and house value, it is not great. For many items, the degree of dissatisfaction is spread evenly throughout the income range. Since a majority of families expressing dissatisfaction could move if they wanted to, this indicates problems may not be those which would require a more rapid replacement rate financed or imposed by the government.

We will need far more information before we can state how many people suffer housing deprivation—defining deprivation as problems they could not solve by altering their consumption pattern or other choices within their existing budget limits. Given this lack of knowledge, it is perhaps presumptuous to say that our housing stock seems to be improving steadily and will continue to improve under the projections of Table 1. However, on several grounds, this appears true. For these various reasons, based upon what we now know about housing deprivation, it does not seem useful to project a demand for added removals.

Comparisons with Other Studies

We can gain some perspective on the probable accuracy of the projections in Table 1 by comparing them with other recent studies and examining the history of such projections. Two cautions are necessary: (a) since all studies use the same basic technique, their results and errors will be interrelated; and (b) the errors in the underlying data are great.

We think of the census as accurate, but upon reflection know it is not. For example, in 1970 it is estimated that the census counted 1,400,000 fewer dwellings than existed. Errors in measurements of the stock and in production can easily be as large as or larger than errors in the projections.

In September 1975, HUD made and described several estimates by others of production needs for the years 1975-80. The range of projections they discussed was from 1,920,000 to 2,550,000 units annually (U. S. Senate). At 2,320,000, our projection falls in the middle of the range.

What are the causes of the differences? Estimates of household formation vary from 1,230,000 a year, which is the pure population growth factor, to 1,640,000 obtained by assuming a continued rapid increase in the headship rate. The 1,420,000 change in households shown in Table 1 is again in the middle of the range, but above the average.

A larger variation exists among these projections in the demand for vacancies. HUD's own estimates show an annual need of about 120,000 for this purpose compared to our projection of 140,000. Among other studies, a more typical estimated need is for an additional 190,000 units annually.

Replacement requirements also differ considerably. Thus HUD shows annual requirements under this heading of 590,000 compared to the 760,000 of this chapter. We are close to the average of other studies, but some run as high as 980,000 annually, even without consideration of substandard units or deprivation. If these are included, the annual replacement demand rises by another 400,000.

Examination of the various studies indicates that unless we have a major depression or some unusual social exhilaration or collapse, it is unlikely for each factor to be at its extreme level. Furthermore, errors are likely to be offsetting. As a result, a range of ±100,000 around our projected production of 2,320,000 units annually for the decade 1975-85 appears to cover most likely outcomes.

We have used these same techniques to make long-term forecasts periodically since 1960. Our errors have all been under 100,000. The largest errors occurred in the projection of vacancies. These differences, however, primarily reflect short-run cyclical movements rather than errors in the projections of long-run demand.

The Amount of Residential Construction

While predictions of housing starts are common, and estimates of expenditures for services not infrequent, estimates of investments in housing are fewer. In estimating investment in the GNP, we must consider, along with the projected number of dwellings to be built, the resources to be spent for each. This problem can be thought of as first measuring the forces changing the type of units demanded and then those altering the amount to be spent for each average new unit. Finally, estimates are also required for investment not directly related to new dwellings.

Figure 1 shows that the factors influencing the demand for space and the demand for investment, while similar, differ considerably. Thus taxes, subsidies, and financing costs and availability influence both the demand for space services and the level of investment, but they need not be the same. Long-term financing influences final demand, while construction financing has more impact on investment. A subsidy to a developer may trigger investment, but has only an indirect effect on demand for space.

Changes in tastes, in housing expenses, in income and wealth, and in relative prices will shift the demand for services. This, in turn, will alter vacancies, sales prices, and rents. Such movements may be primarily absorbed by changes in the value of existing houses or land and have only a slight effect on investment. Because these relationships are complex, they are hard to model. Thus most studies concentrate on either the demand for units or the level of expenditures for housing services.

TYPE OF STRUCTURE

The type of structure demanded, among other factors, depends upon: (a) the type and age of households—single people and the young are more likely to occupy apartments or mobile homes; (b) the relative construction costs of dwellings and their use of land; (c) the expenses of operating different types of units; (d) the location desires of families; and (e) the relative availability of financing. As these factors shifted, the share of single-family structures fell sharply, while the percentage of apartments and mobile homes rose. Since these latter take fewer resources, the number of households sheltered per unit of investment went up.

What significance will such changes have on investment demand over the next decade? Table 2 projects the housing stock and the distribution of new construction by type of unit. The table is based upon the distribution of type of structure occupied by households classified by age and type in 1970. This distribution has been applied to the expected number of households in later years to show a projection of occupied units by type. The estimates of vacancies and removals by type are also based on past trends, but have a larger probable error. Past estimates of these breakdowns are inaccurate.

When we compare this procedure's estimated distribution in 1975 to those derived from updating sample surveys, occupied mobile homes seem to be underestimated, a not surprising result. The rate of change for mobile homes has increased sharply. To allow for this discrepancy, we increase the ratio of households in mobile homes for 1980 and 1985 at the rate of change experienced in 1970-75. The distributions of households by type in Table 2 are based on these augmented ratios.

Even so, this procedure still estimates a level of mobile home sales well below recent trends. There are still many possible reasons for this discrepancy. As new houses have increased in price relative to other expenditures, mobile homes look relatively more attractive. This occurs even though—probably reflecting the inclusion of more services—mobile home relative prices have gone up more than other dwellings. Also the census underreports the increase in mobile homes in the stock. Some are included as regular one-family units, while vacant ones are simply not counted.

For all of these reasons, we have projected a somewhat larger share of mobile homes in future production than would be estimated from expected household formation alone.

We have converted the expected new construction in Table 2 to single-family equivalents, using weights of 0.85 for multifamily units and 0.40 for mobile homes (weights based on relative resource use as shown in the GNP accounts). Comparing the expected change in units either by a simple count or by using single-family equivalents, we find but slight differences in the expected growth rate from 1972-74 to 1975-80 and 1980-85. In both cases, the expected increase in investment demand is between 6 percent and 7 percent for the entire period (not per year).

EXPENDITURES PER DWELLING UNIT

Figure 1 shows many forces which influence the amount invested in a typical dwelling unit. Unfortunately the variables are so numerous and the data so poor that exact statements of causation are difficult. Conversely, so many theoretical relationships exist that anyone can find a few high correlations which signify little if anything about actual causation.

Most studies of housing expenditures have examined family incomes and budgets. They deal with expenses for current housing services rather than with investment. Hundreds of such studies have been performed. They disagree widely. My own published studies estimate that family expenditures on housing services will rise 0.75 percent for each 1 percent increase in family income, and will fall 0.75 percent for each 1 percent increase in the price of housing services relative to the price of other consumption goods (Maisel, Burnham, and Austin). I know of no studies which have successfully contradicted these estimates.

However, as noted, because forces at work in moving from shelter expenditures to construction expenditures are so complex, this knowledge is not too useful in estimating investment. On the other hand, difficulties are also great when we attempt to model construction expenditures directly. The data are inadequate, containing major errors. Estimates are difficult because of varying lags from investment decisions to construction and by shifts among types of structures. Even more problems arise because of extreme cyclical variability.

The Record—Since we are concerned here with the long-run movements in investment, I have taken a simplified long-run approach. I have compared housing starts plus mobile home shipments and the investments in dwelling units to changes in income between the three-year periods, 1947-49, 1963-65, and 1972-74. The averages for these years seem typical. The results of such an examination accord with general knowledge. From 1947-49 to 1963-65, the factors which we believe influence the willingness to invest in housing were favorable. Incomes were rising. Financing terms improved somewhat as small increases in interest rates were offset by longer maturities and lower down payments. Mortgage funds were ample. The relative cost of housing construction fell. Housing rose in peoples' scale of values with the movement to home ownership and larger single-family units. As a result of these forces, expenditures per new dwelling rose faster than average household income. In fact, each 1 percent rise in household income was accompanied by a 1.6 percent increase in the average expenditure per unit.

From 1963-65 to 1972-74, the opposite occurred. All housing expenses such as mortgage interest rates, property taxes, maintenance costs, and construction costs rose in relation to other costs and prices. Land prices also rose rapidly, as did the value of existing units. Credit was rationed in several periods. As a result, real investment expenditures per new dwelling unit actually fell slightly, even though household income continued to rise. The relative decline in expenditures was sufficient so that for the entire twenty-five-year period the growth in unit expenditures was only 0.86 percent for each 1 percent growth in household income.

The Future—Clearly in projecting relative expenditures over this decade, the assumptions made as to the course of interest rates, mortgage availability, relative building costs, and the relative prices of other shelter expenses are extremely significant. I assume that, given the large increases in housing expenses since 1968, market pressures will now work the other way. Housing expenses and costs will improve somewhat compared to others.

The assumption underlying Table 1 is that between 1972-74 and 1980-85 real household income will increase by about 20 percent. Investment per dwelling unit will rise about 15 percent. To this must be added an increase in number and type of units of 6 to 7 percent. As a result, expenditures on new residential dwelling units are estimated to rise from $43.1 billion (in 1972 dollars) in 1972-74 to an annual average of $52.6 billion in 1980-85.

OTHER INVESTMENT EXPENDITURES

The remaining investments in housing shown in our national accounts cover a wide variety of items. They include: additions and major alterations (but not maintenance) to existing units; new nonhousekeeping units such as motels, hotels, or other group quarters; the durable equipment installed in new houses; and payments to brokers for their market function. The private residential investment accounts are reduced by sales of used structures to the government. In 1973-74, these items together averaged $15 billion, or 25 percent of reported residential investment.

Again, we have few theories of the forces causing changes in this type of expenditure. There is a strong suspicion that they contain sizeable errors. From 1947-49 to 1963-65, they virtually doubled in real terms. From 1963-65 to 1972-74, they rose only by 6 percent. We would expect that given the increase in new housing costs, more would be spent in this category. However, such increases do not yet appear in the data.

For Table 1, we have projected a 20 percent increase in real terms for this category from 1972-74 to 1980-85. This would be less than the rate of growth in the earlier period, but far more than in recent years. This results in a total of $14.9 billion (in 1972 dollars), which, added to the estimated investment of $52.6 billion on new dwelling units, gives the final projection of an annual average residential investment of $67.5 billion for 1980-85.

Financing Housing Investment

The fact that the share of resources required by housing in the GNP is projected to decrease does not, of course, mean that no problems will arise. Difficult questions of capacity, skills, technology, and of industrial organization remain. Still the most serious questions are likely in the financing sphere. As in the past, an adequate long-term supply of credit is less likely to be a problem than its instability (Maisel).

A JERRY-BUILT SYSTEM

The source of many of housing's troubles can be found in the jerry-built system of housing finance, composed of a mixture of special institutions, special laws and regulations, and subsidies. To many, the existing system is objectionable because it differs so much from a competitive free market system. To others its most critical fault is its instability. While over the whole period, credit has not been lacking, there have been periodic short-term shortages (Maisel).

Others believe the system is inefficient. The degree to which it is better or worse than other possibilities is unknown. It appears to redistribute income in a quite arbitrary manner—probably from the poor to the better-off. There is always a fair amount of rationing of credit. For example, studies of "red-lining" show major sectors with few if any loans over long periods. In tight-money periods, the number rationed out increases dramatically. The actual costs of borrowing frequently appear unduly large and quite irrational.

There are indications that even under normal circumstances, many families find it difficult to borrow and therefore cannot live in houses which they desire and can afford on the basis of their expected income and wealth. In inflation, the difficulty is compounded (Maisel). There is a technical "inflationary-gap." Consumers cannot borrow because market interest rates contain an inflationary premium, while lenders cannot take into account a probable similar rise in borrowers' incomes. Another difficulty is that many elderly who build up equities in their home still must move because there is no institutional technique for them to borrow against the future (Guttentag).

Probably the greatest concern, however, is that the existing system will fall apart. Fluctuations in monetary policy have an augmented impact on housing credit. There has been a constant worsening of housing instability. If the fluctuations in monetary policy continue and there is no special relief in the housing field, the whole system may self-destruct.

THE CREDIT ALLOCATION SYSTEM

Credit is made available to housing through a system of specialized financial institutions, government subsidies, and government housing agencies. Few realize how complex the system is. The share of the mortgage market dependent on savings and loans and the government agencies has increased rapidly. Savings and loans nearly doubled their share of the mortgage market, making around 40 percent of mortgage loans in the mid-1970s. In 1974, government agencies accounted for over 30 percent of long-term mortgages (Maisel and Roulac).

The dominance of thrift institutions in the mortgage market is based on a set of special regulations and tax subsidies. Most significant is the interest rate ceiling on deposits. This regulation gives the institutions an opportunity to obtain funds at low rates and decreases competition both from commercial banks and among thrift institutions. On the other hand, it causes sharp fluctuations in the flow of deposits as short-term market rates move around the deposit ceiling rates. If the institutions are to pay market rates on their deposits, the amount they earn on their assets must move with the market also. This is not possible under existing regulations. To receive their benefits, the institutions are required to hold mortgages as the bulk of their assets.

The share of the government agencies in the mortgage market has shown the greatest increase of all sectors. They serve both to improve the secondary market for mortgages and also to transfer funds from the bond and money markets to housing.

The growth of the specialized housing institutions has improved availability in capital-short growing sectors and narrowed the spread between mortgages and bonds. The spread between Moody's Aaa bonds and mortgages fell from over 2 percent in 1955 to virtually zero in the mid-1970s.

Federal housing subsidies, whether direct, through interest rates, or by tax expenditures, are well over $18 billion. A small share goes to financial institutions, some to low income groups, and some to rental housing, but the largest share goes to wealthier groups through deductions of property taxes and mortgage interest from incomes subject to tax (Maisel).

EXISTING UNITS AND WEALTH

The financing of housing investment is further complicated by the fact that approximately 70 percent of loans are made to finance the transfer of existing dwellings, and only 30 percent cover new investment. This means that an additional institutional problem exists. Greater attention must be paid to changes in wealth and capital gains than is typical of most investment analysis.

While those in the housing market are aware of the extent to which purchases of new units depend upon profits and savings from prior ownership, there is little discussion of these factors in the literature. This results from the fact that the national accounts and flow of funds pay only slight attention to changes in, and transfers of, wealth.

The Department of Commerce estimates that from 1965 to 1975 the gross value of our housing stock rose by $1,175 billion. The net value increased by over $750 billion, or more than 140 percent. During this period, gross investment was only $450 billion. The actual appreciation in value may have been even greater, because depreciation is estimated arbitrarily on a constant basis.

To the degree that values increase, existing owners have more wealth. The initial increase in value is financed automatically by their larger equity. When properties turn over, additional debt financing is required, but there is no need for additional savings from income. The sellers have capital gains which they can invest, deposit, or lend elsewhere. The capital gains tax on these sales can be easily postponed and eventually avoided. Funds are available unless the sellers increase their current expenditures, but there may be a problem of channeling the funds to the point of need.

Possible Solutions

Because the financing problem is so critical in housing, there is a wide variety of policy proposals, each of which hopefully would improve the underlying situation. While each is the basis of a great deal of debate and analysis, we treat them summarily. For exposition, they can be divided into four groups:

1. Do away with most of the existing system; operate a free market.
2. End inflation and create stability.

3. Reform financial institutions.
4. Alter the government programs; add or subtract some.

A FREE MARKET

Some believe the large numbers of special regulations and institutions in the housing field are inefficient and destabilizing. They would abolish most of the existing system and, if necessary, replace it with direct subsidies. Their view tend not to be based on specific studies or analysis, but rather on their general belief in the efficacy of free markets (Maisel).

Various counterarguments are made. Studies of the housing market seem to show that the existing system does make added credit available and at lower rates. The closing of the interest rate gap is an example. Others believe that a free market could not do the job. They point to the fact that because of large information costs, important sectors have been unable to obtain mortgages, particularly in the past, and some lack credit even with the existing system. They also raise questions as to the dynamic stability of financial institutions under a nonregulated system. Intervention in the past has frequently occurred when instability and losses in the markets were large.

There is also, of course, a major political problem. Irrespective of whether there is a total gain for the economy, it is clear that some groups are better off under the existing system than under proposed ones. They are large and powerful politically. Unless they can be convinced either that they will not lose as a result of changes or that they will lose less, or unless the new proposals compensate them, any changes in the existing system will not be achieved without a struggle.

Finally, it is noted that a special system for housing credit is not unique to the United States. Few countries, if any, operate free housing credit markets. In most, there are special programs and financial institutions similar to those of the United States. One may speculate that this reflects the special characteristics and needs of the housing market. Over time, all types of experiments from free markets to public housing have been followed in different countries; yet most end up with mixed specialized programs.

LESS INFLATION, STABLE MONEY

One fear is that the mortgage market is deteriorating under the twin blows of inflation and increasing monetary instability. Either is sufficient to create great dangers. The increased use of monetary policy results in less "bang" for every buck lost. Those who can protect themselves against credit crunches learn to do so. To achieve any given degree of restraint through monetary policy requires higher interest rates than the last time around.

Each recent cycle has witnessed higher rates, more problems for the thrift institutions, and more problems for housing. Solutions are: less inflation; more dependence on general or specific fiscal policies; or more emphasis on specific, in contrast to general, monetary constraints (Maisel).

A prime need is a recognition of the costs of instability in housing to the overall economy. In the past, many concerned with credit and finance have welcomed instability in housing as necessary to fight inflation. Because housing demand could be lowered so easily through monetary policy, large shifts in mortgage credit were welcomed as stabilizing.

I believe, and have been convinced for twenty-five years, that this theory and action based on it is mistaken under most circumstances. The effect of these policies has been to increase housing costs and prices. While in war or similar periods of extreme demand, the decreased demand from housing has been useful, in normal cyclical movements, the effect has been to accentuate the cycle in resource use and inflation.

Thus a simple decision that housing policy ought to emphasize stability plus actions to implement such policies will aid residential investment and its financing as well as the general economy.

FINANCIAL INSTITUTIONS

Many agree that some changes in existing financial institutions are necessary. Present regulations may not be viable, particularly if technological change speeds up. The problem is to obtain agreement from all interested parties as to what changes make sense. Most proposals have been opposed by some institutions, joined by consumers and housing lobbyists. Disagreements arise because of different estimates of the future.

RESTRUCTURING GOVERNMENT PROGRAMS

Numerous suggestions have been made as to how altered governmental programs can solve the housing finance problem. Since the sums spent are large, since the programs seem to create perverse income distributions, and since they have not increased stability, some changes appear logical.

The factors calling for change should determine their form. New programs should make greater use of the market, improve rather than lessen equity, and operate so as to increase stability. They probably require that more emphasis be placed on the use of existing housing and on conservation than on production.

Variable Rates or Mortgage Rate Insurance—A critical problem arises because of the inability of institutions holding primarily long-term fixed rate assets to alter their deposit payment rates as the market changes. One suggestion to allow institutions to adjust is to introduce variable interest rate mortgages. While their use is growing, variable rate mortgages are opposed by those who feel that they shift too much risk to borrowers. A substitute proposal would enable institutions to convert their fixed income assets to variable ones by contracting with the government, which would assume such risks in place of consumers. The government could either sell interest rate insurance or issue variable rate contracts. In these, the government's and the institutions' income would vary, but in opposite directions, as market rates moved.

Mortgage Annuities—Another useful institutional change would be the introduction of variable-term mortgages tied to annuities for the elderly. These would be loans guaranteeing a fixed or variable income for life. They would enable the elderly to use the equity in their homes as a source of income, with the house passing to the lender upon death or with an earlier sale if this was desirable (Guttentag).

Subsidies—A great deal of dissatisfaction exists over current subsidy programs. They appear expensive, inefficient, and inequitable. A good deal of analytical effort and research is taking place with respect to reshaping the direct subsidy programs. However, far less consideration has been given to the subsidies through tax expenditures and interest rates, which cost the most. The problem is to make a coherent program from expenditures that grew in a completely haphazard manner.

The Housing Agencies—Many proposals entail some reshaping of the policies of the government and government-sponsored housing agencies. They too do not seem to have clear objectives. Most feel they have been useful, but have not lived up to their potentialities. They have failed to promote stability and equity. Proposals for change are to emphasize these goals in their operations. If properly managed, they could be significant forces tending to offset other sources of instability.

Conclusions

Residential investment has constituted between 25 and 35 percent of total private investment and about 4.3 percent of the GNP. Mortgages have been about a quarter of private debt. The share of housing in these totals will probably decrease. The problem of housing differs considerably from other types of investment, but this fact is frequently neglected in discussions of investment and saving.

Under normal economic conditions, the number of housing units demanded over an average period is closely related to demographic factors and replacements. The level of expenditures per unit rises with, but somewhat less than, household income. It is less related to expectations, profits, taxes, and total production than are other types of investment. The critical housing investment problems are the short-run cyclical ones. There have been seven sharp cycles in housing investment since World War II. Starts declined by more than 40 percent on the average. The degree of instability has been increasing. The five years from 1970 to 1974 saw the most violent swing of all.

While other factors play some role, the largest share of the fluctuations is related to changing financial conditions and, in the last cycle, to government subsidy policies. For these reasons, in the analysis of residential investment far more attention has properly been paid to financial institutions and to government policies. There are some cyclical forces related to shifting profit margins in the rental sector and to variations in vacancy rates, but these tend to average out over four or five year periods.

For the decade 1975-85, basic demand is expected to average about 2,450,000 dwellings per year. Of these, roughly 2,000,000 a year would be conventional starts. However, the short-fall in production in 1975 and 1976 has created additional demand for the remaining years. Thus the required average level has risen to 2,100,000 traditional starts plus 450,000 mobile homes. This level of starts, plus increases in the average expenditure per unit, and spending on other items than new dwellings, give a projected annual level of residential investment of $63 billion, or 3.9 percent of the GNP from 1976 through 1985.

Such a level should cause no problems for the economy. However, if fluctuations continue and the actual rates move between 3 percent and 5.2 percent of the GNP, as they have in recent years, the effect on both the housing industry and the economy will be decidedly unfortunate. The fluctuating investment in housing will continue as a destabilizing force on national production and prices. Inflation in rents, in home ownership, and in the general price level will be accentuated.

Recognition of the cyclical problem is at the heart of the interest in reforms in our financial structure and in the government subsidy programs. The overall housing demand for saving and resources is not a problem. Fluctuations and a fear that our thrift system cannot stand the type of pressures experienced over the past ten years are behind proposed changes. Some alterations, particularly in government programs, appear probable. Making significant changes in financial institutions, however, has proven to be an extremely difficult political problem. Some hope that with time this problem will disappear. Others fear that it can only get worse and that reforms are unlikely except in a time of recognized crisis.

References

Board of Governors of The Federal Reserve System, *Ways to Moderate Fluctuations in Housing Construction.* Washington, D.C.: Board of Governors of The Federal Reserve System, 1972.

de Leeuw, Frank and R. J. Struyk, *The Web of Urban Housing.* Washington, D.C.: The Urban Institute, 1975.

Federal Home Loan Bank of San Francisco, *Resources for Housing.* San Francisco, 1976.

Guttentag, J. M., *Creating New Financial Instruments for the Aged.* Solomon Financial Center, New York University, 1975.

Joint Center for Urban Studies of Massachusetts Institute of Technology and Harvard University, *America's Housing Needs: 1970 to 1980.* Cambridge, Massachusetts, December, 1973.

Kristof, Frank S., *Urban Housing Needs Through the 1980s: An Analysis and Projection,* Research Report No. 10, The National Commission on Urban Problems. Washington, D.C.: Government Printing Office, 1968.

Maisel, S. J., "Stabilization and Income Distribution Policies and Housing Production," in *Resources for Housing,* 1976.

Maisel, S. J., J. Burnham, and W. Austin, "The Demand for Housing: A Comment," *Review of Economics and Statistics,* LIII, no. 4 (November 1971).

Maisel, S. J. and S. E. Roulac, *Real Estate Investment and Finance.* New York: McGraw-Hill, 1976.

U.S. President's Commission on Urban Housing, *Report.* Washington, D.C.: Government Printing Office, December 1968.

U.S. Senate, Committee on Banking, Housing, and Urban Affairs, 94:1, *Hearings on Housing Goals and Mortgage Credit: 1975-80,* September 1975.

R. B. Freeman

4

Investment in Human Capital and Knowledge

Introduction

Recognition of the importance of human and knowledge capital in productivity and growth was one of the major achievements in economic analysis in the 1950s and 1960s. While the critical role of trained manpower and the "stock of useful knowledge" in the wealth of nations was not unknown to economists previously (see Marshall, pp. 170-182), it was not until quantitative estimates of the sources of growth (Fabricant, Solow, Denison) revealed that the bulk of increases in gross national product could not be explained by standard labor and capital aggregates that human capital and knowledge achieved center stage.

Spurred more or less directly by the failure of the standard growth accounting model, Schultz argued that human capital was the major omitted factor, accounting for much of the residual in productivity, as well as diverse other phenomena, including changes in physical capital-output ratios over time. Denison accorded the rising educational attainment of the American work force a seminal place in *Sources of Economic Growth,* suggesting that upwards of 42 percent of increases in real national income per person can be attributed to

---

RICHARD B. FREEMAN *is Associate Professor of Economics at Harvard University. He has written widely on problems of human resources, including the books* The Overeducated American *and* The Labor Market for College-Trained Manpower. *He is a consultant to the government of Venezuela on manpower resources, a member of a number of public and private commissions on education and a congressional committee on research and development.*

the growth of schooling (1962, Table 33, p. 240). While Denison's later estimates reduced the contribution of education substantially (to 21 percent of the growth in real national income per person from 1929 to 1969), it continued to be as or more important than capital (1972, Tables 7-8, p. 137). In an important direct test of the human capital-productivity relation, Griliches entered labor skill variables as separate inputs in production functions for agriculture and manufacturing, obtaining significant positive relations between productivity and skill.

Although the "human capital school" has focused more intensely on microeconomic issues in recent years, the incorporation of labor skills into production functions and growth accounting remain one of its major achievements. The analytic stress on the productive role of education may even have contributed to the publicly financed expansion of the education sector in the 1960s.

The economic significance of the second nonstandard form of capital, research-produced "useful knowledge" received considerable attention following Sputnik and the Soviet economic advances of the 1950s and 1960s. While many R & D studies have concentrated on specific innovations (*i.e.*, hybrid corn) or enterprises and are not readily amalgamable into macro-growth accounting, the virtually uniform finding of a large effect of R & D on productivity suggests strongly that economic growth has been substantially raised by investments in knowledge. Crude estimates of the growth implications of industry productivity regressions by Griliches suggest that R & D may have contributed as much as 0.5 percentage points to growth in the 1960s and 0.3 points in the 1970s (1973, pp. 78-79).

The intellectual attention given human and knowledge capital mirrored a rapid increase in investment in education and R & D in post-World War II years. Between 1950 and 1970 the education share of GNP tripled: the vast majority of young persons obtained high school degrees; and many went on to college; over 800 new colleges and universities were established; public subsidization of higher education exceeded $30 billion by 1975. Expenditures for R & D increased more rapidly over a shorter time period: in 1953 the U.S. spent $5.1 billion on research and development, 1.5 percent of GNP; in 1964 over $18.9 billion, 3 percent of GNP. Over the same period employment of scientists and engineers increased by 77 percent and the number of Ph.Ds granted by 71 percent. The comparative advantage which the United States gained in skilled manpower and knowledge-intensive activities showed up dramatically in trade statistics, which revealed that exports tended to be labor intensive (Leontief), labor-skill, and R & D intensive (Keesing). The period from the 1950s to the mid- or late-1960s was a vertiable golden age for education and research, creating a booming job market for scientists, university faculty, and college-trained specialists across-the-board.

The situation underwent sharp change in the late 1960s. R & D spending leveled off and then dropped as a share of GNP. Federal support of basic science in colleges and universities declined in real terms; fellowship support for students diminished; graduate enrollments in physics and other natural sciences fell sharply. Some of the R & D intensive industries, such as aerospace and ordnance which had been growth leaders in the previous decade, contracted. By the mid-1970s, the return to the college investment in terms of income or likely employment in professional occupations dropped to unprecedented lows for new graduates; the proportion of young men choosing college fell and the share of GNP going to education stabilized. In short, the "big push" of investment in education and knowledge of the previous decade ground to a halt.

After the boom of the 1960s and bust of the 1970s, what is the place of human and knowledge capital in the nation's stock of produced means of production? What has happened to the level and return to these forms of investments? What is the likely future course of investments in education and R & D and their potential impact on productivity growth and high employment? How can the government influence the volume and composition of these investments? In what ways, if any, should it seek to influence them?

TOOLS OF ANALYSIS

To investigate these questions I employ the basic equation of growth accounting, which relates marginal increases in the amount of resources to increases in material output. The equation is obtained by differentiating an aggregate production function which, in the case at hand, relates output (Y) to human capital (H); research produced knowledge capital (R); labor (L); and physical capital (K):

(1) $$Y = F(K, K, H, R)$$

Differentiating with respect to the knowledge and human capital inputs yields

(2) $$dY = F_H dH + F_R dR = W_H dH + W_R dR$$

where F_H and F_R are the marginal products of the two inputs, which in certain cases can equal the relevant wages W_H and W_R.

In percentage or log change form (written with dots above variables), (2) can be written in two informative ways:

$$Y = F_H \, dH/Y + F_R \, dR/Y \text{ or as} \tag{3}$$

$$Y = \alpha_H H + \alpha_R R \tag{4}$$

In (3), growth is larger to the extent that either (a) the share of national product allotted to net investment in human capital $[dH/Y]$ and/or net investment in knowledge capital $[dR/Y]$ is larger, or (b) the return or productivity of these investments, F_H and F_R, is larger. Using this formulation, one is led to analyze the effects of these types of investments on economic growth by examining the trends in the share of national product devoted to each type of investment and by examining the trends in their rates of return or productivity. We shall use this procedure to analyze the impact of R & D expenditures on growth because data exists on annual investment in R & D but not on the stock of knowledge capital. In (4), growth is explained in terms of the rate of increase in the stock of human (H) and knowledge (R) capital and their productivity as measured by the share of national income earned by the two forms of capital $[\alpha_H = (W_H H)/Y;$ $\alpha_R \; (W_R R)/Y]$. This decomposition will be used when evaluating the impact on economic growth of investment in human capital since we have data on the stock of this input in the form of the years of schooling of the entire work force.

While the growth accounting approach to productivity analysis provides a useful decomposition of the sources of growth, it has several shortcomings. First, and most importantly, the methodology is not a model of the growth process. It takes as given the changes in supply and marginal products which underly the accounting equations. In a complete model, these elements would be endogenous. Second, the approach deals solely with marginal changes, effectively ruling out possible interesting nonmarginal interrelations among inputs in production. With a linear homogeneous production function and marginal changes, equation (2) tells the complete story about the relation between inputs and growth; with nonmarginal changes (or nonhomogeneous production), the effect of increases in the supply of one input on the productivity of others cannot be ignored. Third, for some inputs, notably knowledge capital, the use of market prices to measure marginal products is suspect. On the one hand, basic research and certain aspects of applied research are nonappropriable, creating externalities which are not valued in the market. On the other, these externalities often enter as "free" inputs into applied research and are valued therein. While the net effect on the market price of all R & D activities is not clear, most analysts believe that the contribution of R & D is undervalued in the market place. In the absence of direct evidence on externalities, little can be done beyond recognizing the potential bias in growth accounting.

These problems notwithstanding, the methodology offers a useful tool for estimating the possible contribution of diverse factors to increases in productivity and will be used in this study.

The Slowdown in the Rate of Increase in Human and Knowledge Capital

Estimates of the quantitative significance of human capital, comparable to those in Schultz's pioneering article, and of knowledge capital in the nation's total stock are contained in Table 1. Empirical and conceptual problems with the various aggregrates dictate the use of several measures. Physical capital is measured by reproducible tangible wealth (the series employed by Schultz in his comparison of human and physical capital), which includes household wealth; and by nonresidential business capital. Human capital is estimated by applying Schultz's cost figures to the distribution of educational attainment of workers to obtain a "cost side" estimate comparable to his. This estimate differs from one obtained by taking the discounted present value of earnings in the work force since human capital is not sold in the market and individuals do not pay full cost. The knowledge capital series are obtained by accumulating expenditures from 1941 to 1975, assuming modest 1941 capital figures, and depreciating the stock at 10 percent per year. Conceptually, it is unclear what rate of depreciation should be used to value knowledge capital. Basic knowledge does not deteriorate physically; as long as there is sufficient investment in education, it is not forgotten; some forms of knowledge may actually appreciate over time through their effect on future research. Still, increased application of particular research outputs to production will reduce the marginal value of output; citations of articles in scientific journals show that they have a short half-life (De Solla Price), suggesting some depreciation. The 10 percent rate used in the table is chosen solely as a measuring rod; until detailed studies of depreciation are available, other rates may be viewed as equally appropriate. Civilian and total R & D are treated separately in the calculations because defense and space research are likely to

TABLE 1. PHYSICAL, HUMAN, AND KNOWLEDGE CAPITAL IN THE UNITED STATES, 1900-1975 *(Billions of Dollars)*

	Physical Capital		*Human Capital*	*Knowledge Capital (with 10 percent depreciation rate)*	
	"Wealth"	*Business Capital (1958 Dollars)*		*Total R & D*	*Civilian R & D*
1900	282	–	63	–	–
1930	735	442	180	–	–
1957	1270	616	535	58	31
1966	–	818	686	135	64
1970	–	973	810	169	85
1975	–	1090 *	997	192	107
		Percent Increases Per Annum			
1900-57	2.7	–	3.8	–	–
1930-57	2.0	1.2	4.1	–	–
1957-66	–	3.3	2.8	10.1	8.6
1966-75	–	4.1	4.2	4.0	6.1

Sources: Column 1, Schultz, "Education and Economic Growth" in National Society for the Study of Education, *Social Forces Influencing American Education* 60th year, Part II (1961), Table 14, p. 73.

Column 2, Series F-480 from U.S. Bureau of the Census, *Historical Statistics of the U.S. Colonial Times to 1970,* Part 1, p. 258 with an update from U.S. Department of Commerce Survey of *Current Business,* March 1974, Table 1, p. 25.

Column 3, Schultz for 1900-57, other years from data in U.S. Bureau of Labor Statistics, *Educational Attainment of the Work Force.*

Columns 4, 5, Calculated from data in National Science Foundation, *National Patterns of R & D Resources* 1953-75, NSF 75-307, Tables B-5 and B-9 with figures from 1941 to 1952 estimated from U.S. Department of Commerce, *Long Term Economic Growth 1860-1965,* Series B53 B56. The initial 1941 total capital stock was estimated to be $9 billion based on estimates for 1929 and 1948 from Kendrick's "The Treatment of Intangible Resources as Capital" *The Review of Income and Wealth,* March 1973, Table 3, p. 119.

* 1974.

have considerably smaller effects on growth and productivity than other R & D.

The major finding in the table is that, after growing much more rapidly than physical capital for many decades, the rate of increase in human and knowledge capital came to approach that of physical capital in the 1960s and 1970s. According to Schultz's estimates, human capital increased by 1.1 percent more per annum than physical capital from 1900 to 1957. By the calculations in Table 1, it increased by 0.5 percent less than physical capital per annum from 1957 to 1966 when the supply of college workers increased only modestly, and by about the same rate as physical capital thereafter (4.2 versus 4.1 percent).

The rate of growth of knowledge capital also declined in the late 1960s, largely because of federal R & D cutbacks. After increasing by 10 percent in the 1957-1966 period, all R & D capital (including space and defense) rose by just 4 percent from 1966 to 1975. Civilian R & D capital declined more moderately but still experienced a rapidly narrowing differential in growth relative to physical capital. From 1957 to 1961 civilian R & D capital is estimated to have grown by 5.3 percent more per annum than physical capital; from 1966 to 1975, by just 2 percent more. While different depreciation rates will yield different estimates of the stock of knowledge capital and different growth patterns, the general trend of decelerating rates of change is clear.

INVESTMENT FLOWS

Additional evidence indicating that the era of especially rapid growth in human and knowledge capital inputs came to an end in the 1970s is given in Table 2, which turns from capital stocks to gross investments in education and R & D. Lines 1 and 2 record the share of GNP going to private and governmental investments in physical capital. Lines 3 and 4 present comparable figures for private and governmental R & D; line 5 records direct expenditures for education while line 6 gives estimates of the income foregone by high school and college students. The final lines of the table report the share of all investment in GNP, exclusive and inclusive of foregone income, in GNP. As foregone income is not counted in GNP, the figures in line 8 are relative numbers rather than shares.

The table reveals several important aspects of investment in post-World War II years. First, there is a clear turnaround in the pattern of growth in the R & D and education share of GNP. From 1950 to 1965, the ratio of R & D to GNP rose sharply, as did the direct and foregone income components of investment in education. In terms of direct spending, less than 5 percent of GNP went for education and R & D in 1950 compared to 9 percent in 1965. As the ratio of foregone income to GNP (line 6) increased from 2.1 to 3.9, total investment in

TABLE 2. INVESTMENT IN PHYSICAL CAPITAL, EDUCATIONAL AND RESEARCH AND DEVELOPMENT AS SHARES OF GNP, 1950-1974

	1950	*1960*	*1965*	*1970*	*1972*	*1974*
1. Private investment	18.8	15.1	16.3	14.3	16.1	15.1
2. Government investment	2.7	3.3	3.8	3.4	3.1	3.3
3. Private R & D	0.5	1.0	1.0	1.2	1.0	1.1
4. Government R & D	0.8	1.7	1.9	1.5	1.4	1.2
5. Direct educational expenditures	3.5	5.0	6.1 *	7.4	7.7	7.3
6. Foregone income of college and high school students	2.1	3.1	3.9	4.1	4.0	3.6
7. Total direct spending (Lines 1-5)	26.3	26.1	29.1	27.8	29.3	28.0
8. Total (Lines 1-6)	28.4	29.2	33.0	31.9	33.3	31.6

Sources: Line 1, U.S. Department of Labor, Employment and Training Report of the President, Table G-3, p. 359.

Line 2, Unpublished data from U.S. Department of Commerce obtained from Table 3.9 Government Gross Free Capital Formation, 1929-1974.

Lines 3, 4, National Science Foundation, *National Patterns of R & D Resources 1953-1975* (NSF 75-307), Table B-5 with 1950 estimated from U.S. Department of Commerce *Long Term Economic Growth 1860-1965,* Series B53, B56 spliced to NSF data.

Line 5, American Council on Education, *A Factbook on Higher Education,* First Issue, 1975, pp. 75-146.

Line 6, Estimated by multiplying the number of students enrolled in high school, college and graduate school by ¾ the earnings of 18-24 year old workers with 8 years of grade school, 4 years of high school, and 4 years of college, respectively. The grade school incomes were adjusted downward to take account of the fewer hours worked by young not enrolled persons. Separate computations were made for men and women. The data are from American Council on Education, *A Factbook on Higher Education, 1975* and the U.S. Office of Education, *Digest of Educational Statistics, 1975,* with incomes from U.S. Bureau of the Census, *Current Population Reports,* Series P-60 Nos. 92, 101. Weeks worked by young persons from U.S. Bureau of Labor Statistics *Special Labor Force Report 174,* Table 3. Precise calculations and data are available on request from me.

* Average 1964 and 1966.

these activities rose more sharply. In the late 1960s and early 1970s, however, the table shows a sharp decline in the R & D and a stabilization in the education share of national product. Between 1964 and 1974 governmental R & D/GNP dropped by 37 percent as space and defense research programs were cut back. The drop in federal R & D caused a major downturn in the science manpower market; the relative salaries of researchers fell sharply; employment of R & D scientists and engineers in industry funded by federal money dropped by

33 percent (from 1963 to 1973); enrollments in physics and natural sciences diminished relative to the size of the student population. At the same time, however, the lower cost induced private companies to increase their employment of R & D workers (by nearly 50 percent), roughly stabilizing the ratio of private R & D spending to GNP given in line 3. To the extent that private R & D has greater productivity effects than space and defense, the alleged dire consequences of the drop in total R & D relative to GNP may be overstated.

The pattern of change in the education share of GNP is more uneven but still indicative of an end to rapid expansion. After more than doubling in the 1950s and 1960s, education/GNP fell from 7.7 percent in 1972 to 7.3 percent in 1974. Within the sector, there was a relative increase in spending for colleges and universities, which is likely to continue as the number of students of elementary and secondary school age falls through the 1980s. In contrast to the increased share of R & D funded by the private sector, private educational institutions declined in importance in postwar years: in 1950, 50 percent of college students enrolled in private institutions; in 1974, 24 percent. As for foregone income, the figures in line 6 show a similar pattern of increase, with a peak in 1970 followed by a decline due largely, it should be noted, to the slow increase in the income of young grade school graduates in the CPS data set used to estimate foregone income. The foregone income of college and graduate students relative to GNP rose slightly in the period.

Even with the turnaround in the pattern of growth in R & D and educational spending, these two activities have become an extremely important and sizeable component in the nation's annual investment budget. In 1950, the ratio of R & D and direct education spending to private investment was 0.27; by 1965, it had climbed to 0.55, and continued to rise to 0.63 in 1974. With the foregone income included in the totals, expenditures on education and R & D relative to private physical capital formation approach 0.90 in the latter years.

Finally, the data in lines 7 and 8 give *no* indication that investment spending, broadly defined, has fallen relative to GNP in postwar years. To the contrary, the figures show rough stability or, if any trend is to be forced out of the data, a moderate increase in the total investment to GNP ratio in the periods considered.

All told, Tables 1 and 2 indicate that after decades of extraordinary growth, konwledge and human capital have come to constitute a large but no longer rapidly expanding segment of the nation's capital stock and annual gross capital formation.

The Economic Decline in the Return to Education

What accounts for this decline in the growth of investment in human capital? To what extent does it reflect a decline in its return as society has accumulated so much? What are the consequences of the decline? Is it possible to pursue policies which would increase its return to the previous levels? To deal with these questions, I shall now turn to an analysis of the changes in the rewards to higher education brought about by the sizeable expansion of the college work force; the supply responses engendered by the "depressed" college market of the 1970s; and then their growth consequence.

One of the major puzzles in the analysis of human capital, first noted by Miller and stressed by Griliches, concerns the pattern of change in the relative income and rate of return to graduates in post-World War II years. Through the late 1960s, the ratio of the income of college to the income of high school workers was stable or modestly increasing, despite the enormous expansion of college and university training. Some analysts sought explanations of the maintained return in the interrelations between educated manpower and other productive inputs, such as capital and R & D.

In the early 1970s, however, the puzzle began to resolve itself as the ratio of the earnings of college to high school graduates fell, particularly among the young. As Table 3 shows, in the span of five years the premium received by twenty-five to thirty-four year old college graduates dropped from 39 percent to 15 percent; over the same period, the real starting pay of new male baccalaureates fell by about 20 percent, while average pay in the economy held roughly even. Tuition and fees and total direct costs of education rose rapidly, with the result that the return to investment in college, the principal "marginal" educational area, fell by perhaps 3 to 4 percentage points. Detailed analyses of the changing market for college graduates in *The Overeducated American* and various articles (Freeman, 1975, 1977) show that the market downturn had effects on job "opportunities" as well as on incomes and occurred despite cyclic forces which operated to improve the relative position of graduates.

The reason for the maintenance of the college to high school income ratio through the late 1960s and the sharp drop thereafter can be readily explained by standard supply-demand analysis. Contrary to widespread belief, the number of college relative to high school graduates in the work force did *not* increase greatly in the 1960s. On

TABLE 3. CHANGES IN THE RELATIVE REWARDS TO COLLEGE, 1949-1974
(All dollars in 1967 constant dollars)

	1949	*1961*	*1969*	*1974*	% Δ *1969-1974*
1. Earnings of men 25-34 years old					
college graduate	5,773	8,334	9,815	8,350	−14.9
high school	4,546	5,979	7,407	7,267	− 1.9
difference	1,227	2,365	2,408	1,083	−55.0
ratio	1.27	1.39	1.33	1.15	−13.5
2. Tuition and fees					
public	153	248	295	341	15.6
private	655	1,011	1,397	1,550	11.0
3. Total cost/pupil	1,182	1,995 *	2,686	2,988	11.2
4. Family income 45-54 year-old heads	6,007	8,342	11,779	11,313	− 4.0

Sources: Lines 1, 4, U.S. Bureau of the Census, *Current Population Reports,* Consumer Income Series P-60, No. 92, Table 1 with ungrouped data adjusted by ratio of ungrouped means in 1967. No. 75, Tables 47, 17 and No. 101, Tables 58 and 25. U.S. Department of Commerce, *Trends in the Income of Families and Persons in the U.S.,* technical paper 8, Table 3. 1949 earnings from H. P. Miller, "Annual and Lifetime Income in Relation to Education, 1939-59," *AER* (Dec. 1960), Table 1.

Line 2, 1969, 1974 from U.S. Office of Education, *Projections of Educational Statistics to 1984-85,* 1975 ed., p. 106. 1961 from U.S. Office of Education, *Projections of Educational Statistics to 1978-79,* 1969 ed., Table 50, p. 107. 1949 from National Science Foundation, *Statistical Handbook of Science and Education* (NSF 60-13), Figure 48, p. 51.

Line 3, U.S. Office of Education, *Digest of Educational Statistics, 1975,* Table 92, obtained by dividing current fund expenditures by respondent degree credit enrollment. Deflator is from U.S. Department of Labor, *Employment and Training Report of the President,* 1976, Table G-6, p. 362.

* An average of 1960 and 1962.

the one hand, the tremendous growth of graduate education tended to delay the labor market entrance of the large college cohorts of the period: from 1958 to 1968, I have estimated that the *net* number of male bachelor's degree graduates appearing on the market actually fell, where net is defined as the number of bachelors, masters, and Ph.D graduates less first-year enrollment in graduate and professional school, and then rose sharply in the early 1970s (Freeman, 1975). Cartter's estimates (1976) of the proportion of bachelor's degree graduates entering the job market tell a similar story: they suggest a small positive annual rate of increase of 1.2 percent through the mid-1960s compared to an 8 percent per annum increase from 1967 to 1973. On the other, there was an enormous expansion in high school education in the period: in 1958 only 18 percent of male workers were graduates; in 1970, 31 percent. As a result, the ratio of the total number of college to high school men was stable through much of the period. In the late 1960s, however, the ratio began to rise, jumping by 25 percent from 1966 to 1975. The supply pressures for a decrease in college-high school income ratios did not become severe until the end of the 1960s—outset of the 1970s.

The pattern of change in demand also helped maintain the return to higher education through 1970. During the late 1950s and early 1960s, in particular, growth of R & D, expansion of education, and of other college manpower intensive activities raised demand for graduates more rapidly than for other workers. While relative demand, as measured by fixed weight indices, show continued shifts in favor of the college-trained into the 1970s, the rate of the shift diminished. In the 1970s the conjunction of fast growth of relative supply and diminished growth of relative demand set the stage for the market turnaround and decline in relative earnings and rates of return, which was observed.

COMPOSITIONAL DIFFERENCES AND SUPPLY RESPONSES

The "new depression" in the college market place did not affect all fields equally. Starting salaries, possibly the best indicator of change (Freeman, 1976) fell especially sharply for doctorate and master's graduates, reducing the return to investments in those areas sharply. Research and academic professions were hard hit, because of the cutback in R & D and the slower expansion of education on the demand side and the large increase in doctorate graduates on the supply side due to the booming market of the 1960s. Elementary and high school teaching was one of the most depressed fields, as the proportion of education graduates obtaining teaching jobs dropped from 74 percent in 1962 to 48 percent in 1974. At the other end of the spectrum, the relative economic position of business-oriented professions, such as accounting and MBA management, improved. In the sciences the bachelor's degree in engineering experienced a "cobweb" upswing while biomedical sciences, whose research support was not reduced during the period, had only a modest downturn.

The change in the relative returns to various investment in education appears to have generated a significant supply response from young persons in the process of choosing their careers. As would be expected of economically responsive decision-makers:

1. The percentage of young eighteen to nineteen year old men enrolling in college dropped sharply, from 44 percent (1969) to 34 percent (1974), apparently in response to the decline in the rate of return (Freeman, 1975), though some believe due largely to the post-Vietnam end of the draft.
2. First year graduate enrollments in natural science and engineering dropped relative to the number of bachelor's graduates; from 1968 to 1973, the number fell absolutely as well, especially in the hard hit field of physics, stabilizing or rising slightly thereafter.
3. The number of graduates in school teaching fell by nearly 20 percent in the 1972-1975 period while the proportion of freshmen planning on education careers declined precipitously, particularly among women for whom teaching had traditionally been *the* college graduate career.
4. In fields with stronger job markets, medicine, biosciences, agriculture, and business-oriented specialties, by contrast, enrollment increased. The number of students seeking M.B.A.s, for example, grew greatly from 1970 to 1974.
5. First-year enrollments in B.S. engineering, which had in 1973 plummeted to its lowest figure since 1949, despite the economic expansion of higher education, rose by 23,000 in the following two years, in accord with the cobweb dynamics that seem to characterize that field.

All told, the decline in the overall return to college training and changes in rewards among fields were accompanied by changes in investment patterns along lines that could be predicted from economic models of career choice. The conjunction of declines in relative earnings and in enrollment propensities have potential consequences for growth, to which we turn next.

GROWTH CONSEQUENCES

The effect of changes in the educational attainment of workers and in the marginal product of schooling on productivity are examined next in Table 4 using a variant of the basic sources of growth equation given earlier:

$$\sum_i a_i \dot{N}_i = \sum_i \frac{N_i W_i}{W} \frac{\Delta N_i}{N_i} = \sum_i \frac{W_i}{W} \Delta N_i \tag{5}$$

where a_i = cost share of ith educational group,
N_i = number of workers in ith group.
$\dot{N}_i$ = percentage change in the proportion of workers in group i,
W_i = wage of workers in i in base period, and
W = average wage in base period.

TABLE 4. COMPOUND ANNUAL PERCENTAGE INCREASES IN THE INCOME OF MALE WORKERS AGED 25+ AND 25-34 DUE TO ADDITIONAL YEARS OF SCHOOLING, 1949-1990

	Men Aged 25+	*Men Aged 25-34*
1949-1961 *	1.0	2.0
1961 *-1969	0.9	0.8
1969-1974	1.0	0.7
1974-1990	0.7	0.2

Source: Calculated by taking income-weighted measures of changes in educational distribution within each period, using annual or other data with initial year income weights, compounding over the period; and taking the compound annual change. Basic data are from U.S. Bureau of the Census, *Current Population Report,* Series P-60, various editions, and U.S. Bureau of Labor, *Educational Attainment of Workers,* various editions. Precise calculations and data are available from me on request.

* 1962 for men aged 25-34.

This equation decomposes the growth in the stock of human capital due to schooling into changes in the proportion of persons in each category multiplied by the base period relative wages. It provides an estimate of the growth in wages that results from changes in the educational distributions. The calculations in the table relate to men aged twenty-five and over and aged twenty-five to thirty-four. They are based on distributions of workers among seven educational categories for the period 1949-1974 and the predicted distribution for 1990; incomes in each year (for which data exists) are used to weight ensuing distributional changes, with the 1974 incomes applied to 1990.

There are three findings. For all men, column 1 shows that increased educational attainment has raised incomes by about 1 percent per year in the period from 1949 to 1974, with *no* sign of a diminished impact. Whatever changes have occurred in the income weights tending to reduce the contribution to schooling have been effectively counterbalanced by the changes in attainment. Among younger workers, by contrast, there is evidence of a declining effect of schooling on productivity. Whereas from 1949 to 1961, the improved educational distribution of twenty-five to thirty-four year old men raised wages by 2 percent per annum, in the 1960s the increase dropped to 0.8 percent and in the early 1970s to 0.7 percent. For both age groups, the projected attainment distribution for 1990 suggests a sharp decline in the impact of improved educational distributions on income: using 1974 income weights and the 1990 B.L.S. projected distribution, education is expected to raise the income of all men by 0.7 points in the 1970s and 1980s and that of men aged twenty-five to thirty-four by just 0.2 points.

The likelihood that investments in the *quantity* of schooling will have a smaller effect on income growth in the future than in the past does not, of course, imply that investments in education need necessarily contribute less to growth. There is some evidence that expenditures on the *quality* of schooling can yield sizeable returns (Stafford and Johnson) as can the amount of time spent on education in a school year (Wiley), though the educational production function literature (see Bowles) has not found much. If there is a high return to more intensive schooling and the nation makes sizeable investments that improve the amount of education in a school year, the contribution of education could remain high. If not, education will be a less important source of growth in the future than in the past, indicative of its more "mature" role as an area for investment in the United States.

The Continued High Rate of Return to R & D

Does the late 1960s-1970s cutback in R & D spending relative to GNP which was documented earlier represent a "silent economic crisis" which will produce slower growth in the late 1970s and 1980s than would otherwise be attained? What is the rate of return to investment in knowledge capital? What is the impact of R & D expenditures on productivity?

Despite a substantive literature on the economic effects of R & D, these are difficult questions to answer. Most R & D studies cover the period of expansion and do not provide estimates of returns in the changed economic setting of the 1970s. Many studies deal with successful innovations and cannot be translated into macro-growth analysis. Few provide estimates of the divergence between social and private marginal productivity. These problems notwithstanding, available knowledge can be used to obtain some crude notion of the effect of R & D-produced knowledge capital on productivity.

As a starting point, Table 5 summarizes the results of a wide variety of estimates of the economic effect of R & D in industry and agriculture. Column 1 gives the name, date, and coverage of the study; column 2 provides a brief description of methodology, distinguishing in particular between four basic types of analyses: those using individual project data (I); those dealing with single company data (II); those comparing the experience of companies with more or less R & D (III);

and those comparing the experience of industries or regions with more or less R & D (IV); column 3 records the estimated rate of return, as given in the relevant publications. Some of the articles report "perpetual" rates of return (the ratio of the estimated gain in output to cost), while others record internal rates of return. The former are relevant for growth analysis and are given in the table unless otherwise stated; the latter are appropriate in project evaluation.

The studies most relevant for growth accounting use cross-industry and cross-company data. They take two basic forms: regression estimates of Cobb-Douglas production functions, in which cumulated or current R & D spending is an explanatory variable; and regression estimates in which total factor productivity (calculated using factor shares and changes in inputs) is regressed on the measure of R & D activity. The production formation approach has the advantage of reducing the danger of error due to problems of measurement of other inputs, especially capital.

The studies differ in various ways, making comparisons difficult and interpretation of differences hazardous. Some try to deal with the timing of R & D (which greatly influences internal rates of return) although the collinearity between R & D over time makes determination of lags tenuous. Others do not. Some studies relate productivity to investment in R & D; others, to cumulated stocks of R & D; and yet others to rates of growth of R & D. Lack of knowledge of depreciation rates and the collinearity of cumulated R & D and R & D in any given year makes it difficult to distinguish between the effect of flows and stocks.

The great diversity in procedures notwithstanding, a general finding emerges: *virtually all analyses of the relation between R & D and productivity have found sizeable returns to investment in knowledge.* In industry, perpetual rates of return range from 30 percent to 50 percent. Since R & D employment and capital are invariably included in the measures of capital and labor inputs, these returns are, in Griliches' words, "excess" in the sense that they are above and beyond the regular output effects of the inputs. Assuming a five year gestation period and a 10 percent rate of depreciation, these perpetual rates translate into internal rates on the order of 20 to 30 percent. In agriculture, similar results are obtained, with especially high perpetual and internal rates of return obtained in the analysis of specific innovations, such as hybrid corn.

To translate the estimated rate of return into the contribution of R & D growth requires a variety of assumptions about parameters for

TABLE 5. SUMMARY OF ESTIMATES OF RETURN TO R & D IN INDUSTRY

Name of Study and Coverage	*Method of Analysis*	*Rate of Return** *(percent)*
1. Minasian (1960) 8 chemical firms, 1948-57	(III) Regression of growth of value added on cumulated R & D and other variables, by company.	48-54
2. Griliches (1973) 85 mfg. industries, 1958-63	(IV) Regression of productivity change on R & D/value added, 5 year lag.	40
3. Griliches (1976) 883 companies, 1957-64	(III) Change in productivity regressed on growth of R & D.	27
	(III) 1963 cross-company production function, with cumulated R & D, capital, employment.	27
	(III) 1963 company productivity as function of cumulated R & D/total assets.	17
4. Terleckyj (1965) 20 mfg. industries, 1919-53	(IV) Regression of total factor productivity on R & D and cyclic variable.	50
5. Terleckyj (1976) 20 mfg. industries, 1948-66	(IV) Regression of total factor productivity on privately financed, government industry, and R & D embodied in purchases.	18 (own) 0 (govt. funded)
6. Mansfield (1968) 10 petroleum and chemical firms, 1946-62; 10 mfg. industries	(II, IV) Rate of growth of productivity and growth of cumulated R & D used to estimate return under diverse assumptions about embodiment of change in capital.	40-60 (petroleum) 7-30 (chemical) 20-62 (unweighted average)**
7. Mansfield *et al.*, 17 industrial innovations, 1960; product and process innovations at single firm, 1960-62.	(I) Social benefit and consumer surplus of innovations compared to cost. (II) Single company estimates of costs and returns.	25 (private) internal 56 (social) 19-55
8. Weisbrod (1971) Time series for polio vaccine.	(I) Related reduced mortality and morbidity to cumulated research spending.	9-13 internal (incl. cost of vaccination)
9. Bailey (1972) 6 pharmaceutical firms, 1954-63	(II) Compares estimated effect of number of new drugs on profits and cost of producing new drugs.	25-35 internal rate (company)

TABLE 5. CONTINUED.

Name of Study and Coverage	Method of Analysis	Rate of Return* (percent)
10. Griliches (1958) Hybrid corn, 1910-55	(I) Relates economic value, including consumer surplus of 15 percent gain in yield to cumulated R & D, with returns and costs valued with 10 percent investment rate.	700 37 (internal)
11. Evenson (1968) Agricultural output, 1939-63	(IV) Productivity index in agriculture on lagged productivity and research spending, 1940-63.	100 (cumulative stock)† 57 (internal)
	Output per unit of input across regressions and time 1937-61.	4,000
	Cross-section production function with research as one factor, 1954-59.	100 (stock) 54 (internal)
12. Peterson (1967) Poultry production by state, 1959.	(IV) Estimate effect of research at state experimentations on poultry output, with other variables.	600 33 internal (with 10 year gestation)
13. Latimer-Parlberg (1965) Agriculture by states, 1959.	(IV) Regression of agricultural output on 10-year lagged cumulative R & D and other inputs.	0
14. Griliches (1964) Agriculture, 39 states, 1949, 1954, 1959.	(IV) Relates output per form to research and extension services and other inputs.	300

Sources: See References at the end of this chapter for references to the studies.

* This column records perpetual average rates of return unless otherwise stated. The perpetual rates are obtained by multiplying the estimated marginal product of a research dollar by 100 percent and thus equal $F_R \times 100$ in equation (3). As indicated in (3) this is the appropriate concept for growth analysis. Project evaluation, however, requires calculation of internal rates, which depend on the time stream of effects and are invariably lower than the perpetual rates.

** These are averages of 9 and 10 industries given for disembodied and embodied technical change from columns 3 and 6 of Table 4.2 of Mansfield's book, p. 71.

† Evenson's regressions relate productivity to annual flows of R & D. Because of collinearity it is not possible to distinguish between the effect of flows and stocks. He divides the flow estimates by 10 to obtain estimates of returns on stock assuming a stock-flow ratio of 10:1.

which little data exists. Some estimate of the depreciation of the stock of R & D is needed to obtain the net investment which creates growth; some decisions must be made about the productivity effects of space and defense R & D; and some estimate of the externalities (across industries or companies, depending on the data set) resulting from R & D must be made. One set of "rough estimates of the contribution of research to growth" has been provided by Griliches (1973), who assumes that about half of R & D is for replacement; that the social return of investments within industries is 30 percent; that there is a 10 percent external effect of private R & D across industry lines; and that space and defense R & D have no spillover effect on productivity. On the basis of these figures, he estimates that R & D in 1966 contributed 34 percentage points to "measured growth" (which excludes knowledge capital as a component of GNP) and that R & D in 1970 contributed 0.19 points to measured growth, a reduction traced to the slowdown in the growth of spending, though he believes that the estimates may be "too high perhaps by as much as 50 percent." Even if that were the case, R & D made a nonnegligible contribution to past growth, despite being a relatively small component of GNP.

The effect of the post-1964 decline in R & D spending relative to GNP is examined further, using an analysis much like Griliches', in Table 6. Line 1 gives the ratio of all civilian and federal civilian R & D to GNP for 1964, 1970, and 1975. It highlights the divergent trend in expenditures for civilian and military purposes and the new importance of federal civilian R & D spending. While the ratio of all R & D to GNP falls sharply from 1964 to 1970 and from 1970 to 1974, the ratio of civilian (nondefense, nonspace) research spending to GNP actually increased significantly in the former period and stabilized in the latter. An important factor in the stabilization in the 1970s is the enormous growth of federal research funds for civilian purposes, a major change in the structure of the research enterprise in the United States. In 1953 just 5 percent of R & D outlays were for federal civilian purposes; in 1975, 17 percent of all R & D and over one-fourth of all nonspace nondefense funds. Line 2 presents estimates of the depreciation of the stock of civilian knowledge capital relative to GNP, assuming 5 percent and 10 percent depreciation rates. These estimates are then subtracted from the gross R & D/GNP figures in line 1 to obtain the net civilian R & D to GNP ratios that affect growth. Line 3 records the net estimates with 0.0 percent, 5 percent, and 10 percent postulated depreciation rates. The final output of the exercise is given in line 4, which multiplies the ratios by an assumed 30 percent return

TABLE 6. ESTIMATED CONTRIBUTION OF R & D TO GROWTH IN 1964, 1970, AND 1975

	1964	*1970*	*1975*
1. Gross R & D/GNP			
total	2.99	2.66	2.41
civilian *	1.34	1.51	1.52
federal civilian	0.33	0.36	0.41
noncivilian	1.65	1.15	0.89
2. Depreciation of civilian knowledge capital/GNP with			
5% depreciation rate	0.54	0.68	0.80
10% depreciation rate	0.79	0.99	1.12
3. Net civilian R & D/GNP			
0% depreciation	1.34	1.51	1.52
5% depreciation	0.82	0.82	0.74
10% depreciation	0.55	0.51	0.32
4. Percentage point contribution to growth with 30% social return			
0% depreciation	0.40	0.45	0.46
5% depreciation	0.25	0.25	0.22
10% depreciation	0.17	0.16	0.10

Sources: Line 1, National Science Foundation, *National Patterns of R & D Resources* (NSF 75-3071) Table 3-5, with GNP from U.S. Department of Labor, *Employment and Training Report of the President, 1976,* Table G-3. Civilian R & D = Total military and space R & D.

Line 2, Calculated from estimated capital stock using data and procedure described in Table 1.

* Nonspace, nondefense spending.

to the R & D investment to obtain the growth contribution. It ignores various accounting technicalities which would be needed to make the estimates consistent with national income statistics (see Griliches, 1973, pp. 78-79) and is designed solely for comparisons of effects over time.

The major result in the table is the finding that because civilian R & D did *not* decline relative to GNP in the late 1960s and early 1970s, the impact of the deceleration of research spending on growth depends critically on the postulated rate of depreciation of the stock of knowledge capital, a parameter about which no real information exists, and on postulated spillovers of the declining military R & D. With a low depreciation rate, such as 0.0 percent and no spillover effects, there are *no* growth retarding effects to the recent cutback:

growth may be less rapid than is possible but will not be less than in the past. With a high 10 percent rate of depreciation, on the other hand, net civilian R & D/GNP falls sharply and the contribution of R & D to growth drops by one-third. Similarly, if (contrary to my assumption) there is a sizeable spillover of military and space technology to civilian productivity, the near halving of the ratio of those funds to GNP will produce a marked fall in the gain in productivity. As we lack knowledge of the appropriate depreciation and spillover rates, the magnitude of the "silent crisis" is difficult to gauge.

Fortunately, the policy question of whether or not additional R & D spending is in the nation's economic interest does not depend on the past contribution of knowledge to growth nor the rate of depreciation of the cumulated stock. It depends solely on the rate of return. *If the high returns found in the 1960s also characterize the 1970s and 1980s, a strong case can be made for raising the R & D share of national product.* If, alternatively, the returns have fallen to equal those on other investments, the issue becomes less clear. While a firm answer must await detailed studies of the 1970s similar to those of Table 5, the high returns found in the studies would have to fall very sharply to overturn the implication that additional R & D is socially desirable. Given the magnitudes of returns in the studies of the past decade, R & D has a long way to reach parity with other forms of investment.

A More Complete Model of the Roles of Knowledge and Human Capital in Growth

As "intangible" inputs, knowledge and human capital are, it is generally recognized, likely to have more complex effects on economic growth than is envisaged in the growth accounting computations which we have discussed thus far. A proper understanding of their role in the growth process requires some consideration of these potential nonstandard routes of impact.

One important way in which human and knowledge capital can affect growth is through their interconnections with other inputs, which alter rates of return and ultimately supplies. It is often claimed, for example, that R & D "creates investment opportunities" for physical capital by expanding technological possibilities and raises demand for human capital by creating temporary disequilibrium to which the more educated are better able to adapt. If these propositions are true, R & D has indirect consequences for growth through physical and human capital formation. While for purposes of growth accounting, the direct effects of increases in inputs may be reasonably ignored, it is important to recognize them in a more complete analysis.

At the same time, there are potential feedbacks of other inputs to knowledge and human capital. One plausible feedback, closely related to the hypothesized dependence of the return to human capital on changes in knowledge, is that the speed with which "best practice" technologies are introduced and thus the value of R & D depends on the education of decision makers. Another important interrelation, shown by Schmookler in his classic *Inventions and Economic Growth,* links increases in patented knowledge in particular types of capital goods to past levels of investment in those machines. Here, the increase in the stock of knowledge is the induced contributor to growth while past investments in physical capital are the underlying causal force. R & D is not the "dynamic" force for growth in the Schmookler model, but rather one of a group of accompanying responses to growth. The hypothesis that physical capital is relatively more complementary with skilled than unskilled labor tells an analogous story for human capital. According to this hypothesis, the growth of the stock of physical capital raises the relative demand for, and return to, human capital.

Interrelations among various components of the stock of knowledge also affect the growth process. The supply of R & D, in particular, is often alleged to "create its own demand," presumably because the productivity of researchers depends positively on the stock of knowledge created by other researchers. If this is the case, "big pushes" in knowledge-creation have the potential for raising growth much more than indicated by marginal analysis, while conversely, slowdowns may have enhanced effects in reducing the R & D contribution.

A major implication of the posited interrelation among inputs is that investments in R & D (or education) can set off "chain reactions" in growth that lead to an extended development spurt of the Schumpeterian type. For example, an R & D-created innovation may alter the returns to various investments in physical and human capital, induce increases in their supply, and change the pattern of interindustrial demand for products. The changes in investments and demands will induce further economic changes and spur widespread growth, with further feedbacks on R & D. In the growth accounting model, such a catalytic effect of a single input is ruled out.

Finally, while monistic explanations of any social phenomenon should be viewed suspiciously, increases in the stock of knowledge can be plausibly viewed as the "ultimate cause" of economic progress. In the absence of changes in knowledge the potential for growth by investing in physical capital, discovering new sources of natural resources, and investing in education eventually appear to run out. These factors face diminishing returns that, at least with current knowledge, are not apparent in the stock of knowledge. The limitation of increased education as a source of growth in the long run has been illustrated graphically by Kuznets, who points out that measured by *years* of training, apprentices in the middle ages had the equivalent of a modern grade school education. If their apprenticeship were increased by eight years, would their contribution to output increase greatly? If all workers in the middle ages had as much schooling as workers today, would GNP reach twentieth century levels? Clearly not. The point is that the difference in *what* is learned, not in the diffusion of middle age knowledge, is the key factor differentiating modern from fourteenth century economies. More positively, one of the most remarkable aspects of the contribution of the stock of knowledge to growth is that even the most abstract scientific work, for instance, non-Euclidian geometry, has historically turned out to have significant consequences that are unlikely to be captured in the simple marginal productivity growth accounting.

Policy Issues and Options

Investments in human and knowledge capital have been among the most important sources of productivity growth. After having risen more rapidly than other investments, these intangible forms of capital are no longer an expanding share of the nation's capital stock nor a leading area of annual gross capital formation. The return to a major component of human capital, college education, appears to have fallen among the young. The return to a major component of knowledge capital, formal research and development, has been found to be quite high in various studies. As the rate of growth of human and knowledge capital decelerates and the return of the former drops, the contribution of these inputs to growth is likely to be less in the future than it was in the past.

Critical questions with respect to investments in human capital relate to: the impact of the future demographic decline of the number of young persons on the level of and return to college training; the extent to which more judicious selection of areas of concentration can raise returns; and the possibility of obtaining a significant impact on productivity growth through investment in efficiency and quality rather than in quantity of schooling.

In the case of knowledge capital, where studies suggest a high return to civilian investments, the central issue relates to the level and institutional form of investments. We are undergoing a major switch in the nation's research budget from military to civilian research activities and in the way in which the federal government supports civilian research. Our major challenge here is to find ways to manage the federal assistance to civilian research activities.

Government's role in the solution of these problems is substantial. Government is a major source of funds for both human and knowledge capital formation. Federal R & D monies have long constituted half or more of the nation's research budget. Federal support of higher education through stipends and grants is substantial. State funded colleges and universities enroll three-fourths of the college students in the United States. Most elementary and secondary school students attend public institutions. Because of the sizeable public role, there is no lack of policy tools for altering the amount or composition of investment in knowledge and human capital. Governmental decisions are a major determinant of the pattern of R & D and educational expenditures.

In years past, the government has not done a good job in the R & D and education markets. Instead of stabilizing the demand and supply for research personnel and highly-trained manpower, the government has induced sizeable swings from shortage to surplus, with consequent wastage of human resources. During the early 1960s, for example, the federal government encouraged expansion of the supply of doctorate and master's scientists and engineers through fellowship support and R & D spending that caused sizeable increases in salaries. When the enrollees graduated in the late 1960s and 1970s, however, federal R & D policies had changed, with a resultant slump in the science manpower market. Similarly, there was an enormous expansion of the college and university system in the period, with little thought given to foreseeable demographic changes which promised to reduce demand for teachers, nor to the potential effect of greatly increased numbers of college graduates on the job market. Greater attention and funds were allotted to expansion of the scale of education than to improving the quality of schooling. While the particular policies which should have been pursued are debatable, it cannot be denied that the government took a myopic short-run view of what are inherently long-run resources and excerbated rather than ameliorated market problems.

A major overhaul in the R & D and educational policy-making process is needed to remedy past weaknesses and deal with changed economic realities.

At the outset, an effort should be made to avoid the deleterious effect of hurky-jurky governmental policies on the job market for R & D personnel and other high-level specialists. The impact of the federal budget on the manpower system should be assessed regularly and stipend and educational expenditures determined in a manner that is consistent with demand-side expenditure forecasts. Program changes which have large manpower consequences ought to be made gradually and some effort undertaken to lean "against the wind" to reduce significant cobweb ups-and-downs. Just as natural resources may be stockpiled to deal with possible future shortages, consideration should be given to maintaining specialists in fields with limited current demand in order to preserve the capability of exploiting unexpected new breakthroughs. Manpower policy regarding human and knowledge capital formation must take a long-run rather than crisis-oriented short-term perspective.

The switch in the nation's research budget from military to civilian activities and, in particular, the new importance of federal funds in civilian research suggest the value of a detailed look at the institutional mechanism for supporting R & D. The nation has no overview mechanism for federally supported civilian R & D, much less for the interrelation between federal and private expenditures. Decisions are made within agencies with regard to the possible contribution of R & D to their missions. While this may be appropriate for applied research and development, there is no reason to believe that it is the best way for supporting basic research. The decline in military R & D, which funded diverse basic research in the past and the applied perspective of civilian mission-oriented research suggests the need for reevaluating the way in which basic "overhead" knowledge is funded. Undirected basic research should be viewed and funded on a comprehensive basis, not as the result of individual unrelated projects. Similarly, there is need to consider alternative ways for performing federally funded civilian research—through industry, national laboratories, or universities—and for guarantees of the diffusion of the knowledge created.

In the case of education, the demise of the "expand, expand" principle of decision-making brought about by the 1970s decline in the college job market should not be replaced by a reflexive movement in the opposite direction. The large number of graduates who have been unable to obtain college level jobs in the 1970s may require retraining in the late 1980s, if, as predicted (Freeman, 1976), opportunities improve then because of smaller graduating classes. A major look at the possibility of intensive rather than extensive investments in education, of improvements in quality, especially in light of the 1964-74 decline in SAT scores, is needed. Even though the return to further quantities of schooling may not be as high as in the past, investment in quality may have substantial payoff.

Finally however the decision-making process with regard to R & D and education is reformed, there is great need for bringing more up-to-date information to bear on policies. If changes in market realities and returns and the effects of programs are monitored regularly and their implications for future possibilities and current policies drawn, better decisions may be made. While even the best knowledge does not permit us to determine what *should* be done, as that depends on social priorities and goals, available information can be used more fruitfully in national policy.

References

ABRAMOWITZ, MOSES, "Economic Growth in the United States," *American Economic Review* (September 1962).

BAILEY, M. N., "Research and Development Costs and Returns: The U.S. Pharmaceutical Industry," *Journal of Political Economy,* 80, no. 1 (Jan/Feb 1972), 70-85.

BOWLES, S., "Toward an Educational Production Function," in W. L. Hansen (ed.), *Education, Income and Human Capital.* National Bureau of Economic Research, 1970, pp. 11-70.

CARTTER, A., *Ph.D.s and the Academic Labor Market.* McGraw-Hill, 1976.

DENISON, E., *Accounting for U.S. Economic Growth, 1929–69.* Washington, D.C.: Brookings Institution, 1972.

———, *The Sources of Economic Growth in the United States and the Alternatives Before Us,* supplementary paper no. 13. New York: Committee for Economic Development, 1962.

EVENSON, ROBERT, *The Contribution of Agricultural Research and Extension to Agricultural Production.* Unpublished Ph.D. thesis. Chicago: University of Chicago Press, 1968.

FABRICANT, SOL, "Economic Progress and Economic Change," *34th Annual Report of the National Bureau of Economic Research.* New York, 1954.

FREEMAN, R. B., *The Overeducated American.* New York: Academic Press, 1976.

———, "Overinvestment in College Training?" *Journal of Human Resources,* Summer, 1975. Reprinted in *Evaluation Studies Review Annual,* Gene V. Glass (ed.). Beverly Hills, California: Sage Publications, Inc.

———, "The Decline in the Economic Rewards to College Education," in *Review of Economics and Statistics* (1977).

Griliches, Z., "Production Functions in Manufacturing: Some Preliminary Results," in *The Theory and Empirical Analysis of Production.* National Bureau of Economic Research. New York: Columbia University Press, 1967.

———, "Research Costs and Social Returns: Hybrid Corn and Related Innovation," *Journal of Political Economy,* 66 (October 1968).

———, "Research Expenditures, Education, and the Aggregate Agricultural Production Function," *American Economic Review,* December 1964.

———, "Research Expenditures and Growth Accounting," in B. R. Williams (ed.), *Science and Technology in Economic Growth.* New York: Wiley, 1973.

———, "Returns to Research and Development in the Private Sector," NBER Conference on Research in Income and Wealth, *New Development in Productivity Measurement,* 1976.

Keesing, D., "The Impact of Research and Development on United States Trade," *Journal of Political Economy,* vol. 75, no. 1 .

———, "Labor Skills and International Trade: Evaluating Many Trade Flows with a Single Measuring Device," *ReStat,* August 1965.

Latmer-Parlberg, "Geographic Distribution of Research Cost Estimates," *Journal of Farm Economics,* 1965.

Leontief, W., "Domestic Production and Foreign Trade; the American Capital Position Re-Examined," *Economica Internazionale,* VII, no. 1 (February 1954), pp. 3-32.

Mansfield, Edwin, *Econometric Studies of Industrial Research and Technological Innovation.* New York: W. W. Norton & Co., 1967.

———, "Rates of Return from Industrial Research and Development," *American Economic Review,* May 1965.

Mansfield et al., "Social and Private Rates of Return from Industrial Innovations," *Journal of Political Economy,* forthcoming.

Marshall, A., *Principles of Economics.* Macmillan, 1959.

Miller, H. P., "Annual and Lifetime Income in Relation to Education: 1939-1959," *American Economic Review,* December 1960.

Minasian, Jora, "Research and Development, Production Functions, and Rates of Return," *American Economic Review,* May 1969.

Peterson, Willis L., "Return to Poultry Research in the United States," *Journal of Farm Economics,* August 1967.

Price, J. de Solla, *Science Since Babylon.* New Haven: Yale University Press, 1961.

SCHMOOKLER, J., *Inventions and Economic Growth.* Cambridge: Harvard University.

SOLOW, R., "Technical Change and the Aggregate Production Function," *Review of Economics and Statistics,* August 1957.

TERLECKYJ, NESTOR, *Sources of Productivity Advance.* Unpublished Ph.D. dissertation. New York: Columbia University, 1960.

———, "Estimating Direct and Indirect Effects of Research and Development on Productivity Growth by Industries," NBER Conference on Research in Income and Wealth, *New Development in Productivity Measurement,* 1976.

WEISBROD, "Costs and Benefits of Medical Research: A Case Study of Polio," *Journal of Political Economy,* Vol. 79.

WILEY, DAVID E., AND ANNEGRET HARNISCHFEGER, "Explosion of a Myth: Quantity of Schooling and Exposure to Instruction, Major Educational Vehicles." Studies of Educative Processes, Report No. 8. Evanston: University of Chicago, Department of Education, 1974.

Martin S. Feldstein

5

National Saving in the United States[1]

A nation's rate of saving is probably its most important macroeconomic characteristic. In this paper I will examine different aspects of the U.S. saving behavior during the postwar period against the background of our saving experience during the previous 50 years. I will then turn to the question of whether the U.S. saving rate should be increased in the future.

The Postwar Savings Experience in Historic Perspective

Before turning to an analysis of the data themselves, it is useful to begin by summarizing the basic conclusions that emerge:

1. The long-term downtrend in the rate of real *net* capital accumulation which was observed before World War II has continued.
2. Although the *gross* national saving rate has been relatively constant, this overall constancy masks important changes in its composition.
3. Personal and corporate saving rates have risen in the postwar period, but growing government deficits have channeled these funds into the purchase of government securities instead of real capital formation.
4. Net investment in owner occupied housing has changed from a major source of personal saving to a significant reducer of personal saving.

MARTIN S. FELDSTEIN *has been Professor of Economics at Harvard since 1960. He is a Fellow of the Econometric Society, a co-editor of the* Journal of Public Economics, *and a member of the editorial boards of the* American Economic Review *and the* Quarterly Journal of Economics. *He has written widely on the economics of taxation and the public sector.*

[1] I am grateful to the National Science Foundation for financial support and to Alison Adams and Larry Summers for assistance and discussions.

5. Social security benefits finance retirement consumption without the real capital accumulation that would accompany private saving. The annual increase in the value of households' "social security wealth" has been larger than all other saving and has been growing in importance.

LONG-TERM TRENDS IN CAPITAL FORMATION

Although the analysis of this section will concentrate on the postwar period, I think it is valuable to begin by looking at the historic trends in capital formation. Because of the special problems of the depression and the war, it is best to focus this historic review and comparison on the period before 1929 and after 1945. Simon Kuznets' (1961) monumental study provides information on gross and net capital formation in the period beginning with 1869. Lines 1 through 6 of Table 1 present decade averages of the gross and net national capital formation rates for the six decades from 1869 through 1928.

Gross national capital formation is equal to total spending on in-

TABLE 1.

		Gross National Capital Formation / Gross National Product (× 100)		*Net National Capital Formation / Net National Product (× 100)*	
Line	*Years*	*Current Dollars*	*Constant Dollars*	*Current Dollars*	*Constant Dollars*
1	1869-1878	19.0	21.8	12.5	14.6
2	1879-1888	19.2	21.3	12.1	13.5
3	1889-1898	21.7	24.5	13.2	15.1
4	1899-1908	21.2	22.4	12.9	13.5
5	1909-1918	19.6	20.5	10.4	10.7
6	1919-1928	19.7	19.5	10.1	9.6
7	1869-1928	20.1	21.7	11.9	12.8
8	1946-1955	16.4	—	8.9	—
9	1956-1965	15.8	—	7.3	—
10	1966-1975	15.2	—	6.8	—
11	1946-1975	15.8	—	7.7	—

Sources: Lines 1 through 7, Kuznets (1961). Capital formation follows Department of Commerce Definition and equals gross private investment including producers durables, construction, net inventory investment, and net foreign investment. Kuznets' constant dollar estimates are based on 1929 prices.

Lines 8 through 11, *Survey of Current Business,* January 1976. No constant dollar estimates for this period are available.

vestment in producers durables, construction (both residential and nonresidential), net inventory accumulation, and net foreign investment. There is no deduction for the depreciation or scrapping of old equipment. *Net* national capital formation is equal to *gross* national capital formation minus depreciation. The gross capital formation rate is the ratio of gross capital formation to gross national product (columns 1 and 2 of Table 1) while the net capital formation rate is the ratio of net capital formation to net national product (columns 3 and 4 of Table 1).

Kuznets' data show no trend in the *gross* capital formation rate through 1928 but a clearly perceptible decline in the rate of *net* capital formation. Stating the same conclusion in different words, the rate of real accumulation of capital declined while the greater depreciation of the larger stock of old capital kept total spending on capital unchanged. The sharp decline in net capital accumulation shows clearly in the comparison between the 12.7 percent average rate for 1869 to 1908 and the 10.2 percent average rate from 1909 to 1928. It is important to emphasize that the rate of capital formation declined long before the beginning of the depression.

The postwar net capital formation rates shown in lines 8 through 11 are based on the recently revised national income estimates prepared by the Department of Commerce. The average net capital formation rate for the thirty-year postwar period is a very low 7.7 percent. Although differences between Kuznets' study and the more recent data in the underlying price indices and in many of the detailed procedures should obviously caution against overinterpreting exact differences, the evidence of a major fall in the net saving rate is clearly striking. The decline within the postwar period will be discussed below when I consider the changing composition of net savings.

The gross capital formation rate has also been substantially lower in the postwar period than it was in the sixty years before the depression. Kuznets found a gross capital formation rate that remained steady at between 19 and 22 percent for individual decade periods from 1869 to 1928. In contrast, the gross capital formation rate for the postwar period has averaged only 15.8 percent. It is clear that essentially all of the 4 percentage point fall in this rate is due to the lower rate of net capital formation, with very little due to a lower rate of replacement investment.

Before leaving this subject, I should comment on the conflict between the change reported here and the evidence of a stable gross private saving cited originally by Denison (1958) and developed more fully by David and Scadding (1974). Note first that there is a difference in the concept of gross saving but one that is not enough to account for the difference between David-Scadding and Kuznets. David and Scadding's measure of gross private saving is equal to gross national capital accumulation plus the government deficit and minus the statistical discrepancy. The statistical discrepancy is never large enough to affect the comparison. The government deficit (including federal, state and local government) averaged 0.9 percent of GNP in the postwar period and was much smaller in earlier years. The David-Scadding and Kuznets-Commerce figures should therefore agree within one percentage point for the postwar period and be even closer for earlier years. This is not the case.

David and Scadding report that the ratio of gross private saving to gross national product has remained essentially unchanged during years of relatively full employment since the beginning of the century. More specifically, they calculate gross private saving rates of 17.7 percent for 1898 to 1916, 14.4 percent for 1921 to 1929, and 15.5 percent for 1949 to 1969. The final figure is consistent with the 15.8 percent gross saving rate reported in Table 1 for 1946 to 1975 but the figures for earlier years do not agree. Their 17.7 percent for 1898 to 1916 is nearly one-sixth smaller than the Kuznets estimates for 1899 to 1918. The Kuznets figures are also supported by a much longer period of previously high gross capital formation values. Moreover, the 14.4 percent rate reported by David and Scadding for 1921 to 1929 is well below the 19.7 percent rate calculated by Kuznets for 1919 to 1928. While I do not feel able to judge the conflicting estimates in detail, I am inclined to support the Kuznets estimates and to believe that there is something about the David-Scadding choice of subperiods that causes them to underestimate gross investment in the early years.

SOURCES OF NATIONAL SAVING

I turn now to examine the changing roles of the different sources of national saving during the postwar period. Table 2 shows that substantial changes in composition have accompanied the quite stable gross national saving rate. Three major changes can be seen. First, personal saving (including private pension saving) has increased sharply, from 26 percent of gross saving in the first postwar decade (1946 to 1955) to 33 percent in the most recent ten years (1966 to 1975). Second, corporate capital consumption allowances account for an increasing share of gross saving, up from 29 percent to 36 percent.

TABLE 2. SOURCES OF GROSS NATIONAL SAVING

Line		*1946-1955*	*1956-1965*	*1966-1975*	*1946-1975*
1	Gross national saving rate	15.8	15.6	15.2	15.5
	Percent of Gross National Saving				
2	Personal saving	26.2	26.1	32.7	28.3
3	Corporate saving	15.4	16.7	13.6	15.2
4	Noncorporate capital consumption allowance	24.4	25.6	23.7	24.6
5	Corporate capital consumption allowance	28.7	34.2	36.4	33.1
6	Federal government surplus	5.5	– 1.6	– 9.0	– 1.7
7	State and local government surplus	– 0.1	– 0.6	3.1	0.8
8	Private saving (lines 2 plus 3)	41.6	42.8	46.3	43.5
9	Capital consumption allowance (lines 4 plus 5)	53.1	59.8	60.1	57.7
10	Government surplus (lines 6 plus 7)	5.4	– 2.2	– 5.9	– 0.9

Source: National income and product accounts as published in *Survey of Current Business,* January 1976. Calculations based on current dollars. The Gross National Saving Rate is defined as Gross National Saving as a percentage of Gross National Product.

Finally, the federal government has changed from a significant contributor to gross saving, accounting for 5.5 percent in 1945 through 1955, to a substantial drain on gross saving by running deficits that averaged 9 percent of gross saving during the most recent decade. Although 1975 was an extreme year, there were deficits in eight of the nine other years in the decade and, for these years, the deficits absorbed 7 percent of gross saving. The shares in lines 8, 9 and 10 show the same results when the detailed components are combined into gross private saving, capital consumption allowances, and the total government budget surplus.

The *net* national saving rate analysis presented in Table 3 shows the cross trends in an even more striking way. Note first that net national saving, i.e., saving net of capital consumption allowances, has fallen from 8.3 percent of net national product in the first postwar decade to only 6.5 percent in the most recent decade. This has occurred even though the personal saving rate (i.e., personal saving as a percentage of disposable personal income, shown in line 5) has increased significantly from 5.8 percent to 7.1 percent. The more comprehensive private saving rate (i.e., personal saving plus corporate retained earnings as a percentage of disposable personal income plus corporate retained earnings, line 6) also shows a steady increase.

The composition of net national saving indicated in lines 2, 3 and 4 resolves the apparent conflict among these trends. The share accounted for by personal saving has increased rapidly, as the government has gone from making a small positive contribution to net saving

TABLE 3. SOURCES OF NET NATIONAL SAVING

Line		*1946-1955*	*1956-1965*	*1966-1975*	*1946-1975*
1	Net national saving rate	8.3	7.0	6.5	7.3
	Percent of Net National Saving				
2	Personal saving	60.0	67.4	87.0	71.4
3	Corporate saving	35.4	41.5	33.7	36.9
4	Government surplus	4.7	− 8.5	−21.1	− 8.3
5	Personal Saving / Disposable personal income	5.8	5.9	7.1	6.3
6	Private saving / Disposable personal income plus corporate saving	8.9	9.3	9.8	9.3

Source: National income and product accounts as published in *Survey of Current Business,* January 1976. Calculations based on current dollars. The Net National Saving Rate is defined as Net National Saving as a percentage of Net National Product.

to having a large negative impact. Corporate saving supplied a rising share of a falling rate for the first two decades; on balance, net corporate saving as a fraction of NNP actually remained constant, until the most recent decade when it fell sharply from its previous average of 2.9 percent of NNP to only 2.2 percent. The government deficits of the past decade have absorbed about one-fifth of net saving; even if the massive deficit of 1975 is excluded, government deficits in the preceding nine years absorbed about one-sixth of net saving. This represents a very sizeable effect on net capital accumulation and a very significant change from the policy of earlier years.

TWO FACTORS AFFECTING PRIVATE SAVING: OWNER OCCUPIED HOUSING AND SOCIAL SECURITY BENEFITS

In the current brief analysis of saving trends it is not possible to analyze why the rate of saving has evolved the way it did. The level and composition of the saving rate reflects a large number of important influences that have changed substantially in both the postwar period and the previous decades. It is instructive to consider a remark that Kuznets (1952) made in his paper on capital formation when he addressed the question of why the saving rate had not risen over time with the general increase in income as might have been expected on the basis of cross-section household data that indicated that the more affluent saved a higher fraction of their income. Kuznets wrote:

> The contrast between the cross-section association of income differences with proportions spent or saved and the association between secular movements in income levels and proportions devoted to expenditures or savings has been, quite unwarrantedly, treated as a puzzle. . . . The general answer to the question as to why savings-income ratios failed to rise with the secular rise in real income per capita is quite simple: because the whole pattern of economic and social life changed. The important task is to distinguish the major components of this change and to measure their relative weight in their impact on the consumption-savings pattern. (p. 522)

I will consider two factors that I believe have been major components of the changing economic and social life that influence the rate of personal saving in the postwar period: the changing growth rate of owner occupied housing and the expansion of social security. (A third factor that might have been singled out is the growth of corporate retained earnings. Inspired in large part by the substantial tax incentives, firms now retain about half of after-tax profits: retained earnings were 48.2 percent of profits after IVA and CCA adjustment for 1966 to 1975. I shall not deal with this issue here because the major *change* in the ratio of dividends to retained earnings occurred before the postwar period: retained earnings were 48.3 percent of profits for 1946 to 1955 and 52.0 for 1956 to 1965. I have studied elsewhere the effect of retained earnings on personal saving and concluded that long-term increases in retained earnings are largely but not completely offset by decreases in personal saving, leaving private saving only slightly higher; see Feldstein, 1973.)

Housing—My interest here is in owner occupied housing as an influence on aggregate saving and not as a component of the use of capital. To indicate its potential importance, it might be noted that the 1975 value of the net stock of all residential capital was $1,313 billion, almost exactly equal to the $1,309 billion value of fixed nonresidential business capital (Musgrave, 1976). Owner occupied nonfarm housing represents $946 billion of the total 1975 residential capital stock. The annual increases in the net stock of such owner occupied housing averaged more than half of total personal saving during the postwar period.

The process of repaying a personal home mortgage may induce some individuals to save more than they otherwise would. Such individuals, unlike the "rational life cycle savers" who dominate textbook discussions of saving, may not have any savings plan but find that they are "forced" to save as they repay their mortgage. The fact that many people reach retirement with almost no net worth other than the equity in their home lends some support to this view but is hardly conclusive evidence. It should be stressed that this is currently only speculation and has not been the subject of systematic research.

Table 4 provides some preliminary evidence on the changing quantitative role of investment in owner occupied housing. The recently completed Department of Commerce estimate of constant dollar net stocks of owner occupied nonfarm housing (Musgrave, 1976) permits a comparison of investment in such housing to total personal saving. The results, shown in line 1, indicate a sharp fall in the relative importance in such investment; the real growth of net nonfarm housing capital has slowed substantially.

The contribution of residential capital accumulation to personal saving should be measured by the net stock accumulation of such housing (i.e., the change in the gross value of the housing stock) *less any increased mortgage debt*. This is shown in line 2 as a percentage

TABLE 4. CONTRIBUTION OF OWNER OCCUPIED HOUSING INVESTMENT TO NATIONAL SAVING

Line		*1946-1955*	*1956-1965*	*1966-1975*	*1946-1975*
1	Net stock accumulation of owner occupied nonfarm housing, percentage of personal saving	85.3	57.3	30.3	57.6
2	Net stock accumulation of owner occupied nonfarm housing less increased mortgage debt, percentage of net stock accumulation of all domestic capital.	11.4	1.7	−16.4	− 1.1
3	Personal net investment in nonfarm homes less increased mortgage debt, percentage of net national saving.	23.5	6.6	−12.0	6.0

Sources: Net stock accumulation of housing and other fixed capital are from Musgrave (1976). Personal net investment in nonfarm homes and the increase in mortgage debt are from *Federal Reserve System Flow of Funds Data.* Net national saving is based on national income data as published in the *Survey of Current Business,* January 1976.

of all net capital stock accumulation. Viewed in this way, residential housing has changed from a positive contributor to personal saving to a net drain on such saving. The same picture emerges in line 3 where the flow of funds financial measure of net investment is used in place of the Department of Commerce measure of net residential capital stock accumulation.

Social Security—For the great majority of Americans, the most important form of household "wealth" is the anticipated social security retirement benefits. The omission of such perceived social security wealth from conventional measures of household assets and of changes in social security wealth from all national income measures of saving tends to obscure the importance of social security in the overall saving process.

Social security wealth is the present actuarial value of social security benefits for which a worker and his dependent spouse become eligible at age 65 (see Feldstein 1974, 1976e, for a description of the method of measuring this in practice). Social security saving in any year is defined as the increase in social security wealth during the year. In one sense, it is quite proper that households' social security wealth and social security saving be excluded from the national income accounts. Although households justifiably feel "richer" when their social security wealth rises, there is no real physical capital accumulation to correspond to this "saving." Social security saving is important not because it contributes to aggregate national saving (it does not) but because it induces individuals to reduce their own personal saving. Social security "saving" is like a government deficit; it provides an alternative to real capital accumulation as a way of providing for consumption in future retirement years. With a government deficit, the alternative asset is a government bond; with social security, the alternative asset is an implicit congressional promise to pay benefits in the future. The national income accounts obscure this by recording a saving flow that is used to purchase a government bond but not recording any measure of the saving that is replaced by social security. If the current implicit social security contracts were replaced by an explicit system in which the government sent "bonds" promising to pay future benefits to all covered workers, the national income accounts should record a corresponding increase in both private saving and the government deficit. National saving would remain unchanged but a more accurate picture would emerge. This is the spirit of the calculations presented in Table 5.

The vast size of social security wealth is shown in lines 1 and 2. By 1971, social security wealth was $2.2 billion at 1972 prices or nearly twice GNP. Social security wealth in constant dollars nearly tripled from 1955 to 1971, rising from 114 percent of GNP to 198 percent in 16 years. (The original study in which social security wealth was estimated [Feldstein, 1974] stopped with 1971; there has actually been a substantial rise in social security wealth relative to GNP since 1971 but a comparable estimate is not available.)

Social security "saving," i.e., the annual increment in real social security wealth, has been larger on average than total real private saving. Moreover, the ratio of social security saving to real private saving has grown from 73 percent in 1946-55 to 152 percent in 1966-71. As a percentage of net national product, social security saving has increased from 5.7 percent in 1946-55 to 12 percent in the most recent 1966-71 period. If the social security "saving" would otherwise have

TABLE 5. THE IMPORTANCE OF SOCIAL SECURITY SAVING

Line		*1946-1955*	*1956-1965*	*1966-1971*	*1946-1971*
1	Social security "wealth," end of period, billions of 1972 dollars.	744	1,507	2,188	2,188
2	Social security "wealth," end of period, percentage of GNP.	113.6	162.8	197.6	197.6
3	Annual social security "saving" as percent of private saving.	73.2	138.0	151.7	116.2
4	Annual social security "saving" as percent of net national product.	5.7	10.3	12.0	8.9

Source: Annual social security wealth estimates were derived by the author; see Feldstein (1974). The estimates are available only through 1971. Social security "saving" is the annual increase in social security wealth. Net national product, personal saving and private saving are based on national income and product accounts published in *Survey of Current Business,* January 1976.

been done as ordinary private saving, social security should be seen as a major government deficit that absorbed savings equivalent to 8.9 percent of NNP in the twenty-five year postwar period. Stated alternatively, this is equivalent to 55 percent reduction of the corresponding potential net saving rate of 16.2 percent. (Table 3 showed an average actual net saving rate of 7.3 percent of NNP. The 16.2 percent is the sum of this 7.3 percent and the average social security saving rate of 8.9 percent of NNP.)

The assumption that all of the social security saving would otherwise have been accumulated as private saving is obviously extreme. Some individuals would have saved little or nothing even in the absence of social security. Moreover, the observed private saving rate reflects not only the depressing effect of substituting social security wealth for ordinary wealth but also the positive effect on saving that results from the increase in planned retirement (and therefore retirement saving) that results from social security. It is important therefore that the empirical research that is beginning to accumulate does indicate that increases in social security wealth do substantially reduce private saving; see Feldstein (1976b) for a summary of this research. I shall return to some of the implications of this in the next section.

Does the United States Save Too Little?

There has recently been renewed widespread interest in the question of whether the United States should increase its rate of capital accumulation. Those who favor such an increase often note that the U.S. saving rate is lower than the rate in almost any other industrial nation.[2] While this in itself is neither good nor bad, it should arouse interest in the question of whether the U.S. saves too little.

Much of the recent discussion about the possibility of a "capital shortage" consists of the claims of conflicting authorities who point to alternative projections of "likely investment demand" and conclude that future saving will or will not be adequate for the projected investment. Those who foresee a capital shortage often bolster their case for particular government remedies by arguing that more capital is needed to prevent either unemployment, inflation, an adverse balance of trade, or some combination of these three. Frankly, I think that all such analyses fail to ask the right question about our national saving rate.

To know whether the U.S. does save too little we must ask: If we increase our rate of saving and therefore of capital accumulation, would the resulting higher level of consumption in the future more than compensate for the reduced consumption today? In other words, would the future reward justify the current sacrifice? The first part of this section shows how this question can be answered and why I believe the answer is "yes." I turn then to ask *why* the U.S. saves too little. Finally, I comment in more detail on the nature of the recent arguments about the possibility of a "capital shortage."

To avoid unnecessary confusion, let me hasten to distinguish my view that the future reward of greater consumption would justify the current sacrifice from the common but technically false assertion that an increase in the rate of saving is desirable because it causes an increase in the rate of growth of national income. Although a higher saving rate does cause a temporary increase in the rate of growth of income, it is better to regard this as a transition to a higher level of income. Eventually the rate of growth returns to its original value; a permanently higher saving rate does not buy a permanently higher rate

[2] For the 24 O.E.C.D. members other than the United States, gross fixed capital formation averaged 24 percent of gross domestic product in the period 1962 through 1973. Measured in this way, the U.S. rate of capital formation was only 17 percent. By contrast, the rate of Japan was 33 percent.

of growth. It is true that the transition takes a very long time so that the movement to a higher income level looks very much like a slightly higher rate of growth for a generation or more. But looking at the "growth" effect of a higher saving rate is bound to make a change in saving seem unimportant. For example, a one-fifth increase in the net saving rate—from 7.5 percent of net national product to 9 percent—would raise the equilibrium level of national income by about 10 percent. If this increase in income is completed in 40 years, it would add less than one quarter of one percentage point to the growth rate during this transition period and nothing thereafter (even though the saving rate continued at its new and higher level). Looked at in this way, there is little gained by the permanent 1.5 percentage point increase in the saving rate. But it should be clear from the fact that the saving rate has *no* permanent effect on the rate of growth that it is wrong to assess the importance of saving in terms of the rate of growth. The importance of saving must be seen in terms of the substantial effect of a higher saving rate on the level of income, i.e., in terms of the real return that the nation earns on that extra saving.

Since my subject is a very big one, let me be clear about some of its limits. I will consider only the accumulation of physical capital, excluding the issues of education and research. I am also not concerned with short-run considerations, neither the current state of the economy nor the general Keynesian concern about unemployment caused by an excess of desired saving over desired investment. I recognize that a large increase or decrease in saving would have unsettling short-run effects and that any major change in the saving rate should be accompanied by an appropriate mix of monetary and tax policy during the period of transition.

COMPARING THE REWARD WITH THE SACRIFICE

A higher saving rate would mean that we would consume less today but more in the future. For many, the fruit of a higher saving rate would be a higher standard of living in retirement. For others, the reward would come in preretirement years in the form of home ownership and other forms of consumption. To say that we now save too little is essentially equivalent to saying that it is worth foregoing some more consumption today to get this greater addition to future consumption.

In general, we economists assume that such decisions can be left to individuals to make for themselves. We do not ask whether people spend too much on tables and not enough on chairs. Why then should we ask whether they spend too much on current consumption and not enough on future consumption? The answer that I will emphasize in this chapter is that the individual saving decisions are subject to the powerful distorting influences of public policy through tax rules and social security. It is necessary therefore to look beyond the individual decisions and compare explicitly the benefits and costs of additional saving.

The first step in answering our question is to estimate the rate of return that the *nation* would earn on additional saving, i.e., the rate that would be available as a reward for individual saving in the absence of taxation. Each of us can then decide whether at that rate of return he would want to save more than he currently does. If everyone would want to save more if that rate of return were available on additional saving, there would implicitly be unanimous agreement that the nation now saves too little. Even though the current tax rules require each of us to share the reward from saving so that no one can earn the pretax national rate of return on his own saving, it is in terms of that pretax rate of return that the desirability of an increase in saving must be assessed.

The National Rate of Return on Private Investment—In measuring the national (or social) rate of return on private investment we want to summarize the effect that foregoing a dollar's worth of consumption now would have on the income available for consumption in the future. We can regard this as the internal rate of return on today's marginal private investment; this rate is to be measured in real terms and before tax. Of course, we are interested not only in the return on additional saving today but also in the marginal internal rates of return that will prevail in future years. We want to know the size of the sustained increase in the national output that would result from a sustained increase in the capital stock.

We can only approximate this marginal internal rate of return concept by the available aggregate national income and capital account data. There would be problems with any aggregate even if it were constructed in exact conformity with the appropriate theory for a representative capital good. In practice, further problems arise because arbitrary accounting conventions are used to value depreciation and scrapping. Despite these limitations, I believe that the national income and capital account data can provide a useful estimate of the current rate of return and an assessment of any significant trends.

I will measure the available national rate of return on private investment by the ratio of the capital income to the value of the capital stock in the nonfinancial corporate sector. Capital income is defined to include the net interest paid by corporations. The capital stock includes inventories as well as fixed reproducible capital. Two alternative measures are developed. The net return, r_n, subtracts current depreciation in measuring capital income and measures the capital stock net of accumulated depreciation. The gross return, r_g, does not subtract depreciation in measuring capital income but measures the capital stock net of accumulated scrapping. Feldstein and Summers (1976) show that each measure is equivalent to the internal rate of return measured under a particular technological assumption.

We are fortunate to have new Department of Commerce data that reports capital income and the capital stock in constant dollars. The old tax accounting measures of depreciation at historic cost have been superseded by new measures of economic depreciation at replacement cost. Nominal inventory profits have been purged of the distorting effects of inflation. Table 6 presents the estimated net and gross rate of return for overlapping decades from 1950 through 1975.

The average net rate of return was 12.4 percent for the entire period 1946-75. The gross rate was very similar, 11.3 percent. Both rates are quite similar in each of the decade intervals as well.

The lower rate for the most recent decade suggests the possibility of a permanent decrease in the rate of return or even the beginning of a secular decline. In a widely cited paper, Nordhaus (1974) has pointed out the recent decline and suggested that it can be explained by the higher capital intensity that resulted when investors shifted funds into the corporate sector because their perception of the risk

TABLE 6. RATES OF RETURN ON CORPORATE CAPITAL, 1950-75

Period	*Net Return* (r_n)	*Gross Return* (r_g)
1946-55	0.135	0.118
1950-59	0.126	0.117
1956-65	0.124	0.116
1960-69	0.134	0.122
1966-75	0.112	0.104
1946-75	0.124	0.113

Source: Feldstein and Summers (1976). See text for definitions.

of such investment had declined. Alternatively, a permanent decrease might reflect the end of the "capital scarcity" that was due to low rates of capital formation during the depression and the war. I frankly doubt both such effects.

Such interpretation of the recent evidence ignores the cyclical nature of profit rates. Larry Summers and I have analyzed the annual values of r_n and r_g in the postwar period (Feldstein and Summers, 1976). We find that there is absolutely no evidence of a downward trend in the period through 1969. While the profit rate fell substantially in the following six years, we believe that this reflects the abnormal experience of an imported inflation, of price controls and of a sharp recession. Indeed, the adverse effect on profits of a low rate of capacity utilization that can be inferred from the experience before 1970 is sufficient to explain the seeming downward trend in profits for the period through 1975. Moreover, the rate of profit began to recover in 1975 and now looks as if it will be up substantially again in 1976.

It seems most appropriate to conclude that the national rate of return on private corporate investment is about 12 percent and shows no evidence of a permanent or secular decline. Such a rate of return implies that sacrificing $1.00 of consumption now would permit a $2.00 increase in consumption after only 6 years. If saving for retirement from age 45 to 64 is increased by $100 per year, retirement consumption from age 65 to 80 could rise by $750 per year. These numbers look to me like a high potential reward for increased saving.

Let me now look briefly behind the assumption of a single rate of return to be earned on all new investments. If markets function freely and properly, all rates of return are equalized (after adjustment for risk, a subject to which I will return below). In practice, there are several important distortions in our economy that cause unequal rates of return on different types of investment: the corporation income tax, the exclusion of state and local interest payments from taxable income, the local real property taxes, the special tax treatment of both owner occupied and rental housing, etc. The differences in *pretax* national rates of return arise because investors move capital among investments until the *after-tax* individual rates of return are equalized in all types of investments. With different tax rates for different types of investment, equal after-tax rates of return imply unequal pretax rates of return.

A closer look at the corporation income tax will illustrate the nature of this distortion. If the corporation income tax were the only distortion and if corporations issued no debt, the national rates of return on corporate investment (r_{corp}) and noncorporate investment ($r_{noncorp}$) would have to satisfy $r_{noncorp} = (1 - t_{corp})r_{corp}$ where t_{corp} is the corporation income tax rate. In fact, the difference between r_{corp} and $r_{noncorp}$ is less than this indicates because investments are partially financed by debt; indeed, with 100 percent debt finance of *marginal* investments, the two rates would be equalized because interest payments on debt are deductible in the calculation of taxable corporate income. The differential is further reduced because the personal income tax is not levied until dividends are paid out, a feature that makes the corporate income tax into a tax shelter rather than an extra burden for high income shareholders.

What is the implication of these unequal national rates of return on different investments? Additional saving would expand capital in all of its uses, the actual allocation depending on differences in the rates at which incremental capital lowered rates of return. The national rate of return on the additional saving would be a weighted average of the individual rates of return, the weights being the shares of the new capital going to each use. While a proper calculation of this type remains to be done, it would most likely indicate a weighted average return below the 12 percent calculated above for the corporate sector but, I believe, not very far below. Moreover, since these differences in rates of return are largely a reflection of deliberate tax policies, they may to some extent reflect the government's perception that some apparently low yielding investments deserve subsidy because of social externalities. The most obvious case is the subsidy of state and local borrowing for the provision of public services. Housing may be subsidized vis-à-vis corporate investment because of presumed neighborhood externalities, etc. Dr. Pangloss would say that all social rates of return when properly measured to include externalities have been equalized by a wise tax policy.

While most economists who review the evidence will agree that the current return on corporate investment is approximately 12 percent, there are some who fear that any substantial increase in the capital-labor ratio might substantially reduce the marginal product of capital. Even a very large increase in capital would have little effect if its marginal product behaved as the commonly assumed Cobb-Douglas technology implies: a 10 percent increase in the ratio of capital to labor would decrease the return from 12 percent to 11.2 percent, while a 20 percent increase would lower the return to 10.6 percent. Although studies using time series data often suggest a much lower elasticity of substitution and therefore a much greater sensitivity of the return to the capital-labor ratio, the weight of the evidence based on cross-section data and long time-series indicates that the Cobb-Douglas response is the preferable assumption. This is supported by the long-run constancy of factor shares. The time series analyses are biased by the effects of cyclical variation in capacity utilization, wage setting and profitability.

There is finally the problem that the rates of return available to savers involve an element of risk that makes the average rate discussed here greater than the corresponding "certainty equivalent" rates, i.e., the riskless rate that investors would regard as equal in value to the 12 percent average with its accompanying risks. I will not deal with the problem of assessing a certainty equivalent but will make only two comments. First, a large part of the national return on investment accrues to the government as tax receipts; this both pools a very large number of individual risks and spreads the remaining risk over the entire population. For this part of the national return, the mean can be treated as equal to its certainty equivalence. Second, the difference between the individuals' net of tax mean yield and the corresponding certainty equivalence must also be borne in mind in evaluating their rate of consumption time preference. It is to this general subject that I now turn.

Preference for Present and Future Consumption—At one level of analysis each of us can ask himself whether he would want to sacrifice more present consumption if he could obtain a 12 percent rate of return. I for one would answer "yes." But as economists we would also like to say something more general about the rate at which others would be prepared to substitute future consumption for present consumption. If the amount of future consumption that individuals require to forego a dollar's worth of present consumption is less than the rate at which investment produces future consumption from current capital investments, we should save more. Stating the same thing more succinctly, *the U.S. saves too little if the rate at which individuals discount future consumption is less than the national rate of return on private investment.*

If there were perfect capital markets and no taxes on capital income, it would be a simple matter to infer the rate at which everyone discounted future consumption. Even if individuals have very different tastes, everyone would borrow or lend until his own marginal rate of substitution between present and future consumption were equal to

$1 + i$ where i is the market rate of interest. Equivalently, everyone's rate of time discount (d) would equal the market rate of interest. With no taxes, this rate would also equal the marginal product of capital.

The existing personal and corporate income taxes put a wedge between the national return on capital and the net rate received by savers. As a first approximation, everyone equates his rate of time discount to the net of tax rate of return that he receives. The substantial tax "wedge" makes the consumption discount rate (d) substantially less than the pretax national rate of return on additional investment. The size of this discrepancy and the amount of capital accumulation that would be required to eliminate it are indicators of the extent to which the U.S. currently saves too little.

A simplified analysis of the corporate and personal income taxes will illustrate the size of this discrepancy; I abstract here from noncorporate investment. With no corporate debt finance a corporation tax at rate t_c and a personal income tax at rate t_p imply that $d = (1 - t_p)(1 - t_c)r$ where r is the national (pretax) rate of return. Understating the tax rates as $t_p = 0.3$ and $t_c = 0.4$ overstates d; still, a national rate of return of 0.12 corresponds to $d = 0.05$. Inflation tends to raise the effective tax on capital income even further and therefore to widen the gap between d and r. This occurs because the tax laws deal with nominal interest rates, nominal depreciation and nominal capital gains instead of the corresponding real magnitudes; see Feldstein, Green, and Sheshinski (1976). Because interest payments are a deductible expense in calculating taxable corporate income, the use of debt finance reduces the effective rate of corporate income tax. If $100b$ percent of investment is financed by issuing bonds, the rate of time preference will satisfy $d = (i - t_p)[(1 - t_c)r + t_c bi]$ where i is the interest rate paid by the corporation; with $B = 0.5$, with $i = 0.05$ (without inflation), $t_p = 0.3$ and $t_c = 0.4$, $d = 0.057$. The net return received by investors and therefore their rate of time discount of future consumption is less than half of the corresponding pretax national rate of return.

As I noted above, replacing the mean values that I have been discussing with corresponding "certainty equivalents" yields would lower both r and d. Using certainty equivalent yields would increase the relative difference because the current absolute difference between the means reflects the portion collected by the government which is pooled and spread and which therefore need not be reduced (or reduced very little) in going from a mean rate to a certainty equivalent rate.

A more realistic analysis would recognize that most individuals do not save by buying corporate stock but by accumulating pension reserves or savings account deposits. Although pension funds receive favorable tax treatment, their equity investments are still subject to the corporate income tax. The low rates of return imposed by Federal Reserve Regulations on bank depositors implies both that their rate of time discount is reduced and that the marginal return on the investments financed with these funds are below the national return on corporate investment. To the extent that individuals buy higher yielding assets and also accumulate bank deposits, the difference reflects both a liquidity premium and a willingness to sacrifice higher return to eliminate some types of risk.

I turn finally to the difference between the interest rate paid to savers and the rate charged to borrowers. It is occasionally argued that the rates of time discount discussed above are too low for at least those individuals who borrow at consumer credit interest rates that reach 18 percent or even higher. Of course, these are nominal rates and the corresponding real rates are now approximately 13 percent. Many individuals can and do borrow at lower interest rates on mortgages and car loans. For most people the consumer credit rates are so much higher than their time preference rate that they do not borrow at all. There is also a process of adverse selection at work, making default rates high among those who borrow at high rates. To the extent that this default risk is anticipated by the borrower, the contractual interest rate overstates the expected rate and therefore the rate of time preference. In short, I believe that, for the vast majority of individuals, the very high borrowing rates are irrelevant as indicators of the rates of individual time preference.

There is a quite different way to think about comparing and aggregating consumption at different dates, which may be of interest to some readers of this chapter. It can be found in Appendix 1.

Distributional Issues—Critics of increased saving often ask: "Why should we save more to benefit the next generation? They will be richer than we are." This line of argument is quite irrelevant. Although we *can* save more in order to *give* more wealth to the next generation, additional saving can also be purely selfish. We can save more in order to enjoy a higher standard of living in our own retirement or in later preretirement years. At that time we can *sell* the capital stock to the next generation and consume its value. If each generation chooses to save more *for its own retirement years,* the capital stock will be *permanently* higher. This happens even though each individual saving decision is purely selfish.

The question of whether the United States should save more is really a question of whether government policies should be changed to foster more saving. The particular choice of policies would influence the distribution of the benefits and costs of increased saving. For example, if the government raised taxes now in order to reduce the outstanding public debt, the benefits of this method of achieving any particular change in current capital formation would accrue to future taxpayers who would no longer have to pay taxes to finance interest payments.

There is a basic distributional consequence of the increased capital stock that results from additional saving. A substantial increase in the aggregate capital stock would raise the marginal product of labor and lower the marginal product of capital. Workers would be made better off and capital owners would see a fall in their capital income unless they increased their own saving. The magnitude of such redistribution would not be terribly important, however. For example, a Cobb-Douglas technology implies that a 10 percent increase in the capital labor ratio would raise labor incomes by about 3 percent and would depress the rate of return by about 7 percent, e.g., from 6 percent after tax to 5.6 percent.

WHY DO WE SAVE TOO LITTLE?

We save too little as a nation for two quite different reasons. First, the personal and corporate income taxes greatly reduce the reward for saving. Second, social security provides an alternative to private saving as a means of providing for consumption after retirement.

I have already explained how the corporate and personal income taxes on capital income reduce the net reward that savers receive for postponing consumption. If the government financed the same public spending by a tax that exempted capital income, the net reward to savers would rise and the nation's rate of saving would increase. If a consumption tax were substituted for our current income tax in a way that keeps the present value of everyone's life-time tax burden unchanged, there would be a change in the timing of aggregate tax collections. National saving would increase by the amount of the rise in private saving only if the government adjusted its net surplus to keep real government consumption unchanged. A tax on "labor income" (defined to include the receipt of gifts and bequests) has the same effect on personal consumption but a yet different timing of tax receipts; see Feldstein (1976a).

I have discussed elsewhere (Feldstein, 1976a) in some detail the sense in which the tax-induced reduction in saving entails a welfare loss and therefore the sense in which we can be said to do "too little saving" because of the tax on capital income. Reducing the tax on capital income would require an increase in the tax on labor income to keep total government receipts unchanged. The welfare gain that would result from removing the saving distortion would be partly offset by a welfare loss that would result from a greater distortion of labor supply. My previous calculations indicate that, with plausible but conservative parameter values, the welfare gain would outweigh the loss; using Boskin's (1976) estimate of the response of saving would increase the net welfare gain beyond the value that I obtained. We save "too little" because of taxes in the sense that both saving and economic welfare would increase if the taxes on capital income were reduced and replaced by a tax on consumption with equal yield and equal progressivity.

The effects of social security on saving and on welfare are more complex. As I have explained elsewhere (Feldstein, 1974, 1976b,c), social security affects saving in two countervailing ways. For someone with fixed retirement plans, the availability of social security benefits unambiguously reduces the amount of private saving; because social security operates on a pay-as-you-go basis, i.e., uses tax receipts to finance concurrent benefits, there is no extra public saving to offset the decline of private saving so national saving falls by an equal amount; in particular, if the combination of the social security tax and the benefits that it finances has no income effect, the social security program will reduce saving during the individual's working years by just enough to leave consumption during retirement unchanged. More generally, however, there is a second effect of social security that would in itself tend to increase personal saving. By providing transfer payments to older persons who retire, social security induces the aged to reduce their supply of labor. This reduction in working years and the resulting increase in the period of retirement induce additional saving. The net effect of social security on the saving of the nonaged (and therefore eventually on the aggregate net saving of the population) is theoretically indeterminate and depends on the relative strength of the traditional "saving replacement effect" and the new "induced retirement effect." The relative importance of these two effects depends on a variety of factors: the extent of the change in retirement, the duration of retirement in the absence of social security, the distribution of lifetime consumption over the individual's life, etc. There is now a growing body of econometric studies using both aggregate data and household survey data that shows that social security does substantially reduce private saving. I have reviewed these studies in Feldstein (1976b) and report new household evidence in Feldstein and Pellechio (1976).

While many readers may find these empirical analyses of the effect of social security on private saving sufficient to confirm the primary conclusion, some readers may find the more theoretical exposition which is contained in Appendix 2 to be of additional assistance.

FOUR WRONG REASONS FOR SAVING MORE

I would now like to contrast the reason that I have emphasized for saving more—that the benefits greatly exceeded the cost—with the types of arguments that have been prominent in the recent debate about the "capital shortage." Most prominent is the notion of a "capital gap" between likely saving and investment. Then come arguments that a higher saving rate would reduce both unemployment and inflation and would improve our balance of trade. In general, these arguments are not valid. But their prominence in the public debate requires at least brief attention in the current paper.

The Capital Gap—The public's attention was drawn to the issue of a "capital shortage" by cries of alarm from the Secretary of the Treasury, the Chase Manhattan Bank, and several leading business publications. In May 1975, Treasury Secretary Simon testified to the Senate Finance Committee that "investment needs between 1974 and 1985 will range from $4 trillion to $4.5 trillion," estimates that are now a familiar part of the capital shortage litany. He then compared this with the $1.5 trillion capital investment during the period from 1962 through 1973 and concluded that "our capital investment needs in the coming years are approximately three times the level of the recent past."

The shortfall of $2.5 trillion implied by these figures is both alarming and misleading. The capital requirements of more than $4 trillion are projected in the prices of future years, based on a 5 percent rate of inflation. It makes no sense to compare future capital spending measured in these depreciated dollars with actual past capital spending when the price level was lower than it is now.

If we do the calculations with constant 1974 dollars instead, the Treasury's $4.2 trillion estimate implies $3.15 billion in 1975 prices. The $1.5 trillion of actual gross investment from 1962 through 1973 represented annual rates that were about 14 percent of GNP. If this rate continues, actual investment from 1974 through 1985 would, on the Treasury's assumption, total $2.94 trillion in 1974 prices. The net shortfall would be only $210 billion, a far cry from the common figure of $2.5 trillion. This gap could be closed by an increase in gross savings of less than one-tenth, i.e., less than 2 percent of GNP.

There is another sense in which all such projections of a capital "gap" are misleading. As an economist, I am puzzled that experts appear to be predicting that the demand for capital will continually exceed its supply. Usually when there is excess demand for some good, its price rises until demand and supply are equal. In the capital market, the interest rate and the cost of equity capital should increase until they are high enough to force firms to tailor their aggregate investment demands to the available supply. There will be no shortfall of investment funds because the demand for funds will shrink to the available supply. This has been pointed out explicitly in the Report of the Council of Economic Advisers (1976), and in Bosworth, Duesenberry and Carron (1975), Friedman (1975), Sinai and Brinner (1975), and other recent analyses. Sinai and Brinner define a shortage to exist if the future investment demand cannot be financed at a "reasonably stable" interest rate. It is not at all clear why the *current* rate of interest should be identified as a standard in this regard, however.

Full Employment—A quite different notion of a capital shortage is offered by those who believe that the capital stock is too small to provide full employment and that an increase in savings and investment would provide the capital equipment "necessary" to employ the unemployed. Such a view of unemployment is contrary to both the Keynesian analysis that unemployment can be eliminated by a higher level of aggregate demand and to the neoclassical view that the high "permanent" rate of unemployment in the United States reflects adverse incentives that result from government policies and labor market institutions. In the long run, which is the focus of this chapter, the size of the capital stock is irrelevant to the level of employment. In the long run, the capital intensity of production rises or falls as the availability of capital or labor increases or decreases relative to each other. Among developed countries, a higher ratio of capital to labor does not imply a lower long-run rate of unemployment.

At best, the notion that more capital can lower the unemployment rate could be rationalized in terms of a temporary situation in which there is no unused excess capacity and in which there is no opportunity to use existing capital in a more labor-intensive way. Under such short-run circumstances, an increase in available capital would be a prerequisite for more employment. Neither of the two conditions holds at present: there is substantial evidence of excess capacity and the capital stock can always be used in a more labor-intensive way by greater reliance on multiple-shift working.

Moreover, it is clear that any such argument for more capital to reduce unemployment confuses the occasional desirability of a *temporary increase* in the capital stock with the desirability of a *permanently higher* saving rate and correspondingly larger capital stock.

Price Stability—A similar confusion of temporary increases in investment with permanent increases in the capital stock underlies the price stability case for increased saving. Since some price increases occur when the demand for particular products exceeds capacity output, selective temporary increases in capacity could eliminate this potential source of inflation. But a permanently higher saving rate and a correspondingly higher capital stock would not reduce the frequency or severity of bottlenecks and excess demand. While the larger capital stock would permit a higher level of output, it would also raise the level of wages and capital income and therefore the demand for that output. There would in short be no change in the extent of excess capacity and no greater ease in preventing temporary inflationary shortages.

International Competitiveness—A larger capital stock would increase the productivity of U.S. workers. For any given level of real wages, greater productivity means lower prices. And with fixed exchange rates, lower prices mean more exports and fewer imports. This line of reasoning is used to argue that a higher saving rate will improve the long-run balance of trade and, by reducing imports and increasing exports, will "prevent the loss of American jobs to foreign workers."

It should be clear that the argument is faulty at several points. Higher productivity should increase real wages. The level of prices will depend on (among other things) the ratio of the money supply to the level of output and not on productivity or other such "real" variables. Exchange rates do not actually remain unchanged in the long run even when exchange rates are officially "fixed" and certainly vary quite rapidly under the current system of "managed floating" exchange rates. The domestic price level can therefore change without affecting exports and imports. And, finally, if the domestic labor market functions efficiently and aggregate demand is maintained, there will be no relation between the level of net exports and the level of domestic employment.

If there is a relation between capital accumulation and export performance, it should be both temporary and weak. An increased rate of saving causes productivity to grow more rapidly during the transition to a new equilibrium capital intensity. With productivity rising more rapidly, it may *institutionally* be possible to have a lower rate of price inflation because the rate of nominal wage increase does not rise fully with the rate of productivity growth. In addition, exchange rates may not rise rapidly enough to eliminate export surpluses, in part because countries use reserves to delay such changes. And the resulting strong net exports are both a direct stimulus to domestic production and a factor that induces a reserve-conscious government to maintain a high level of aggregate demand. It is clear that this effect of a higher saving rate is at most temporary and is more appropriately viewed as only one among many ways of achieving temporarily both high demand and a favorable balance of payments.

Concluding Comments

The existence of this conference is ample evidence that economists and others are asking whether the United States now saves too little. In the first part of this paper I presented evidence that the rate of real net capital accumulation has fallen steadily throughout the past century and that it continued to fall during the postwar period. I later noted that the U.S. gross capital formation rate is one-third lower than the average of all other OECD countries. Although both types of statistics should motivate a concern about our saving rate, neither constitutes a reason for saving more.

I have explained in some detail that the real reason to increase our saving rate is that the reward for additional real saving that the nation as a whole would receive would be well worth the current sacrifice. The reason that our private saving rate is now too low is to be found in our method of taxation and in our social security program. During the past decade, the actual saving rate has been further depressed by an almost continuous government deficit. Finally, I have tried to distinguish my line of analysis from what I regard as spurious arguments about a capital "gap" and about the potential contribution of a larger capital stock to full employment, price stability and the balance of trade.

There now seem to be four principal ways in which public policies can be used to achieve a higher national rate of saving: government surpluses, changes in tax rules, changes in the structure of social security benefits and financing, and reform of the regulation of financial institutions. I hope that future economic analysis will focus on defining the appropriate mix of these four options.

Appendix 1: Comparing Present and Future Consumption

This appendix presents a way to think about comparing and aggregating consumption at different dates which is quite different from that presented in the main body of the text.

The marginal rate of substitution between consumption at different dates is (in cardinalist language) the ratio of the corresponding marginal utilities of consumption. Ignore for the moment the fact that future consumption is less certain because of the probability of intervening death and psychologically less attractive because of what Pigou (1920) referred to as the "faulty telescopic faculty" that causes future pleasures to appear smaller than they are in reality. The marginal utility of consumption nevertheless falls through time because real consumption per capita rises. If, over the relevant horizon, consumption grows exponentially at rate g and the elasticity of marginal utility with respect to consumption is a constant of $-m$, the marginal utility will also fall exponentially at rate gm. The marginal rate of substitution therefore satisfies $MRS_{s,\, s+1} = e^{gm}$. Since this derivation ignores both the individual probability of death and the psychological myopia and idealizes the change in consumption as a constant exponential growth, the resulting marginal rate of substitution is best thought of as representing a "planner's time preference" that is appropriate if we wish to ignore the distribution of consumption among individuals including the distribution among individuals of different generations. To distinguish this from the individuals' time preference rate d, I will denote this by δ. Thus, viewed in this way, $MRS = (1+\delta) = e^{mg}$. As a quite accurate approximation for the relevant orders of magnitude, δ is mg. Note that δ will be less than d by the annual probability of death and by the discounting of future utility that individuals would later recognize as irrational.

A numerical example will help to fix these ideas. Since per capita consumption is growing at about $g = 0.02$, we find $\delta = 0.02m$. If a 10 percent increase in consumption causes its marginal utility to decrease by 20 percent, $m = 2$. The appropriate value of m is clearly a matter of introspective judgment; I think of m as between 0.5 and 1.5 and would find values of m much in excess of 2 to be quite implausible. Even with $m = 2$, $\delta = 0.04$. A reasonable adjustment for the probability of death and for Pigovian myopia would still leave d at no more than 0.07.

Thus, this direct utilitarian approach, like the analysis of the prevailing net-of-tax asset yields, implies that the rate of time discount of future consumption is probably about half of the gross social return on additional private investment.

Appendix 2: Social Security and Private Saving

To illustrate the nature of the welfare loss that occurs when an increase in social security depresses private saving, I shall consider an increase that is small enough to leave unchanged the national rate of return and the rate of time preference. Samuelson's (1958) model of overlapping generations is a convenient framework for this analysis. To avoid additional cumbersome notation, I will assume that each generation lives for one "year" or, equivalently, that the rates of return and of time preference are "per generation." Samuelson shows that if the aggregate real income grows at rate n, social security "pays" an implicit rate of return of n, i.e., for each one dollar of social security taxes that individuals pay during their "working year" they will recetive $1+n$ dollars of benefits in retirement during the "next year." The substantially higher return that has been enjoyed by U.S. social security annuitants represents a transition phase that is rapidly coming to an end; see Feldstein (1976d). If the one dollar of taxes had instead been invested in real capital accumulation, the return would have been r dollars. The individual investor might receive less than r *directly* because of the taxes he pays but the remainder comes indirectly because of the greater taxes that the government collects. The individual thus loses $r-n$ dollars during the "retirement year" per dollar of tax paid (rather than invested) in the previous "working year." The discounted value of that loss at the time that the tax is paid is thus $(r-n)/(1+d)$, where d is the individual's rate of time discount.

Consider now a decision to increase social security taxes and benefits by S at time $t = 0$ and to raise this increment annually at rate n as national income grows. There is an immediate gain of S to the generation of retirees who receive the initial transfer without paying any extra tax and a net loss to the present generation of workers and to each future generation; for those who are working in future year t the value of the net loss is $[(r-n)/(1+d)]$ $S(1+n)^t$. The immediate gain of the initial retirees can be compared to the current and future losses by discounting these losses at the time preference rate δ that is appropriate for intergenerational comparisons of consumption. The net loss is thus:

$$L = \frac{r - n}{1 + d} \cdot S \sum_{t=0}^{\infty} \left(\frac{1 + n}{1 + \delta}\right)^t - S. \tag{1}$$

The future losses have a finite present value only if the discount rate (δ) exceeds the rate of growth of national income (n); I shall make this convergence assumption even though it is not necessarily satisfied: Recall that δ may be regarded as the rate of decline of the marginal utility of consumption *per capita* while n is the rate of growth of *aggregate* income. With a population growth rate of $\pi = .02$, a real *per capita* consumption growth rate of $g = .02$ and a marginal utility elasticity of $m = 2$, we have $\delta = .04$ and $n = g + \pi = .04$. In this case, the future losses have an infinitely large present value, limited in reality only by the eventual limit to population growth.

With the assumption of convergence, equation (1) implies that the present value loss per initial dollar of tax increase is:

$$\frac{L}{S} = \frac{r - n}{\delta - n} \cdot \frac{1 + \delta}{1 + d} - 1. \tag{2}$$

Since $r > n$ and $r > d \geqq \delta$, the loss is clearly positive.

Readers familiar with Samuelson's analysis may wonder why he reached the very different conclusion that social security would raise the welfare of every generation. Unlike the current analysis, Samuelson assumed that no capital goods exist so that real saving and investment is impossible. By extension, whenever r is less than n, the "loss" of each future generation is actually a gain and social security unambiguously raises welfare by reducing real investment (see David Cass and Menahem Yaari, 1967). But in the realistic case of $r > n$, the loss depends on the relative magnitudes of r, n, δ and d. For example, if $r = d = \delta$ there would be no present value loss in the case being considered although each generation of workers would lose $(r - n)/(1 + d)$. With no tax distortion ($r = d$) but with $d > \delta$, there would be a loss per dollar of initial tax increase of $(d - \delta)(1 + n)/(1 + d)(\delta - n) > 0$.

The issue of optimal social security benefits is of course more complex than this simple discussion implies. But the analysis is sufficient to illustrate the basic point: in reducing private saving, social security causes the substitution of a low-yielding implicit intergenerational contract for real capital investment with a higher social yield.

References

BOSKIN, MICHAEL J., "Taxation, Saving and the Rate of Interest," Working Paper Series No. 135. National Bureau of Economic Research, Inc., 1976.

BOSWORTH, BARRY, JAMES DUESENBERRY AND ANDREW CARRON, *Capital Needs in the Seventies.* Brookings Institution, 1975.

CASS, DAVID AND MENAHEM YAARI, "Individual Saving, Aggregate Capital Accumulation, and Efficient Growth," in Karl Shell (ed.), *Essays in the Theory of Optimal Growth.* Cambridge, Mass., 1967.

Council of Economic Advisers, *Economic Report of the President.* Washington, D.C.: Government Printing Office, 1976.

David, Paul A. and John L. Scadding, "Private Savings: Ultrarationality, Aggregation, and 'Denison's Laws,'" *Journal of Political Economy,* 82, no. 2, part I (March/April 1974).

Denison, Edward F., "A Note on Private Saving," *Review of Economics and Statistics,* 40 (August 1958), 261-67.

Feldstein, Martin S., "Tax Incentives, Corporate Saving, and Capital Accumulation in the United States," *Journal of Public Economics,* 2 (1973), 159-71.

———, "Social Security, Induced Retirement and Aggregate Capital Accumulation," *Journal of Political Economy,* 82, no. 5 (September/October 1974).

———, "Welfare Loss of Capital Income Taxation," *Journal of Political Economy.* Forthcoming, 1976a.

———, "Social Security and Saving: The Extended Life Cycle Theory," *American Economic Review,* 66, no. 2 (May 1976), 77-86, 1976b.

———, "Social Security and Private Savings: Intergenerational Evidence in an Extended Life Cycle Model," in Martin Feldstein and Robert Inman (eds.), *The Economics of Public Services.* An International Economic Association Conference volume. Forthcoming, 1976c.

———, "Facing the Social Security Crisis," mimeo, 1976d.

———, "Social Security and the Distribution of Wealth," *Journal of the American Statistical Association.* Forthcoming, 1976e.

Feldstein, Martin S., Jerry Green, and Eytan Sheshinski, "Inflation and Taxes in a Growing Economy with Debt and Equity Finance." Harvard Institute of Economic Research Discussion Paper 481, 1976.

Feldstein, Martin S. and Anthony Pellechio, "Social Security and Household Wealth Accumulation: New Microeconomic Evidence." Forthcoming, 1976.

Feldstein, Martin S. and Lawrence Summers, "The Rate of Profit: Falling or Cyclical?" Forthcoming, 1976.

"The $4.5-Trillion America Needs to Grow," *Business Week,* September 22, 1975, pp. 42-48.

Friedman, Benjamin M., "Financing the Next Five Years of Fixed Investment," *Sloan Management Review,* Massachusetts Institute of Technology, 16, no. 3 (Spring 1975), 51-74.

Kuznets, Simon, "Proportion of Capital Formation to National Product," *American Economic Review,* XLIII, no. 2 (May 1952), 507-26.

———, *Capital in the American Economy.* Princeton: Princeton University Press, 1961.

Musgrave, John C., "Fixed Non-Residential Business and Residential Capital in the U.S., 1925-75," *Survey of Current Business,* 56, no. 4 (April 1976), 46-52.

New York Stock Exchange, *The Capital Needs and Savings Potential of the U.S. Economy,* September 1974.

Nordhaus, William D., "The Falling Share of Profits," *Brookings Papers on Economic Activity,* Washington, D.C.: Brookings Institution, 1:1974, pp. 169-208.

Pigou, A. C., *The Economics of Welfare.* London: Macmillan and Company, 1920.

Samuelson, Paul A., "An Exact Consumption-Loan Model of Interest with or without the Social Contrivance of Money," *Journal of Political Economy,* LXVI, no. 6 (December 1958), 467-82.

Sinai, Allen and Roger E. Brinner, *The Capital Shortage.* Lexington, Mass.: Data Resources, Inc., 1975.

Tax Foundation, Inc., *The Challenge of Tax Reform: 4. Capital, Taxes, and Jobs,* New York, 1976.

Wachtel, Paul, Arnold Sametz, and Harry Shuford, "Capital Shortages: Myth or Reality," *Journal of Finance,* May 1976.

Wallich, Henry C., "Is There a Capital Shortage?" *Challenge,* September-October 1975, pp. 30-36.

Weidenbaum, Murray L., "Saving, Investment, and Capital Shortages," *Astronautics and Aeronautics,* December 1975.

Leonall C. Andersen

6

Regulation and the Achievement of Productivity Growth and High Employment

Introduction

In recent years a large number of government regulations regarding the conduct of private economic activities have been added to an already extensive body of existing regulations. The extent of the recent increases in the number of regulations and their complexity is suggested by the ever-growing size of the Federal Register. Regulatory agencies have been required to publish their regulations in the register since 1937. That year from a size of 3,450 pages, it increased to 35,591 pages in 1973, to 45,422 pages in 1974, and to 60,221 pages in 1975.

PURPOSES OF REGULATIONS

The purposes of the regulations have been to produce benefits to individuals in our society from the achievement of a number of objectives. Some objectives of earlier regulations were a "living wage," "fair prices" to consumers of the services provided by public transportation companies and public utilities, and "pure" food and drugs. More recently, higher standards of achievement than in the past have been set with regard to such objectives as worker "health and safety," "equal" employment opportunity, consumer product "safety," and environmental "protection."

LEONALL C. ANDERSEN *is Economic Advisor to the Federal Reserve Bank of St. Louis. He has also been Professor of Economics at the University of Missouri in St. Louis. Dr. Andersen has served as Senior Staff Economist to the President's Council of Economic Advisers.*

The usual reason given for imposing regulations is that in many instances our relatively free market system puts out "products" that are deemed by some individuals to be "undesirable." The president of Chrysler has provided an example of such a "product," the pollution of the air by automobiles. He argues according to an article by John J. Riccardo in the *New York Times* (July 20, 1976), that, a

> . . . large part of the public will not voluntarily spend extra money to install emission control systems which will help to clean up the air. Any manufacturer who installs and charges for such equipment while his competition doesn't soon finds he is losing sales and customers.

In this case, it is argued that only by adopting a regulation requiring emission control devices on all automobiles will individuals receive a benefit in the form of cleaner air. Such an argument is incomplete, however, because it ignores the costs to individuals in terms of the achievement of other objectives which they give up as a result of the regulation.

COSTS OF REGULATIONS

The regulations adopted to achieve these objectives are of three general types—control of specific prices, mandated use of resources, and prohibition of the use of certain materials. An example of the first type is the program controlling the price of oil produced from existing wells. An example of the second type is the devices required on all new automobiles to reduce air pollution. An example of the third is the ban on DDT in pesticides.

In a market economy, in which prices are free to change, and resources are free to move from market to market, and in which use of resources is unrestricted, consumer market decisions determine the allocation of resources. By restricting changes in some prices and the free movement or use of resources, regulations result in an allocation of existing resources different from that which would have prevailed otherwise. Such a reallocation of resources counter to individual market decisions imposes costs on them in both the present and the future.

Present Costs—The regulations impose a present cost on individuals in terms of foregone consumption opportunities *for a given rate of production*. A smaller proportion of existing resources is allocated in the present to the production of the types of goods and services that would otherwise be produced in markets and a larger proportion to meet the objectives of regulation.

An example of a present cost to individuals is the added equipment required on automobiles to meet the standards imposed by regulations regarding cleaner air and safer automobiles. It has been estimated that in 1973, purchasers of new cars produced in the United States paid over $3 billion extra because of these regulations. The regulations thus reallocate in the present a considerable amount of existing resources from the production of goods and services—production that would have met other demands of consumers in the market—to the production of items mandated by the regulations.

Future Costs—The regulations also may impose a future cost on individuals. If the induced reallocation of resources retards productivity growth and/or impedes achievement of a high level of employment, future growth of production for the market would be slower than otherwise. In such an instance, individuals would experience foregone consumption opportunities in the future because of the *slower growth in production.*

An example of a future cost to individuals is the reallocation of resources to meet the standards mandated by regulations imposed on business firms regarding environment protection and employee safety. It has been estimated that in 1973, $3 billion of capital outlays by business firms were directed toward meeting these requirements. To the extent that such outlays resulted in smaller outlays for other additions to the physical capital stock of business firms and did not increase worker productivity, growth of productivity in the production of goods and services for the market and, hence, future growth of such output, would be less than otherwise.

POINTS TO BE COVERED

This chapter analyzes the influence of some present regulations on the growth of private sector output for the market, as related to the achievement of productivity growth and high employment. First, the analytical framework is presented. Next, the influence of regulations is analyzed within the framework. Then, some proposals for a regulatory strategy are given.

Analytical Framework

In our market economy, there are three major influences which underlie growth of private sector output for the market. The first one is growth in population of labor force age—the potential number of individuals available for employment. The second one is the preferences of individuals regarding work and leisure and regarding consumption in the present and consumption in the future. These preferences are important determinants of the number seeking employment and of growth in capital which underlies productivity growth. The third one is the influence of the existing body of laws and regulations on market decisions made in the private sector. For a given state of these three influences, market forces determine growth of private sector output.

This analysis is concerned with the last influence. There are many laws and regulations which influence growth of private sector output, for a given growth in population of labor-force age and a given state of individual preferences. Among these are tax laws, government programs for income redistribution, laws providing subsidies to various lines of economic activity, and laws which have set up what is commonly called "regulatory agencies." Attention is focused here mainly on the last one.

The assumptions of a given growth of population of labor-force age and a given state of individual preferences are maintained throughout the analysis and will not be mentioned further. Laws other than those regarding regulatory agencies, with one exception, are treated in a similar manner.

REGULATION, MARKET FORCES, AND GROWTH OF OUTPUT

Growth of output reflects growth in employment and productivity. In a market economy, prices adjust over time to equate the amount of labor services demanded and the amount supplied and the amounts of human and physical capital demanded and the amounts supplied. Consequently, both the long-run growth of employment and the production of human and physical capital are determined by the interplay of market forces. In addition, market prices adjust in such a manner as to allocate existing resources to their most efficient use in production; that is, output is maximized for given consumer market demands. Since capital accumulation and efficiency in the use of resources exert an important influence on productivity growth, that too is determined in the market. To the extent that regulations impede the normal functioning of markets, growth of employment and/or productivity, hence, growth in output, would be less than would otherwise be the case.

DIAGRAM OF FRAMEWORK

A simplified version of the market forces influencing growth of private sector production for the market is presented in Figure 1. The items presented are summary measures of the market influence, operating through the price mechanism, of changes in the factors that jointly determine growth of output. Although there are many market channels involving price changes by which the underlying factors influence growth of output, the diagram shows only a few of these so as not to complicate it unduly. The arrows show these channels and the direction of influence. The diagram is used in subsequent analysis to identify some of the major points at which the regulations influence growth of output.

Referring to the diagram, the top four boxes on the left-hand side are summary measures of the market influence of factors determining "man-hours worked in the private sector," and the bottom three boxes are summary measures of the influence of the factors determining "output per man-hour worked in private sector," more commonly called productivity. The growth rate of "private sector output," at prevailing prices, equals the sum of the growth rates of these two summary measures. The two boxes on the upper, right-hand side are summary measures of the market influence of factors determining the allocation of given output to "physical capital accumulation" and "human capital accumulation."

An important aspect for the analysis shown in the diagram is the interdependence in the market (a feedback channel) between output and the amount of physical and human capital accumulation. Associated with a prevailing set of market prices are an amount of output and an amount of capital accumulation. The latter amount influences growth of productivity and, subsequently, growth of output.

Inflence of Some Current Regulations on Growth of Private Sector Output

It is virtually impossible, at this time, to measure the magnitude of the market influence of current regulations on growth of private sector output. So instead, their net direction of influence is investigated. In many instances, however, even ascertaining this is very complicated because of the highly interrelated nature of our market economy. For purposes of discussion the analysis is organized around

Fig. 1. Factors Influencing Long-run Economic Growth

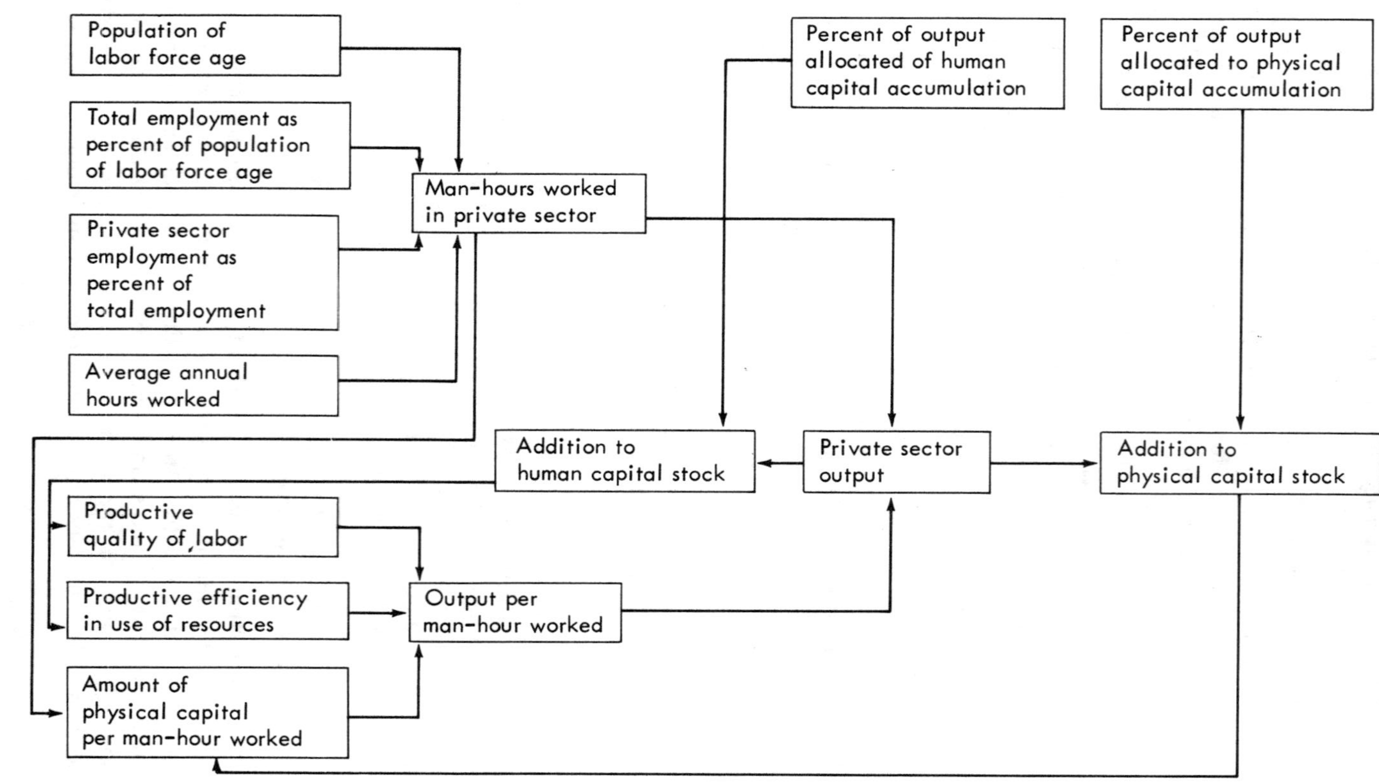

the influence of regulations on growth of private sector employment and productivity. Although growth of productivity and employment are interdependent, the influence of regulations on each one is analyzed separately. Not all regulations are discussed, but several specific ones are used as illustrations.

INFLUENCE ON GROWTH OF PRIVATE SECTOR EMPLOYMENT

The regulations can exert an important market influence on growth of private sector employment, measured by "man-hours worked." Two market channels of influence involve induced changes in market prices over time, which result in changes in (1) "total employment as percent of population of labor-force age" or in (2) "private sector employment as percent of total employment" (see Figure 1). An induced change in one of these two summary measures (for example, "total employment as percent of population of labor-force age"), all other summary measures remaining unchanged, influences growth of private sector employment in the same direction. The following discussion uses this partial analysis.

Reduction in Growth of Private Sector Employment—On the one hand, some regulations tend to reduce growth of private sector employment, at a prevailing real wage, from what it would have been otherwise. For example, a recent study at the Center for the Study of American Business estimated that the 1966 increase in the minimum wage had by 1972 resulted in teenage employment being 320,000 lower than otherwise. This result follows, at prevailing prices of goods and services, from a mandated minimum money wage higher than the potential productive contribution of these relatively unskilled individuals. A similar result could also be expected for other prospective workers who are relatively unskilled. Consequently, at a time, as in recent years, when teenagers and other unskilled entrants into the labor force are increasing faster than growth of population of labor-force age, "total employment as percent of population of labor-force age" will tend to rise slower than otherwise.

Some analysts also argue that the Equal Employment Opportunity Program tends to hold back the filling of job vacancies, at a prevailing real wage, because employers have to engage in an extensive search for candidates who meet the qualifications of both the program and specific jobs. In many instances, finding such a match of qualifications is difficult. During such a search, therefore, these jobs remain vacant.

In these instances, any expansion of this program or a more stringent administration of its provisions will tend to reduce "total employment as percent of population of labor-force age."

Another factor tending to hold back growth of private sector employment is the amount of government employment required to administer the regulations. It has been estimated that the administration of current regulations by the twenty-four major regulatory agencies require over 100,000 government employees, many of whom would have otherwise sought private sector employment at prevailing real wages. This number is about the same as the combined employment of McDonell-Douglas and Coca-Cola in 1973. Increases in the number of government employees required to administer the regulations tend to reduce "private sector employment as percent of total employment."

Increases in Growth of Private Sector Employment—On the other hand, the regulations may tend to increase private sector employment because of the reporting burden placed on private business. For example, in June 1974, there were 5,146 different types of approved government report forms, excluding tax and banking forms. It has been estimated that over 130 million man-hours a year were required to fill out these reports. This number of man-hours is equivalent to about 65,000 employees working a forty-hour week, or approximately the number employed by General Dynamics in 1973. To the extent an increasing reporting burden is met by additions to payrolls of business firms and not by reallocating those already employed, "private sector employment as percent of total employment" increases.

INFLUENCE OF REGULATIONS ON PRODUCTIVITY GROWTH

Obviously, if as a result of the regulations private sector productivity growth is retarded significantly, there would be a considerable reduction in growth in the amount of goods and services produced. For example, a one percentage point reduction in the rate of productivity growth, other factors unchanged, means an equal reduction in the growth of private sector output. If this reduction in productivity growth is maintained for ten years, the amount of production would be more than 10 percent lower than otherwise by the tenth year.

Channel through Human Capital Accumulation—For a prevailing amount of "private sector output," there is a channel of market influence on productivity (other factors constant) running from the "percent of output allocated to human capital accumulation," to "additions to human capital stock," to "productive quality of labor" and "productive efficiency in the use of resources" (see Figure 1). Slower growth in these last two summary measures, other factors unchanged, reduces growth of productivity.

Human capital accumulation in the form of an enhanced "productive quality of labor" has been retarded by regulations. Workers gain skills from on-the-job training and work experience, but the 320,000 teenagers and others who were not employed in 1972 because of the minimum wage were denied such gains. Improved health of workers also contributes to the "productive quality of labor." Medical advances thus contribute to human capital accumulation. An American Enterprise Institute study points out, however, that the 1962 amendments to the Food and Drug Act have tended to delay the introduction of drugs that have proved to be effective by about four years, thereby retarding improvement in the "productivity quality of labor."

Channel through Physical Capital Accumulation—For prevailing "private sector output," according to Figure 1, there is a channel of the market influence of the regulations (other factors constant) on productivity growth running from "percent of output allocated to physical capital accumulation," to "additions to physical capital stock," to "amount of physical capital per man-hour worked." A reduction in the growth of this last summary measure, other factors unchanged, tends to reduce productivity growth. The net direction of the influence of the regulations on growth of "amount of physical capital per man-hour worked" is not clear, however.

For example, it has been reported that over the past four years, 350 foundries closed down (a reduction in the stock of physical capital) because it was not profitable for them to meet the requirements of the Environment Protection Agency and the Occupational Safety and Health Administration. On the other hand, some firms found it more profitable to meet those requirements than to close down, and, therefore, added to their stock of physical capital. A recent McGraw-Hill survey indicates that planned capital outlays of industry to meet the requirements of OSHA increased 17 percent from 1975 to 1976 and those to meet the requirements of EPA increased 7 percent. In these two cases, the net direction of influence depends on the relative sizes of the two results.

Another complication in ascertaining the net direction of the influence of the regulations on "physical capital accumulation" is that they do not have a uniform impact on all industries. For example, it has been reported recently that in the petroleum industry, in which regulated prices are below free market prices, the number of seismic exploration crews (an indicator of future development of petroleum resources) decreased in the past two years. But this does not necessarily mean that the total amount of physical capital accumulation will be less in the future than otherwise, because resources available at prevailing prices and interest rates for production of physical capital will tend to flow to unregulated industries.

There is one situation in which there would be an unambiguous, negative direction of influence on "physical capital accumulation." This would be a situation in which there was great uncertainty throughout business regarding the effect of regulations on the future net return to be realized from adding to the stock of physical capital. Such uncertainty would follow from the long stretched-out procedure involved—the passing of legislation, the adoption of regulations, the administration of the regulations, and the testing in courts—before their impact on net returns becomes clear.

Channel through Productive Efficiency—The regulations also exert an influence on productivity growth in the private sector through their impact on the "productive efficiency in use of resources" (see Figure 1). If, other factors unchanged, they result in a less efficient allocation of existing resources in production than would have otherwise prevailed in markets, productivity growth in terms of market goods would also be less.

An example of such a reallocation of productive resources is that which has occurred in the petroleum and natural gas industry, because present price controls and the threat of additional controls and other regulations in the future have reduced expected returns from their present operations. It has been reported that oil companies are shifting their use of resources from oil production to mining and manufacturing, from developing new sources of hydrocarbons to developing existing oil and gas reserves, and from exploring and producing natural gas which is sold in controlled interstate markets to developing that which is sold in the relatively uncontrolled intrastate markets. Also, the Federal Energy Administration estimated in late 1975 that if price controls on old oil were lifted, the recoverable reserves of oil would be doubled, because it would then be profitable to allocate resources to secondary and tertiary recovery processes to meet consumer demands.

Another example is the mandated use of resources. It has been estimated that industrial outlays to meet worker safety and noise standards will range up to $40 billion over the coming five years. The head of a large construction firm located in St. Louis has reported that, in building a plant which uses polluted water from the Mississippi River for cooling purposes only, the Environment Protection Agency required the addition of equipment to return "clean" water to the river. These types of additions to physical capital do not increase the amount of market oriented output for a given input of labor.

Or, take the case of the reporting requirements mandated by regulators. As was noted earlier, it has been estimated that the filling of the number of reports in existence in 1974 required over 130 million man-hours. Such an increase in labor input would not increase the amount of market oriented output for a given stock of physical capital.

There is also evidence that recent regulations have resulted in a smaller percent of output than otherwise allocated to technological development. By increasing the costs of implementing new technology or by reducing their expected returns, regulations tend to deter innovation. In such a case, growth in the "productive efficiency in the use of resources," is less than otherwise.

For example, despite the increasing trend growth rate of "private sector output" since the late 1940s, the pace of innovation in American technology has slowed in recent years, according to an analysis by Dr. Jerome B. Wiesner, president of Massachusetts Institute of Technology. Among the ever-increasing deterrents to creative change in American science and industry, Dr. Wiesner cites increasing government regulation.

Furthermore, much of current research has been directed toward meeting the regulatory requirements placed on American business, thereby reducing the amount of research in other lines. For example, Paul F. Chenea, vice president for research laboratories at General Motors, reported in *Business Week* (June 28, 1976), "We've diverted a large share of our resources—sometimes up to half—into meeting government requirements, instead of developing new materials, better manufacturing techniques, and better products. . . ."

Educators have pointed out that proposed new federal regulations on discrimination against handicapped students, while good in intent, will result in a considerable reallocation of resources used in producing education. The resulting reallocation of given resources would result in a less efficient production of education. According to a statement issued by the American Council on Education and ten other associations in opposition to the proposed regulations:

> If prior experience with such all-embracing antidiscriminatory programs is considered, one could reasonably predict that the end result will be sheaves of unread, unnecessary paper, uneven and inconsistent enforcement . . . expenditure of scarce institutional resources on the technicalities of enforcement, a staggering back-log of complaints, and the diversion of administrative and faculty talent. [*The statement concluded*] . . . that the case has not been made to support the proposition that an extensive federal regulatory scheme is essential to secure the education or rights of handicapped students.

Feedback Channel through Output Growth—There is also a feedback channel of the influence of regulations on productivity growth, for a prevailing "percent of output allocated to capital accumulation" (see Figure 1). Regulations for minimum wage and equal employment opportunity have tended to reduce employment growth and, therefore, growth of output. The regulations which were cited as tending to reduce the rate of improvement in the "quality of labor" or the "productive efficiency in use of resources" also have tended to reduce output growth. The slower growth in output in these cases, other factors unchanged, tends to reduce the "additions to human capital stock" and the "additions to physical capital stock." As a consequence, growth of productivity is less than otherwise.

EVALUATION OF INFLUENCE OF REGULATIONS

According to the preceding arguments, the market influence of some current regulations have tended to reduce growth of private sector output for the market from what it would have been otherwise. A foremost influence has been that associated with regulations which have resulted in a less efficient use of resources in production than would have prevailed in markets. Other important influences are those associated with regulations which have tended to retard growth of private sector employment and growth in human capital accumulation.

Proposals for a Regulatory Strategy

An implication of the preceding analysis is that regulations have imposed costs to individuals, which could be considerable, in the form of foregone consumption opportunities. Given the apparent desire of members of our society to achieve the benefits they have come to associate with the regulations, along with their growing concern regarding the costs, a regulatory strategy for the future appears warranted.

CONSIDER ALL INDIVIDUALS

Since the costs of regulation are widely distributed (foregone consumption opportunities affects us all), a regulatory strategy should take into consideration the viewpoints of all individuals. Such has frequently not been the case in the past. Many regulations have been adopted because of the vigorous agitation of "narrowly based" interest groups, the ascendancy of "advocate politics," and the "campaigns" of the news media. Frequently, purported benefits have been emphasized but costs have been ignored or belittled. Consequently, regulations resulting from such efforts have not reflected the considered judgment of all individuals if the relevant information had been made available.

A case in point is that of the agitation in the early 1970s to prevent the building of the Alaskan pipeline. Zealous conservation groups, activist members of Congress, and "social-minded" elements of the news media proclaimed to the public that great benefits would accrue from maintaining a wilderness, but they showed little interest in mentioning possible costs to individuals. As a result, there was considerable public opinion in opposition to building the pipeline. But when the oil embargo of 1973 highlighted the possibility of considerable costs if the pipeline was not built, public opinion quickly changed and the pipeline was permitted.

RELY FIRST ON MARKETS

The reason given for the necessity of regulation always is the contention that our market system produces too many undesired "products." An example cited of such a "product" was pollution of the air by automobiles. Just because this may happen in some cases does not necessarily mean that detailed regulation is appropriate in all cases. Our market system, operating within the context of a general body of laws, is self-regulatory in most instances. Moreover, markets provide for an allocation of resources based on the considered judgment of individuals. Full advantage should be taken of these features of our market system before regulations are adopted.

Market Provision of Information—In many instances, private organizations have evolved which provide information regarding product quality and safety to consumers. Examples of such organizations are Underwriters Laboratory, United States Testing Laboratory, Consumers Union, and Better Business Bureaus. Based on information provided by such private organizations, consumers can make informed market decisions regarding which product to buy. Competition in the markets for sales, in turn, imposes sanctions on firms which produce a product found to be of poor quality or one that is not safe.

A regulatory strategy should take into consideration this provision of market information by private organizations. In cases in which such information is not provided, however, it would be appropriate for government to provide it, but then individuals should be allowed to make their own market decisions. An example of such information provided by government is that regarding the tar and nicotine content of various brands of cigarettes.

Market Incentives from Laws—Our market system operates within the context of a general body of law defining individual rights. Within this body there are laws establishing liability for violations of the rights of others. The possibility of having to pay damages for such violations provides, in many instances, incentives for business firms to conduct their activities in a "socially desirable" manner.

An example of such an incentive provided by law is that one who is injured by a product found to be faulty can receive compensation from the producer. Many firms, therefore, carefully test a product before selling it and set quality standards for its production. For instance, a St. Louis manufacturer of power mowers for Sears requires that its grass-catchers trap steel ball bearings and six-penny nails traveling at a speed of 192 miles per hour. The reason cited for this requirement by the firm's president is "the ever costly product liability laws," not any existing regulation.

Another example is that a worker found to have been injured on the job as a result of employer negligence can receive compensation. As a result, many firms have established job safety programs. Also, those who insure firms against worker liability claims have hired safety engineers who give safety advice to employers and conduct safety training sessions for employees. The possibility of higher insurance rates or the loss of coverage because of too many claims provides an incentive for firms to provide a safe work environment.

Present regulatory strategy appears to ignore the influence of liability laws on market behavior of firms. Oftentimes, detailed regulations, much of which is unnecessary given the laws, have been imposed. As a result, unnecessary costs have been imposed on individuals. For instance, OSHA and CPSC have required manufacturers of ladders to affix an increasing number of safety and warning labels on their products, including a three-inch strip giving the user twenty-two different instructions on how to use a ladder safely. There is considerable doubt that such warnings and instructions will reduce injuries, because after centuries of experience with ladders 80 percent of injuries still are related to their improper use.

In another example, OSHA has imposed many detailed regulations on industry regarding worker health and safety. They have ignored the fact that many firms have excellent programs in this regard. For instance, Du Pont Company has had an excellent worker safety record, but last April it was slapped with numerous fines, all of which were related to violations of detailed safety standards and none to any actual injuries.

IMPOSE REGULATIONS ONLY WHEN SELF-REGULATION FAILS

Only in cases in which the self-regulatory feature of markets fails to protect the rights of individuals can an argument be made for imposing a regulation. An example of such a case is the violation of the rights of people living in Duluth before Reserve Mining began to discharge into Lake Superior waste containing asbestos fibers which are believed to cause cancer.

But in such cases, regulations must meet the test of "cost-benefit" analysis. This analysis, however, is not a perfect solution because it is highly subjective. Individuals make their judgments on the basis of personal values and perceptions of costs and benefits. Moreover, it is frequently impossible to arrive at a collective judgment in any other manner than that expressed in markets. Be that as it may, steps can be taken to assure a better use of cost-benefit analysis in a regulatory strategy. The result would be a shifting of emphasis away from the usual question at present of "either/or" to the more relevant ones of "more or less" and "how."

A regulatory strategy in cases in which self-regulation fails must provide individuals with relevant information regarding costs and benefits so they can make informed judgments. Up to now, however, the development of estimates of the costs and benefits associated with the various regulations have often been made in a rather haphazard manner. Moreover, the attention of individuals has generally been directed more at the purported benefits than at the associated costs.

Estimating Costs—The importance of giving proper consideration to costs in a regulatory strategy has been emphasized by Murray L. Weidenbaum, a noted authority on government regulation of business. He points out that, ". . . if we ignore the costs, we are bound to operate in the zone of overregulation." Such overregulation produces costs to individuals greatly in excess of any perceived benefits.

In developing the costs associated with a regulation careful consideration must be given to the interrelated nature of our market economy. Only by doing so, as was argued earlier, can anything close to reliable estimates of the present and future costs of a regulation be developed. This would be a marked departure from current practices, in which costs, if presented at all, are presented to individuals for only a narrow segment of our economy. Even in those instances, little attention is given to future costs.

The regulatory strategy, if undue costs to individuals are to be avoided, should provide estimates of the overall costs associated with a whole body of regulations instead of just providing estimates for individual regulations. The reason for doing so is that, although the costs to individuals may be relatively small when taken separately, they may be relatively large when taken as a whole.

Weidenbaum presents a striking example of such a situation. He reports that one large oil company is required to file approximately 1,000 reports annually to thirty-five different federal agencies. It has 100 full-time employees whose work is centered around meeting federal regulations, at any annual cost of $3 million. Expanding this situation to all oil companies probably would indicate a large amount of resources, that would have been used otherwise in producing goods and services for markets, were being devoted to meeting the requirements. While the resulting cost to individuals of meeting all regulations is quite large, the cost of any one regulation would most likely appear to be relatively small.

Estimating Benefits—The strategy should provide information regarding the benefits to individuals associated with a regulation. Such estimates should be derived from "hard" scientific evidence and not from casual evidence or personal introspection, as has frequently been the case in the past. In other words, the procedures of scientific methodology must be adhered to rigorously in developing estimates of benefits.

A brief review of the steps involved in the scientific method will help to place in proper perspective the use of scientific inquiry in estimating the benefits of a regulation. For example, take the test hypothesis, "Certain ingredients in aerosol spray adhesives do not cause birth defects." To test this hypothesis, experiments would be set up to provide evidence rejecting it. (In science, a hypothesis can only be found false, it never can be proven true.) If such evidence is not found, the test hypothesis is provisionally accepted. On the other hand, if such evidence is found, the test hypothesis is rejected and the alternative hypothesis, "Certain ingredients in aerosol spray adhesives cause birth defects," is provisionally accepted.

Further testing is required, however, before a decision can be given with any degree of certainty. But even then, it is the nature of scientific inquiry that a hypothesis may be accepted when it is actually false, or it may be rejected when it is actually true. It is important, therefore, to remember that this procedure is not infallible for developing estimates of benefits.

The above analysis carries three important implications for developing estimates of benefits to be presented to the public. The first implication is that, given the uncertainty inherent in science, any conclusions regarding the benefits of a regulation should be subject to only a reasonable doubt. The extent of doubt frequently is not conveyed to the public, however. Dr. James P. Lodge in *Business Week* (June 21, 1976) gives the following tongue-in-cheek example: "All too often a scientist's statement, 'Under highly unrealistic laboratory conditions, I have a small amount of evidence to suggest that lifetime exposure to elephant hide could, with 5 percent probability, cause cancer' becomes the newspaper headline, 'Scientist says elephants cause cancer.' " Given this misleading information an easily frightened public calls for government regulation.

The second one is that information based on preliminary results of an investigation, as has happened in the past, may prove to be unnecessarily costly to individuals if it leads to a regulation. Subsequent testing may not corroborate the preliminary findings and, therefore, costs would have been incurred without any resulting benefit. Take the case of the above mentioned test hypothesis. On August 20, 1973, the Consumer Products Safety Commission accepted the alternative hypothesis on the preliminary findings of one academic researcher and banned certain brands of aerosol adhesive spray. Subsequently the ban was lifted on March 1, 1974, when more careful research failed to corroborate the initial findings.

While this may appear to be a trivial example, it does illustrate the potential for misinformation. Such misinformation may prove costly, however, even in a trivial case. For instance, in the case of the ban on aerosol spray adhesives, a number of pregnant women who had used the adhesives underwent abortions for fear of producing babies with birth defects.

A third implication is that, even if an initial finding is corroborated (that is, there is only reasonable doubt), the extent of risk to individuals should be presented. For example, in the summer of 1973, the National Cancer Institute reported that TCE, a solvent used in the manufacture of decaffeinated coffee, may be the cause of cancer. Certainly, one would not want to recommend a regulation of this information, if there was only a very low probability (great doubt) that it was correct. But in this case, even if the probability was high (little doubt) that the information is correct, the risk to an individual of getting cancer from drinking decaffeinated coffee is very small. The reason for this is that the amount of TCE given to test animals was equivalent to a human being drinking fifty million cups of decaffeinated coffee every day for his entire lifetime, certainly not a very large risk.

ADMINISTRATION OF REGULATIONS

Suppose that, on the basis of sufficient information and an apparent failure of market self-regulation, the collective judgment of individuals is that the benefits derived from a regulation outweighs its associated costs and Congress legislates accordingly. The question then arises regarding the proper administration of the regulation.

Setting Standards—Given the uncertainty discussed earlier regarding the "truth" derived from scientific evidence, there are two procedures for developing regulatory standards from such evidence. They can be illustrated by referring to two alternative procedures in law for determining guilt—one is "presumed innocent unless proven guilty beyond a reasonable doubt," or is "presumed guilty unless proven innocent beyond a reasonable doubt." The choice between these two procedures depends on society's evaluation of the consequences of a wrong decision—punishing an innocent person or not punishing a guilty one. For example, in our country, law is based on a presumption of innocence because society has held it worse to punish an innocent person than not to punish a guilty one.

The choice between these two procedures in setting regulatory standards is illustrated by the current controversies regarding the use of psychological and other tests in hiring employees and the use of red dye no. 2 in food production. In the first controversy, the Justice and Labor Departments support a new equal employment guideline that if a battery of tests does not eliminate minorities disproportionately, it would be presumed legal (presumption of innocence). The EEOC, on the other hand, wants to stick to its present requirements that each step in the employment process be justified as nondiscriminatory (presumption of guilt) regardless of final hiring patterns. In the second controversy, the food industry has challenged the FDA's ruling which banned red dye no. 2 in food production unless it can be proven not to cause cancer (presumption of guilt).

Since bans on employment tests and red dye no. 2 would impose costs on individuals, the procedure chosen for setting standards should be related to the seriousness of the consequences of a wrong decision. While the consequences of the presumption of innocence may be small relative to the costs in the case of employment tests, they may be relatively large in the case of red dye no. 2.

The setting of standards should also take into consideration implications for the use of resources. Take the case of setting standards for auto bumpers. In this case, the greater the required ability of auto bumpers to withstand an impact, the greater is the amount of steel required to meet the standard. In addition, the weight of an automobile increases as more steel is used and, consequently, more gasoline is required per mile traveled. Thus, while the benefit to individuals may increase with an increase in the standard, there is also an increase in the costs in the form of less production of other market goods and services using steel as a raw material and/or using petroleum for energy.

The above analysis carries two implications for setting regulatory standards such that the cost to individuals is minimized. The first one is that a standard should seek to use the smallest amount of resources necessary to produce a given level of benefits. For example, OSHA has proposed an industry-wide standard of a 90 decibel maximum noise level. This standard is to be met wherever feasible through the "installation of engineering and administrative controls," with personal protective devices to be used only as a "last resort." According to a CWPS study, meeting this standard by engineering and administrative controls would be about seven times more costly, per additional worker protected, than by the use of personal protective devices. Thus, cost considerations would mitigate against OSHA's recommendation.

The second one is that the setting of a standard should be carried to the point where the *increase* in benefits equals the *increase* in cost. This is illustrated by organized labor's proposal of a maximum noise standard of 85 decibels instead of 90. The Labor Department has estimated that the 5 decibel reduction in the maximum noise level permitted would entail an added cost of $8.5 billion. This proposal should not be accepted if the added benefits are less than the added costs.

Coordinating Regulations—In setting standards for a regulation, consideration should be given to avoiding conflicts with the standards of other regulations, so as to avoid undue costs to individuals. For example, the desulfurization of coal to reduce air pollution requires the use of lime. But a by-product of lime is large quantities of solid waste in the form of calcium sulfate. Disposal of this waste creates water pollution problems. As a result, a regulation requiring desulfurization of coal entails two costs, not one. They follow from the use of resources to desulfer coal and from the additional use of resources required to meet the standards set regarding water pollution.

Limiting Requirements—The requirements of a regulation should be limited to only those necessary to achieve its objectives. In the past, many regulators have imposed on an operation minute requirements which, oftentimes, are trivial in the sense that they are unnecessary to achieve the objectives. But these requirements must be met nevertheless and, as a result, there is an unnecessary cost to individuals.

For example, John J. Ahern, director for security for General Motors, reported recently that his company had invested $79 million and the equivalent of 1,100 man-years to satisfy OSHA requirements in 1974 alone. Commenting in *Business Week* (June 14, 1976) on these outlays, Ahern said, "We had a good safety program going long before anybody ever heard of OSHA, and we haven't seen any effect from all the money that has been spent, so far as any reduction to our accident rate is concerned." It can thus be seen that in this case the diversion of capital and labor resources away from the production of other goods and services imposed a considerable cost on individuals but produced few benefits, if any.

Conclusion

Current regulations have imposed a considerable cost on individuals in the form of foregone consumption opportunities, both in the present and in the future. These costs have resulted from the market influence of the regulations which has produced slower growth of private sector productivity and employment than would have prevailed in markets. Consequently, growth of private sector output has been slower than it would have otherwise been.

A regulatory strategy should first take into consideration the self-regulatory feature of our market system before imposing a regulation. In cases in which market self-regulation fails to protect the rights of individuals, information should be presented regarding the costs and benefits of a regulation so that individuals can make a considered judgment. The administration of a regulation should always seek to minimize its cost to individuals for a given level of benefits.

Daniel M. Holland

7

The Role of Tax Policy

Given this book's theme—Capital for Productivity and Jobs—it would seem that tax policy, particularly in the form of modifying the relative importance of different taxes in the total revenue structure, would be one of the most fruitful areas for innovation and change.

Of course, there is little illumination in the "insight" that since taxes exercise a deterrent effect on both investment and saving, if we do away with taxes or lower them substantially, we will be helping growth. Tax revenues support government expenditures, so a level of taxation something very close to what we have is, in effect, voted by the community when it decides its expenditure budget. But that budget can be financed in many different ways. And some taxes deter savings, and/or investment more than others. Why should we not design the tax mix with these crucial economic activities in mind?

For example, families in the upper income classes appear to save more on average and at the margin than families in the lower income classes. Under the progressive income tax, high savers are taxed at higher rates than lower savers. Under a proportional tax on income (or a tax on sales) that raised the same revenue as the present progressive tax, other things being equal, savings would be greater.

In the last several years changes in taxes have been the most prominent policy prescription in discussion of "the capital shortage."

Daniel M. Holland, *Professor of Finance at the Sloan School of Management, M.I.T., has been consultant to more than a dozen organizations in public and business finance, including the U.S. Treasury, AT&T, AID, and the World Bank. He has written several books and many articles on public finance, and is editor of the* National Tax Journal.

A New York Stock Exchange study (1974) of capital needs and savings potential, for example, recommended:

1. replacement cost depreciation,
2. a higher investment credit,
3. abolition of "double-taxation" of distributed earnings,
4. lower taxes on capital gains, and
5. a cut in corporate income tax rate.

Much the same set of proposals appeared also in an analysis of economic prospects by General Electric (1975) and in a long-term forecast by Michael Evans, Chase Econometric Associates (1975).

But students of public finance have generally not been sanguine about changes in tax structure designed to encourage savings or investment. While the scholarly fraternity is not unanimous about the point, their publications exhibit a clear central tendency. The record is replete with reservations and caveats on the use of taxation as a tool for this purpose.

In part the reservations come from a conflict between objectives. Thus a progressive income tax has distributional effects considered preferable to a proportional tax on income or purchases. The progressive tax, it is held, accords more closely with "ability to pay."

The concern with equity should not be taken lightly. While impossible to define with objective precision, there is a widely-shared belief in income as the relevant measure of "ability to pay" and a progressive schedule, with rates of tax rising with income, as the "equitable" pattern of sacrifice for the community.

The present tax structure in our country—all taxes levied by all levels of government—however, has a pattern of distribution that is most meaningfully described as proportional over almost all of its range. A definitive distribution of the tax burden by income classes lies beyond our knowledge of tax incidence and the available data. Joseph Pechman and Benjamin Okner (1974), whose study is the most comprehensive that exists, face up to the unsolved problems of incidence by providing estimates based on alternative assumptions which encompass the range of possible results for each major tax. Then they combine the burden of each of the taxes to arrive at a measure of the effective rate of the entire structure of taxes (total taxes/total income) for the United States population arrayed by deciles in ascending order of income.

For a number of taxes, alternative incidence assumptions are an accurate reflection of the state of our knowledge. Therefore, there are many possible different distributions of the tax burden among income groups. Pechman and Okner developed eight which they felt covered the range of reasonable possibilities. In Table 1 we reproduce two of them. Variant 1c combines the most progressive assumptions; variant 3b, the least progressive. Note, for example, in variant 1c how the corporation income tax, which is assumed to fall half on stockholders and half on owners of capital generally has a progressive distribution, while in variant 3b, in which half the corporate tax is assumed to be shifted forward via higher prices of what consumers buy, the effective rate of tax declines as income rises.

The important conclusion from Table 1 is that under even the most progressive set of assumptions the total tax burden is only mildly progressive. And the vast mass of the population that falls between the lowest 20 percent of incomes (first and second deciles) and the top 10 percent (tenth decile) are subject essentially to a flat rate. (The difference between 21.7 percent on the third decile and 23.3 percent on the ninth can hardly be significant.) And under the least progressive group of assumptions, the tax structure is essentially proportional over the whole range. The individual income tax is the only solidly progressive element. Substitute a proportional income tax or a sales tax for the personal income tax, and the tax structure in its entirety would be sharply regressive. Compare the income level distributions for the individual income tax and sales and excise taxes in Table 1.

There is another reason why students of public finance are skeptical of changes in tax structure to encourage savings and investment. They doubt the efficacy of tax measures for this purpose. Substituting a flat rate tax for the present income tax would be a major feat of fiscal engineering. In fact, it may be beyond the capacity of our governmental institutions to accomplish. But would it be worth doing?

How different are the savings propensities of rich and poor? How great an increase in intended savings would major tax adjustments accomplish? To what degree would an increase in desired saving result in higher capital formation? Clearly there is room for substantial difference of opinion.

What Can We Expect from Tax Changes?

SAVINGS

In general, there has been a central tendency in the judgments of students of public finance which holds that tax changes—even severe and traumatic changes—would have only modest effects on savings and/or investment.

Useful in the discussion of these opinions are the data of Table 2. Lines 2 through 4 give the magnitudes of the major items of the present federal tax structure (on a National Income and Product Accounts basis) and line 1, their total. Lines 6, 7, and 9 give the components of Total Gross Saving (line 10), with Personal Saving and Gross Business Saving summing to Gross Private Saving (line 8).

A broad basis for the belief that tax modifications would have little effect on savings has been provided by Paul David and John Scadding (1974, pp. 236 and 246). After carefully reviewing the evidence on Gross Private Saving (GPS), they conclude from the constancy of the ratio GPS/GNP over time that: "The total of private saving has been almost totally insensitive to the share of output absorbed by the public sector, given the level of output." (Additionally, the ratio of GPS to GNP has been insensitive to the relative importance of different taxes in the total tax take.) David and Scadding also concluded that the nature of the response of individuals to taxes and changes in the government's budget surplus (or deficit) "leaves fiscal policy no scope to affect the accumulation of capital." On the basis of the historical record they have developed an explanation of economic conduct consistent with the conclusion that neither the *level* of taxation nor its *composition* affects private saving or investment.

Theirs is the strongest statement of the ineffectiveness of tax structure changes for raising the level of saving and/or investment. But many scholars, with reference to particular modifications of the tax structure, have reached substantially the same conclusion.

Here are some examples:

Joseph Pechman (1971, p. 65) in a general statement of the case concluded as follows:

> Consumption taxes can be avoided simply by reducing one's consumption. This means that an expenditure tax encourages saving more than does an equal-yield income tax that is distributed in the same proportions by income classes. In practice, where the income tax is paid by the large mass of the people, much of the tax yield comes from income classes where there is little room in family budgets for increasing saving in response to tax incentives. As a consequence, the differential effect on total consumption and saving between an income tax and an equal-yield expenditure tax is likely to be small in this country.

Dealing with the same kind of comparison, Richard B. Goode (1976, pp. 67-68) provided a numerical estimate of the effect that might be expected.

> Subject to the limitations of the data and methods, my estimates for 1960-61 indicate that the difference between the impact on saving of the

TABLE 1. EFFECTIVE RATES OF FEDERAL, STATE, AND LOCAL TAXES, BY TYPE OF TAX, VARIANTS 1C AND 3B, BY POPULATION DECILE, 1966 *(Percents)*

Population Decile	*Individual Income Tax*	*Corporation Income Tax*	*Property Tax*	*Sales and Excise Taxes*	*Payroll Taxes*	*Personal Property and Motor Vehicle Taxes*	*Total Taxes*
			Variant 1c				
First	1.1	1.7	2.1	8.9	2.6	0.4	16.8
Second	2.3	2.1	2.6	7.8	3.8	0.4	18.9
Third	4.0	2.2	2.6	7.1	5.4	0.4	21.7
Fourth	5.4	1.9	2.1	6.7	6.1	0.4	22.6
Fifth	6.3	1.7	1.8	6.4	6.3	0.3	22.8
Sixth	7.0	1.5	1.6	6.1	6.2	0.3	22.7
Seventh	7.5	1.6	1.7	5.7	5.8	0.3	22.7
Eighth	8.3	1.8	1.8	5.5	5.4	0.3	23.1
Ninth	8.8	2.2	2.2	5.0	4.8	0.3	23.3
Tenth	11.4	8.1	5.1	3.2	2.2	0.2	30.1
All deciles	8.5	3.9	3.0	5.1	4.4	0.3	25.2

Population Decile	*Individual Income Tax*	*Corporation Income Tax*	*Property Tax*	*Sales and Excise Taxes*	*Payroll Taxes*	*Personal Property and Motor Vehicle Taxes*	*Total Taxes*
			Variant 3b				
First	1.2	6.1	6.4	8.9	4.5	0.4	27.5
Second	2.0	5.4	5.1	7.5	4.5	0.4	24.8
Third	3.9	5.0	4.6	6.8	5.4	0.4	26.0
Fourth	5.1	4.4	3.8	6.5	5.7	0.3	25.9
Fifth	6.0	4.1	3.3	6.2	5.8	0.3	25.8
Sixth	6.7	3.9	3.2	5.9	5.6	0.3	25.6
Seventh	7.3	3.7	3.2	5.6	5.4	0.3	25.5
Eighth	8.0	3.7	3.2	5.3	5.0	0.3	25.5
Ninth	8.4	3.9	3.2	4.9	4.5	0.3	25.1
Tenth	11.9	5.2	2.9	3.3	2.5	0.2	25.9
All deciles	8.4	4.4	3.4	5.0	4.4	0.3	25.9

Source: Joseph A. Pechman and Benjamin A. Okner, *Who Bears the Tax Burden?* The Brookings Institution, Washington, D.C., 1974, p. 61.

Note: For this table the U.S. population is ranked from low to high incomes and partitioned by tenths. Those in the first decile are the lowest 10 percent of income recipients; those in the tenth decile are the top 10 percent of income recipients. The numbers in the body of the table are effective rates of tax computed by calculating the amount of tax paid by the average family in each decile as a percent of the average income in that decile.

TABLE 2. FEDERAL GOVERNMENT REVENUE AND NATIONAL SAVINGS DATA, 1975

Item	*Amount (in Billions)*
1. Total receipts of federal government (National Income and Product Account)	$286.5
2. Personal tax and nontax receipts	125.7
3. Corporate tax accruals	42.6
4. Indirect business tax and nontax accruals	23.9
5. Contributions for social insurance	94.3
6. Personal saving	84.0
7. Gross business saving	171.6
8. Gross private saving (6 + 7)	255.6
9. Government surplus (+) or deficit (–)	–64.4
10. Total gross saving (6 + 7 + 9)	191.2

Source: Survey of Current Business, July 1976.

progressive individual income tax and that of a flat-rate consumption tax is an unimpressive 6 percent of the yield (30 percent for the income tax compared with 24 percent for the consumption tax). On the assumption that this relationship was still applicable in 1970, replacement of the entire individual income tax by a flat-rate consumption tax would have increased private saving by about $5 billion. This sum is equal to about 9 percent of actual personal saving in 1970 and 10 percent of total net investment.

And later in his analysis (pp. 72-73) Goode gave this assessment of the possible impact of a change in savings of this magnitude.

Many discussions have, I think, greatly exaggerated the possible differences in the influence of alternative taxes on work incentives, private saving, and investment. Careful theoretical analyses and factual evidence on the subject are inconclusive. Moreover, the contribution that additional saving and investment can make to the growth of an economy such as that of the United States may be less than is often supposed. According to Denison's estimates, net investment was responsible for only about one-fifth of the growth of potential national income over the period 1948-69—0.80 percentage point a year out of 4.02 percentage points. If these estimates are combined with mine, it appears that even had the progressive income tax been replaced by a flat-rate on consumption, net saving in that period would have increased by an amount sufficient to have raised the annual growth rate by considerably less than 0.1 percentage points.[1]

[1] Goode noted a number of caveats. For one thing, some scholars see capital formation as having a more powerful effect on growth. For another, a consumption

At an earlier date Richard A. Musgrave (1963, pp. 67-69) estimated for 1959 that if the personal income tax were replaced by a flat rate tax on consumption designed to raise the same amount of revenue, savings would have increased by $5.5 billion—about 7.4 percent of Gross Private Saving, or 24 percent of Personal Saving. He observed that while this constituted a substantial change in saving, generating it "would turn the U. S. tax structure as a whole into a highly regressive system." But he noted further (p. 70) that equity should not be an issue because even major changes of the kind discussed would have a slight effect on growth. Replacing the income tax by a proportional tax on consumption would not generate a sufficient increase in saving to finance a 0.5 percentage point increase in growth.[2]

George F. Break (1974, p. 195) distinguished between the short-run and long-run initial impact on savings.[3] With the data for 1960, he estimated that the substitution of an equal yield sales tax for the federal income tax would increase personal saving (initial impact concept) by 10.5 percent in the long-run (by 3.8 percent in the short-run).

Very recent work by Michael J. Boskin (1976) and Martin Feldstein suggests the possibility of a considerably more powerful savings response (Boskin) and greater efficiency gains (see below) to be had from substituting a tax on consumption for the personal income tax. But this research is still in process and not completely "proved out." (Moreover, of course, a wholesale change of this kind is not in the political cards.) Ours remains a fair summary of the prevailing scholarly opinion.

---

tax and an income tax are likely to have different effects on the various forms of saving. In particular, the consumption tax would tend to enhance the savings of the highest groups vis-à-vis those of lower income, and because the top income recipients hold much more of their wealth in corporate stock and ownership of nonincorporated business (while low income taxpayers saving takes the form of additions to bank accounts or equity in a residence). It is plausible that investments in business assets or claims contribute more to innovation and growth than investments in one's own home; for example, the consumption tax would tend to contribute additionally to economic growth over and above its effect on the level of savings *per se*.

[2] The $5.5 billion increase in saving would, he estimated, finance a 0.25 percentage point increase in growth.

[3] Break (p. 193) pointed out that the change in saving, dependent on the response of investment, cannot in general be considered equal to the change in consumption. However, under the assumption that personal income remains unchanged, the change in consumption can be considered to be matched by an equal change (opposite in sign) in saving, which he calls the initial impact.

INVESTMENT

As to the other side of the coin—investment—the prevailing state of opinion reflects the diversity of explanations of the investment process. Most "models" of investment identify the following as determinants of investment:

1. Induced demand via changes in output,
2. The availability of funds and the cost of capital, and
3. The rate of return investments can be expected to earn.

But they differ with respect to the importance of each of these factors in the explanatory schemes. Thus predictions of tax effects span a wide range of possibilities.

Robert E. Hall and Dale W. Jorgenson (1967, p. 413) analyzed the effects on investment of a number of structural changes introduced in the corporate income tax since 1954—accelerated depreciation, shorter guideline depreciable lives, and the investment credit. From their empirical study they concluded that the effects on investment of:

1. "accelerated depreciation are very substantial,"
2. "the depreciation guidelines of 1962 are significant," and
3. "the investment tax credits of 1962 are dramatic and leave little room for doubt about the efficacy of tax policy in influencing investment behavior."

Employing the same data but with a different specification of the investment function, Robert Eisner (1969, p. 387) concluded quite the contrary, *viz;* that "no statistically significant role for the tax incentive is found in any of the estimates."

While Charles W. Bischoff (1971, pp. 124-25) found that: "The investment tax credit adapted in 1962 has probably directly stimulated more investment spending than the policy has cost the government in taxes." But, ". . . the data give no support to the hypothesis that accelerated depreciation has any effect at all in investment."

From a sample of seven studies cited by Lester Thurow (1971, p. 33) to the question: "By how much would a 1 percent cut in the effective corporate tax rate stimulate investment in plant and equipment," two would have answered zero; one, $800 million; and the other four would have put it at $300 million, $400 million, or $500 million (these are 1958 dollars).

Allen S. Blinder and Robert M. Solow (1974, pp. 92-93) summarize where things now stand this way:

> One might have hoped that the succession of investment incentives in recent years would have produced what economists are always looking for —a "controlled experiment." After all, we have seen accelerated depreciation (1954), relaxed depreciation guidelines (1962), the investment tax credit (1962), repeal of the Long amendment, which had required firms to deduct the amount of the credit from the depreciation base (1964), reduction of the tax rate on corporate profits (1964), suspension of the investment tax credit (October 1966), and its later resumption (originally scheduled for December 1967, but actually occurring in March 1967). Perhaps it is an indication of the vanity of such hopes that no consensus has yet emerged on the quantitative effectiveness of such fiscal devices in controlling plant and equipment purchases.

The findings of a recent study by Andrew F. Brimmer and Allen Sinai (1976) suggest that tax measures would have a modest effect on investment. They have a model of investment spending which takes account of financial variables, availability of funds and cost of capital —as well as the expected profitability of investment. And because it is imbedded in a complete model of the economy, feedback effects of tax policies can be estimated.[4]

For the nonfinancial corporate sector Brimmer and Sinai explore the effects of three changes in corporate tax structure.

1. An increase in the investment tax credit from 10 to 12 percent.
2. A two-stage reduction of the corporate tax rate from 48 to 42 percent.
3. Indexing book depreciation to the current rate of inflation for plant and equipment.

Their findings are summarized in Table 3. Over a five-year period, 1976-1980, a 20 percent increase in the Investment Credit would have meant a revenue loss of $10.1 billion, would have been responsible for an increase in capital expenditures of $6.9 billion, and would have generated sixty-eight cents of investment for each dollar of revenue loss. The cut in corporate rates from 48 to 42 percent (in two stages) would have caused an $11 billion increase in capital expenditures over a five-year period at the expense of a revenue loss of $32.5 billion. Thus it would have increased investment spending by thirty-four cents for every dollar of revenue loss. By this latter ratio, replacement cost depreciation would be a more powerful stimulant, increasing investment outlays by $1.68 for every dollar of revenue loss. But its aggre-

[4] For example, increased investment in business equipment and plant could cause interest rates to rise which would discourage investment in residential construction.

TABLE 3. ESTIMATED REVENUE LOSS, INCREASE IN CAPITAL EXPENDITURES, AND BENEFIT-COST RATIO FOR THREE CHANGES IN TAX POLICY, 1976-1980 *(Dollar Amounts in Billions)*

Item	*Increase in Investment Credit*	*Cut in Corporate Tax Rate*	*Replacement Cost Depreciation*
Revenue loss	$10.1	$32.5	$ 6.6
Increase in capital expenditure	6.9	11.0	11.1
Benefit-cost ratio	0.68	0.34	1.68
Average annual increase in capital expenditure	1.4	2.2	2.2

Source: Andrew F. Brimmer and Allen Sinai, "The Effects of Tax Policy on Capital Formation, Corporate Liquidity and the Availability of Investable Funds: A Simulation Study," *Journal of Finance,* May 1976, pp. 287-308.

gate effect on investment spending would have been of the same order of magnitude as the other two tax changes, an increase of $11.1 billion over the five-year period.

While Brimmer and Sinai present as one of their findings the "clear conclusion . . . that additional business tax reform would bring a significant improvement in capital formation" (p. 307), they also note that "the tax incentives provided only a modest stimulus to the overall rate of capital spending" (p. 299). And they also express a preference for macro-policy:

> However, the adoption of a tax incentive is not necessarily the best way to enhance the growth of physical capacity. A more effective strategy could be the pursuit of macro-economic policies designed to raise aggregate demand and reduce the excessively high level of unemployment. A monetary policy more liberal than the one the Federal Reserve seems to be following would be particularly appropriate. (p. 307)

About the Brimmer-Sinai paper Benjamin M. Friedman (1976, p. 310) commented:

> . . . the quantitative effects of their three tax policies on plant and equipment investment are tiny. The issue is not so much that these effects are so small as to strain economists' credulity. More importantly, they are small enough to strain policy makers' willingness to play the game. In today's political climate, can anyone seriously expect Congress to lower the corporate tax rate from the present 48 percent to 42 percent if the pay-off

for doing so is to raise investment by only $2 billion per year (on a base of $110 billion in 1958 dollars)?

Brimmer's and Sinai's judgment that macroeconomic policy is a more efficient tool than changes in tax structure for encouraging investment is complemented by Musgrave's (1961, p. 57) conclusion that:

> Under conditions when investment responds to an increase in the supply of loanable funds, the required increase in saving is provided for best by an increase in the level of tax rates (preferably first bracket rate of income tax) and a budget surplus, rather than by changes in the composition of the tax structure so as to move the burden from saving to consumption. This preference arises because the surplus approach is more neutral with regard to tax equity, and because it is more flexible and adaptable to changing economic conditions.

A Promising Possibility

The earlier examples of possible major changes in tax structure—substitution of a sales tax for an income tax or a proportional rate to replace the present progressive rate schedule—can hardly be considered currently relevant possibilities.

More pertinent and promising, however, is the proposal to abolish the corporate income tax and treat corporate earnings for tax purposes as we do income from partnerships and proprietorships. In the pure form of the "partnership" method, each stockholder would include his *pro rata* share of corporate earnings in taxable personal income, and be taxed currently on it. To the extent that corporations retain earnings, the basis of valuation of shares for capital gains purposes would be increased by the excess of imputations over dividend receipts. (If dividend payments exceeded earnings, the basis would be stepped down by the difference.)

A major change, not precisely of this nature but well along the road to it, was proposed in the summer of 1975 by Secretary of the Treasury William Simon (1975, pp. 3843-3883). In supporting his proposal—which would, in effect, relieve distributed earnings of the corporate tax—the Secretary offered a number of arguments, but placed particular emphasis on saving and its role in economic growth.

> Our tax system, like any tax system which relies on an income tax, is biased against saving. . . . In general, our tax system inhibits savings because it promises to take away a substantial part of the income from any amounts saved, thus reducing the incentive for saving . . . (p. 3849).
>
> Therefore . . . after many months of deliberation we have concluded that the most important step we can take to achieve greater savings through

> the tax system is to move toward the elimination of the double tax which presently is imposed on income from assets used in the corporate form of business (p. 3846).

While integration of the corporate and personal income tax would be a highly desirable tax reform for a number of reasons, it is not at all clear that it would lead to a substantial expansion of saving. On this question Martin Feldstein (1973, p. 170) concluded that, in general, integration would leave total savings substantially the same, with increased personal saving offsetting decreased corporate saving, because the two forms of saving are close substitutes.

> The parameters of the consumption function imply that households see through the corporate veil and adjust their personal savings to changes in corporate savings. The current system of corporate income taxation, which induces corporations to retain a high fraction of earnings, therefore appears to have little if any effect on the aggregate volume of capital formation.
>
> This suggests that integration of the corporation tax and the personal income tax would not reduce to total rate of capital accumulation.

More recently, Feldstein (1975) has analyzed the particular proposal put forward by Secretary Simon in some detail. Taking account of the various ways in which saving would be affected—the decrease in corporate saving, the increase in personal saving by stockholders due to higher dividends, the effect of additional taxes to offset the lost corporate tax revenue, and the response to an increase in the net rate of return to saving (which in theory, could be an increase or decrease in aggregate saving)—he reached the conclusion that ". . . there is no way to know at this time whether integration is more likely to increase or decrease aggregate capital accumulation."

But the proponents of integration have not generally based their case solely on salutary effects on capital accumulation. There are a number of other cogent reasons in support of this change in tax structure. And both Simon (1975) and Feldstein (1975), whose paper I have drawn on, have presented them forcefully.

Full Integration Preferable

In principle, full integration, *i.e.*, thorough-going application of the "Partnership" method (or its equivalent) to include stockholders' *pro rata* share of corporate earnings whether distributed or retained, should be the objective. The Simon proposal, however, which is limited to distributed earnings would still leave a major distortion in the tax structure—in effect an undistributed profits tax. An undistributed profits tax has particularly adverse effects on small companies which rely on retained earnings to finance growth. And a major inequity would exist; the tax on retained earnings would constitute an extra burden that varies in relative severity inversely with the stockholders' income.

Viewing the problem as "double taxation" obscures the fundamental inequities. With corporate earnings taxed at the corporate level when made and the personal level when distributed, what results is differential taxation of stockholders. Distributed earnings are always "overtaxed," but to a diminishing extent, the higher the stockholders' income, while retained earnings are either over or under taxed, and again, the severity of the differential declines with income.

To explain: Take two stockholders, A in the twenty percent bracket and B in the sixty percent bracket; assume for arithmetic convenience, that the corporate tax rate is 50 percent and let A and B each own 100 shares in a corporation that earns $2.00 per share before tax, and pays out all its net income. Both A and B "bear" a corporate tax of $100, and, in addition A pays $20 on the dividends he receives while B pays $60. A's total tax is $120; B's is $160. Had there been no corporate tax, the personal income tax on $200 of earnings would have been $40 for A and $120 for B. So the "extra" tax on distributed earnings is $80 ($120 – $40) for A, or 40 percent of corporate earnings, while the "extra" burden is $40 ($160 – $120) for B, which is 20 percent of his corporate earnings.

With respect to retained earnings, currently $200 earned on behalf of a stockholder but not distributed to him would be subject to $100 corporate tax when made and no tax at the personal level. (We neglect possible future capital gains taxes for simplicity.) Had the $200 been taxed as personal income, A would have paid $40 and B, $160. A, therefore, is overtaxed on retained earnings and B is undertaxed.

Only full inclusion of distributed earnings and full imputation of retained earnings in personal income—the "Partnership" method—would remove over and/or undertaxation for all stockholders. And only the "Partnership" method (or equivalent) would negate income tax distortion of the corporate dividends versus retention decision.[5]

Efficiency Gains from Integration

Currently, as we have noted, the tax structure encourages retention. The tax system not only raises revenue, but it distorts economic decisions, causing retained earnings to be "too high" and external

[5] For an extended discussion see Holland (1958) or McLure (1975).

finance "too low" relative to the level that would prevail under a neutral tax system. Stockholders will acquiesce to investment financed with retained earnings that earn *lower rates of return before tax* than they might have earned elsewhere, because of the lower tax on retained earnings vis-à-vis dividends, permitting *higher (or, at the margin, equal) after-tax returns.* The stock of capital is employed less efficiently than under a neutral tax system. Full integration by equalizing taxes on distributed and retained earnings would remove this distortion, and increase the efficiency with which we employ the available stock of capital.

Presently, corporate earnings are subject to a higher tax than earnings in the noncorporate sector. People will not invest in one sector, if they can earn more in another. At the margin, then, rates of return earned by investors *after tax* are the same in the corporate and noncorporate sectors. But *before tax* they are higher in the corporate sector. Were tax considerations not distorting its allocation, capital could be shifted from lower-yielding investments in the noncorporate sector to higher-yielding investments in the corporate sector. The economy is deploying its capital stock inefficiently. Were corporate earnings simply taxed as part of personal income, we would get more value of output from the same capital stock.

Integration, then, would make for more efficient employment of our existing capital stock. The stock, of course, is very large relative to annual capital formation. A modest increase in the efficiency of its allocation could have a more powerful effect on the value of the economy's output.

Arnold Harberger (1966, p. 116) has estimated the order of magnitude involved here. His calculations suggest that the "efficiency cost of the existing pattern of taxation" comes to something like one half of one percent of national income. Currently that would be on the order of \$6 billion.[6]

With returns to equity included in the corporate tax base and interest payments deductible in computing taxable income, the present system encourages debt as against equity finance. Integration would remove this distortion also.

Full integration, as noted above, would require that the basis of stock for capital gains purposes be stepped up by the excess of imputations

[6] Harberger's estimated property taxes, which are concentrated in the noncorporate sector, are considered along with the corporate income tax to be capital income. The distortion due to the corporate tax alone, is, therefore, somewhat higher than \$6 billion.

over current receipts (*i.e.*, by the amount of retained earnings). This would go a long way toward "unlocking" those investors who presently have unrealized capital gains on their present holdings, see more desirable investment opportunities, but who are deterred from making the portfolio changes because they would incur a capital gains tax. Under full integration, to the extent that the rise in stock price is due to reinvested earnings, the basis having been stepped up commensurately, there would be no taxable capital gain if they switched.

Finally, we note that full integration by bringing corporate earnings under the personal income tax could enhance the role of our primary revenue measure, help to stem the erosion of its scope, and permit a broader tax base and lower rates of personal income tax.

Distortions, *i.e.*, inefficiencies in resource use, can be expected whenever substitutable activities are subject to differential taxation. Within the personal income tax a large variety of distortions *are* created by special provisions, for example, exemption of state and local government bonds, or the noninclusion of the imputed income from owner-occupied homes (although the interest and property tax costs of that investment are deductible), and the itemized exemptions, *e.g.*, deductibility of interest, etc.

A courageous program of income tax base broadening that brought more income under regular tax treatment would tend to undo these differentials, thus bringing efficiency gains. Moreover, as George F. Break and Joseph A. Pechman (1975, pp. 128 and 131) have shown, marginal rates of income tax could come down to a maximum of 50 percent or very close to it for a fully integrated income tax. The cut in marginal rates would be a source of additional efficiency gains.

And if marginal rates were brought down to 50 percent, a major obstacle to full integration would be removed. With marginal rates now as high as 70 percent there is great concern about the constitutionality or political feasibility of requiring stockholders in the top tax brackets to include in income and pay a tax on their *pro rata* share of retained corporate earnings. The concern arises from the fact that they will incur a tax liability but will not have received sufficient funds to pay it. While there are good grounds for arguing that this concern is misplaced,[7] it is nonetheless widespread.

If the maximum marginal rate of personal income tax was 50 percent and the personal income tax on corporate earnings was withheld at a rate of 50 percent, almost all stockholder taxpayers would get

[7] See, for example, Holland (1975).

refunds if their "grossed up" corporate earnings were included in income, and no stockholder would be required to pay any additional tax on their corporate earnings.[8]

Summary

While tax changes figure prominently in policy proposals for the "capital shortage," the evidence to date suggests that major changes in the tax structure (so severe as to be ruled out politically) would have a modest effect on the rate of savings or investment. The effect of likely changes in taxes would be still weaker.

However, a meaningful payoff in terms of efficiency and productivity could come from tax changes which would induce more efficient utilization of the capital stock we now have. Currently a major source of distortion and efficiency in this connection is the corporate income tax. If the corporation income tax were abolished and corporate earnings taxed as personal income (and other taxes increased sufficiently to maintain government revenues) important efficiency gains would result in:

1. the employment of the capital stock,
2. the division of corporate earnings between distributions and retentions,
3. the weight of debt and equity in the structure of corporate finance, and
4. investors' management of their portfolios.

Further, *full* integration—aboliton of the corporate income tax *and* taxation of corporate earnings (both distributed and undistributed) currently as part of stockholders' personal income—would make our tax system more equitable. Overtaxation of distributed corporate earnings and the over or under taxation of retained corporate earnings would end.

Basic to a good income tax structure is the condition that all income, from whatever source derived, be taxed at the same rate. If this requirement is not met, tax differentials, as we have seen, will induce

[8] This was the way the Canadian Royal Commission (the Carter Commission, 1966) proposed to achieve integration. The Commission's proposal would achieve substantially the results of the Partnership method by providing for a withholding rate on corporate earnings at the maximum personal marginal rate, grossing up retained earnings, the withheld tax a credit against personal taxes due on the grossed up amounts, and the "basis" for stocks increased by grossed up retentions. With the withholding rate at the maximum personal rate almost all taxpayers would get refunds if their grossed up corporate earnings were included in personal income. Hence, the Carter proposal is tantamount to the Partnership method *de facto*.

an inefficient allocation of resources. If this requirement is met the tax system becomes more equitable, in the sense that persons with the same income pay the same tax.

With respect to income taxation, then, the policy most appropriate for the issue—full integration of the corporate income tax—is also the tax policy required for the broader objective of a "good" tax structure. A modification of the tax structure that serves both the goals of equity and economic efficiency is doubly blessed.

References

BISCHOFF, CHARLES W., "The Effect of Alternative Lag Distributions," Chapter III in Gary Fromm (ed.), *Tax Incentives and Capital Spending*. Washington, D.C.: The Brookings Institution, 1971.

BLINDER, ALAN S. AND ROBERT M. SOLOW, "Analytical Foundations of Fiscal Policy," in *The Economics of Public Finance*. Washington, D.C.: The Brookings Institution, 1974.

BOSKIN, MICHAEL J., "Taxation, Saving and the Rate of Interest," OTA Paper 11. Office of Tax Analysis, U.S. Treasury Department, April, 1976.

BREAK, GEORGE F., "The Incidence and Economic Effects of Taxation" in *The Economics of Public Finance*. Washington, D.C.: The Brookings Institution, 1974.

BRIMMER, ANDREW F. AND ALLEN SINAI, "The Effects of Tax Policy on Capital Formation, Corporate Liquidity and the Availability of Investable Funds: A Simulation Study," *Journal of Finance,* May 1976.

DAVID, PAUL A. AND JOHN L. SCADDING, "Private Savings: Ultrarationality, Aggregation, and 'Denison's Law,'" *Journal of Political Economy,* March/April 1974.

EISNER, ROBERT, "Tax Policy and Investment Behavior," *American Economic Review,* June 1969.

EVANS, MICHAEL K., *Long-Term Forecast: The Next Ten Years, Inflation, Recession, and Capital Shortage*. Chase Econometric Associates, 1975.

FELDSTEIN, MARTIN, "Corporate Tax Integration and Capital Accumulation," Harvard Institute of Economic Research, Discussion Paper Number 47, October, 1975 (Unpublished).

———, "The Welfare Cost of Capital Income Taxation," *Journal of Political Economy,* forthcoming.

FRIEDMAN, BENJAMIN M., "Discussion" (of Brimmer-Sinai paper), *Journal of Finance,* May 1976.

GENERAL ELECTRIC, *Economic Prospects: 1975-85* (1975).

Goode, Richard, *The Individual Income Tax* (revised edition). Washington, D.C.: The Brookings Institution, 1976.

Hall, Robert E. and Dale W. Jorgenson, "Tax Policy and Investment Behavior," *American Economic Review,* June 1967.

Harberger, Arnold C., "Efficiency Effects of Taxes on Income from Capital," in Marion Krzyzaniak (ed.), *Effects of Corporation Income Tax,* pp. 107-17.

Holland, Daniel M., *The Income-Tax Burden on Stockholders,* National Bureau of Economic Research. Princeton: Princeton University Press, 1958.

———, "Some Observations on Full Integration," *National Tax Journal,* September 1975, pp. 353-57.

McLure, Charles E., Jr., "Integration of the Personal and Corporate Income Taxes: The Missing Element in Recent Tax Reform Proposals," *Harvard Law Review,* January 1975.

Musgrave, Richard A., "Effects of Tax Policy on Private Capital Formation," Research Study Two in *Fiscal and Debt Management Policies,* a series of studies prepared for the Commission on Money and Credit. Englewood Cliffs, N.J.: Prentice-Hall, Inc., 1963.

New York Stock Exchange, *The Capital Needs and Savings Potential of the U.S. Economy: Projections through 1985,* 1974.

Pechman, Joseph A., *Federal Tax Policy* (rev. ed.). Washington, D.C.: The Brookings Institution, 1971.

———, and Benjamin A. Okner, *Who Bears the Tax Burden?* Washington, D.C.: The Brookings Institution, 1974.

Simon, William E., Statement to the House of Representatives, Committee on Ways and Means, July 31, 1975, Hearings Before the Committee on Ways and Means, 94th Congress, First Session, on the subject of Tax Reform, Part 5, pp. 3843-3883.

Thurow, Lester C., *The Impact of Taxes on the American Economy.* New York: Praeger Publishers, 1971.

INDEX

D

E

F

I

J

K

L

M

N

O

P

U

V

W

ABOUT THE AMERICAN ASSEMBLY

The American Assembly

Columbia University

About The American Assembly

The American Assembly was established by Dwight D. Eisenhower at Columbia University in 1950. It holds nonpartisan meetings and publishes authoritative books to illuminate issues of United States policy.

An affiliate of Columbia, with offices in the Graduate School of Business, the Assembly is a national educational institution incorporated in the State of New York.

The Assembly seeks to provide information, stimulate discussion, and evoke independent conclusions in matters of vital public interest.

AMERICAN ASSEMBLY SESSIONS

At least two national programs are initiated each year. Authorities are retained to write background papers presenting essential data and defining the main issues in each subject.

A group of men and women representing a broad range of experience, competence, and American leadership meet for several days to discuss the Assembly topic and consider alternatives for national policy.

All Assemblies follow the same procedure. The background papers are sent to participants in advance of the Assembly. The Assembly meets in small groups for four or five lengthy periods. All groups use the same agenda. At the close of these informal sessions, participants adopt in plenary session a final report of findings and recommendations.

Regional, state, and local Assemblies are held following the national session at Arden House. Assemblies have also been held in England, Switzerland, Malaysia, Canada, the Caribbean, South America, Central America, the Philippines, and Japan. Over one hundred institutions have co-sponsored one or more Assemblies.

ARDEN HOUSE

Home of the American Assembly and scene of the national sessions is Arden House, which was given to Columbia University in 1950 by W. Averell Harriman. E. Roland Harriman joined his brother in contributing toward adaptation of the property for conference purposes. The buildings and surrounding land, known as the Harriman Campus of Columbia University, are 50 miles north of New York City.

Arden House is a distinguished conference center. It is self-supporting and operates throughout the year for use by organizations with educational objectives.

The background papers for each Assembly are published in cloth and paperbound editions for use by individuals, libraries, businesses, public agencies, nongovernmental organizations, educational institutions, discussion and service groups. In this way the deliberations of Assembly sessions are continued and extended.

The subject of Assembly programs to date are:

1951—United States–Western Europe Relationships
1952—Inflation
1953—Economic Security for Americans
1954—The United States' Stake in the United Nations
—The Federal Government Service
1955—United States Agriculture
—The Forty-Eight States
1956—The Representation of the United States Abroad
—The United States and the Far East
1957—International Stability and Progress
—Atoms for Power
1958—The United States and Africa
—United States Monetary Policy
1959—Wages, Prices, Profits, and Productivity
—The United States and Latin America
1960—The Federal Government and Higher Education
—The Secretary of State
—Goals for Americans
1961—Arms Control: Issues for the Public
—Outer Space: Prospects for Man and Society
1962—Automation and Technological Change
—Cultural Affairs and Foreign Relations
1963—The Population Dilemma
—The United States and the Middle East
1964—The United States and Canada
—The Congress and America's Future
1965—The Courts, the Public, and the Law Explosion
—The United States and Japan
1966—State Legislatures in American Politics
—A World of Nuclear Powers?
—The United States and the Philippines
—Challenges to Collective Bargaining
1967—The United States and Eastern Europe
—Ombudsmen for American Government?

1968—Uses of the Seas
—Law in a Changing America
—Overcoming World Hunger
1969—Black Economic Development
—The States and the Urban Crisis
1970—The Health of Americans
—The United States and the Caribbean
1971—The Future of American Transportation
—Public Workers and Public Unions
1972—The Future of Foundations
—Prisoners in America
1973—The Worker and the Job
—Choosing the President
1974—The Good Earth of America
—On Understanding Art Museums
—Global Companies
1975—Law and the American Future
—Women and the American Economy
1976—Nuclear Energy
—Manpower Goals
—Capital Needs in America
1977—Corporate Conduct
—The Performing Arts

Second Editions, Revised:

1962—The United States and the Far East
1963—The United States and Latin America
—The United States and Africa
1964—United States Monetary Policy
1965—The Federal Government Service
—The Representation of the United States Abroad
1968—Cultural Affairs and Foreign Relations
—Outer Space: Prospects for Man and Society
1969—The Population Dilemma
1972—The Congress and America's Future
1975—The United States and Japan